DON'T EVEN THINK ABOUT IT

Paperback ISBN: 978-1-932113-58-7
Copyright 2010-2024
Published by High Home Endeavors: Books
and in Conjunction with Wolfpack Publishing

All rights reserved.

OTHER TITLES BY W. HOCK HOCHHEIM

Dead Right There
Fightin' Words
Dead Right There
Blood Rust: Death of the China Doll
My Gun is My Passport
Last of the Gunmen
American Medieval
The China Alamo
Be Bad Now
Impact Weapon Combatives
Knife Combatives
Training Mission Series One through Five
The Great Escapes of Pancho Villa
Face the Muzak
Takedown the Take
The Horse Killers
Swellen's Reckoning
Swellen's Orphans

TABLE OF CONTENTS

Foreward: Then Came Bronson, There Goes Hock	7
Chapter 1: It's You Who Is On Fire	11
Chapter 2: My First Dead Body	17
Chapter 3: And Dats Da Punishment Arm Break	21
Chapter 4: The First Guy I Knocked Out	27
Chapter 5: The First Time I Was Shot At	33
Chapter 6: The Night I Killed Myself	37
Chapter 7: The First Time I Shot At Someone	41
Chapter 8: Basic Soldiers and Cops	49
Chapter 9: What to Wear? When?	55
Chapter 10: The First Days	63
Chapter 11: The First Time I Was Officially Shot At	69
Chapter 12: Seven Men Down	77
Chapter 13: Car 54. Car 54. Be On The Lookout for a Tornado	95
Chapter 14: A Tale of Two Qounset Huts	101
Chapter 15: My Longest, Worst Fight	113
Chapter 16: Me and ROK Marines	127
Chapter 17: This War! T.C. Gaston's Follow Me Order	133
Chapter 18: The Knights. The Duel. The Fair Lady. The First Murderer I Caught in Texas	137
Chapter 19: How To be Sued For 1,75 Million	143
Chapter 20: The Bouncer Jump	155
Chapter 21: Me and the Lone Ranger	159
Chapter 22: Some Gunplay and Some Fitsicuffs! Night of the Mad Pay-tre-ons	163
Chapter 23: Harvey, Give me The Shotgun	169
Chapter 24: The Barefoot Policeman	177
Chapter 25: Nightmare Near Elm Street	183
Chapter 26: This'll get Your Goat	195
Chapter 27: The Illegal Immigrant Thing	199
Chapter 28: The Man Whose Head Was On Fire	207
Chapter 29: The Case of the Sleeping Gunman	211
Chapter 30: The Tireless Chase! Roll Over Beethovan	217
Chapter 31: The Great Train Stoppery	223
Chapter 32: Bad Night at the Broken wagon	229
Chapter 33: Fiery Grab-Assing!	235
Chapter 35: Christmas Throat Punch	243
Chapter 36: CPR at Sambos	249
Chapter 37: Knife Fight and the Jailhouse SuperBowl Ring	255
Chapter 38: A Roach Story	261
Chapter 39: Me and John Paul Hale, from Fistfights to His Death	267

Chapter 40: Caught in the Water Channel	281
Chapter 41: Everything But the Kitchen Sink	287
Chapter 42: Shoot the Car! I Need Me Some Relief!	293
Chapter 43: The Mudslide Fight at Hospital Hill	297
Chapter 44: Car as a Coffin	307
Chapter 45: Most Dead	313
Chapter 46: Splitten' hairs	319
Epilogue	323

"Taking a trip?"

Foreword: Then Came Bronson, There Goes Hock

Do you remember how the old Steve Martin movie, "The Jerk," started out? Steve says, "I was born a poor black child." A great opening line for any so-called biography. Or, how about the classic Bill Cosby comedy routine album title from many years ago, "I Started Out as a Child?"

I have read many biographies. And in these biographies, we are always subjected to the same beginning chapters. Like, "Billy was born on a farm ... his mother was ... his father did ... in high school, he....Billy was a...." And so on. Yawn. These were always the sleeper parts of biographies for me. A necessary evil I guess. The intellectual beard-strokers would say, "How else can we (beard-stroke) ... can we (beard-stroke) ... understand the true core, introspective motivations and inspirations of the subject?"

Yup, I get it. Still, though, I usually speed-read through all the "growd' up on a farm," first girlfriends, and high school stories even though I do understand the overall arguments for their inclusion. But for me, if it's not unusual or interesting, I break speed-reading records and zip through those early parts. (How many times must we reread the "Buds" experience in SEAL biographies?

That leaves me with ... me. What of my book?

What then of my motivation? I'll admit I have been asked with some frequency, "How is it that you became a police officer?" Or worse, not how, but "why?" The answer will come here.

But first, this book is not really a biography. If I thought the early-day stories were interesting, shocking, or had so-called teaching moments of their own, I used them here. The mundane? No.

So here goes a breaking-the-speed-limit origin. I will tell you briefly that I also did start out as a child; but I was not born a poor black child like Steve Martin, though some colors were indeed involved. Blue. Blue, and not cop blue. A sweaty blue, as in a collar. I was born the son of a blue-collared New York City factory worker who was also a World War II vet who landed on the beaches on D-Day and slogged all the way to Berlin under Patton's command. But for the following decades of his life, he made metal cans for vegetables at a machine press. Decades in the blue-collar, smelly, oily, and machined trenches making cans. I believe my dad, like so many quiet WW II vets, thought he was lucky to be alive; and after the war, he settled in for any normal routine he could find and was damn happy to have it.

I grew up on the Hudson River right across from Manhattan, New York City. I can't think of a conscious moment during those years that I wasn't planning on leaving there. "Escape" is a better word. I would pace the edges of Jersey and Palisades Cliffs of the Hudson River overlooking at the spectacular west-side view of Manhattan. That view, I can say, was one of the wonders of the world; but I was not in the least drawn to those bright lights. I simply was not meant for that dense a turf. The whole world that surrounded New York City awaited.

So, I was drawn to the way West. I was more inspired by the wild adventures of books and movies and the primitive television of the day. I escaped the Northeast Coast with plans like seen in old TV shows such as "Then Came Bronson".

This Bronson show wasn't very successful with the general public as it lasted but one year, but it was very successful as kind of a cult show to this day. It starred Michael Parks, and he has acted in films such as "Kill Bill." I watched "Then Came Bronson" show as a young teen, and I saw his troubled young man's escape on a motorcycle. I plotted and waited to do the same. I knew my only cut-rate chance would be just like his, atop an affordable motorcycle with a sleeping bag, a duffle bag of clothes, and a transistor radio.

In the beginning of every episode, Bronson pulled up to a red light. A down-trodden businessman in a fedora, shirt, and tie was in a car next to him. He gazed over at Bronson and eyed the sleeping bag and camping gear on the bike.

"Taking a trip?" asked the driver.

"Yup," Bronson said.

"Where to?" questioned the driver.

"Wherever I end up I guess," Bronson replied.

"Man, I wish I were you!" the driver concluded, shaking his frustrated head.

And MAN, did I wish I was Bronson, too. Escape. Adventure. Romance. I so wished I was him. On a Harley right after high school, I did become him for a few years. Then came Bronson, and there went Hock.

I do have to tell some interesting, formative recollections; but my life really began the day I rode my motorcycle out of New Jersey on the Fourth of July right after I finished four ugly, uncomfortable, and odd years in high school. College? Who had money for college? I burned rubber with $100 in my pocket.

I like to say that so far I have lived four different

lives. Those first years I was growing up and then traveling like Bronson on a motorcycle, living here and there for a few years. The second life was all my years in the military, police work, private investigations, security, and raising kids. A third life began, finally happily married to Jane Eden and teaching hand, stick, knife, and gun combatives all over the world. Thirty great years. Fourth life? Jane died of "window-maker" heart attack in July, 2023, and a new version of my life began. Four completely different environments, missions, people, wives, and lives.

Yes, I will recount a few some important youthful stories to keep the beard-strokers happy and try to keep you entertained.

Reviewing all these stories, I do realize many of them do not always put me in the "best light." Just consider them lessons to be learned in life and police work. But good or bad light, I have caught me some pretty bad criminals along the way.

This is book one, the early and patrolman years. Book two is "Dear Right There," about my investigation and detective years.

But it all started out in the NYC Metro area. And there went Hock...

Chapter 1: It's You Who is On Fire

Our tenement apartment building was ravaged by a fire two days before Christmas way back in the 1950s. This put us homeless on the streets of Union City, New Jersey. I was about five years old. Our apartment had been two rooms, a kitchen and a living room. No walls. One big open area. My parents opened a couch into a bed, a "hide-a-bed" as they called it, right in the kitchen-dining room area to sleep. I had some kind of small fold-away bed, too. The apartment was one small open area with a bathroom about three or four stories up. Millionaires had elevators. We had creaky stairs. My grandparents lived upstairs.

The fire is one of my earliest memories. My mother, grandmother, and a wee, small boy (me) were walking up Bergenline Avenue when my mother spotted thick smoke in the late afternoon sky ahead of us.

"Look, Momma, look at that smoke!" my mother said to my grandmother.

"Oh, I hope it's not our place!" my grandmother said.

I heard that. I remember that. I remember that because it was indeed our building. Within minutes, as we got closer and closer, we knew it was. My grandfather had been napping upstairs on his couch. The fire-truck sirens woke him up; and he ran upstairs to the sixth floor, broke down a locked door, and rescued a crazy old invalid lady. He threw her over his back and ran down the stairs. Firemen saw this and helped him at about the second floor. They said she screamed and grabbed at all the banisters along the way down.

Then he spent the rest of the time helping firemen with the hoses on the fire trucks behind the building. I still vaguely remember seeing him in one of those white tank muscle shirts and dress pants, covered in soot, and helping the firemen. His t-shirt was tucked in. He wore a dress belt. Even at 5, I was impressed with my grandfather that day. I guess I learned what "impressed" meant, what the feeling meant. He was a hero at least that day. He was pretty much a loser in life, an ignorant, unemployed, or poorly employed drunkard in fact, but not that afternoon. The inconsistency of heroism. According to Julius Caesar, "All glory is fleeting." But I remember.

The building was quickly gutted. An old tinderbox. We lost everything. We retreated to the nearest safe street corner with the rubberneckers. And another first memory of mine of mine was seeing my father walking down a side street to us. He got the call at work about the fire at his factory job, and they let him off. He took the bus up Hudson Boulevard from Jersey City. It was dark by then. Flames, sparks, and smoke curved over the side street. He was just a silhouette on the city sidewalk under this blazing red overhead show, but I recognized his walk.

An Italian guy owned a furniture store on that corner. He and his wife let us wait outside the store in the vestibule after my dad got there. My mother was typically hysterical. My dad, ever the WW II vet used to the slog of life, was calm. I remember his crouching down to a squat and lighting a cigarette with his big, heavy lighter, the flames and smoke in the distance. Years later I saw a photo of him in his scrapbook down in that same squat at a calm moment at the Battle of the Bulge. His forearm was resting on his knee, the ever-present Camel cigarette dangling in his open hand. The cigarette brand that would eventually kill him years later.

The fire raged on, and we couldn't leave. We didn't own cars! And we didn't have anywhere to go if we did. Our relatives lived miles away; and they were also poor folks in small, tiny, shared apartments. The store owner and my dad towed some old used furniture out of the store and into the dirty hallway outside his front doors. The owner had to eventually lock up the store and go home. That night after the fire was extinguished, we slept out there on two or three used couches under some mover's blankets. Unable to fall sleep on a small couch, I saw my dad pee in the street in the middle of the night. Later, I did the same. I lay there on the couch looking out at the empty midnight street. I guess a sense of fleeting detachment stuck with me from that moment. Plus, I saw the calm of my father. The heroics of my grandfather. My hysterical mother. My first real memories of life came from that night.

They took up a collection at the can factory for us. I remember that. We begged and borrowed for a week or two here and there, much of which I can't remember except for feeling like a refugee. It was a moving blur. You know, there weren't many hotels back then, not like there are today. And I don't know what we did that actual Christmas Day. Where did we go? There was no official Christmas that year. My parents cobbled it all together and got another apartment on a street closer to the Hudson River in a small city called West New York.

I have some revealing flashbacks of that place, too. It was there in our new digs that I had another vivid, rare, and early memory. I was still about five years old, and my mother stopped in a neighborhood corner candy store for something, with me in a low tow. My eyes spotted artwork of a book cover on a shelf of books and newspapers. I picked it up and thumbed through it.

"Dick Tracy?" my mother asked over my shoulder.

It was a paperback book collection of Dick Tracy comic strips. A book of cartoons with speeches in balloons, big guns, punches, racing cop cars, and very weird-looking bad guys.

"Ya want that book, Walta?" ("Walta" is how a Yankee pronounces "Walter.")

"Yeah." ("Yeah" is how a young Yankee kid says "yes.")

So my mother put down a real silver nickel on the counter and bought that book for me.

I tried to look over the amazing pictures as we walked home. I couldn't read yet. I knew I had to learn and find out what they were saying in those balloons! I recall my dad reading me some of the stories. Every toy and book I'd had was burned in the fire, so this Tracy book was pretty important to yours truly. My only book! My first book I remember. Dick Tracy.

Eventually I could read the adventures. I read and reread the Tracy book many times. While other kids read fairy tale stories and how Dick and Jane pushed Spot around in their red wagon, I worried about how

Tracy could thwart a crime wave in his city or rescue Sam or Tess. I learned that Dick Tracy was in color and on the cover of every Sunday New York Daily News because the comics section wrapped the newspaper. Tracy's hat was yellow! And he was still on the job in the newspaper, even after the last page of my worn paperback book. He was a detective cursed with never-ending cases. like years of my life would be. I am pretty convinced that this early exposure to Dick Tracy left an imprint on me for police work and, even more specifically, becoming a detective in the Army And in Texas.

In the 1980s, my parents came down to Texas for a Christmas visit; and we all went out to see Warren Beatty's movie version of Dick Tracy. I couldn't help but think that something had come full cycle with that matinee. Exactly what piece of irony that would be called, I don't know but something made a circle. A cycle.

I think about that fire just about every Christmas. Not every Christmas, but many, especially as I get older. I think about sleeping in that dirty hallway of the furniture store. I learned that things could go to hell in a minute, blow up, burn up, and disappear. Best not cling too dearly to things (and, well … for the longest time, people, too). Best not. I learned that you could look up in the sky and see smoke and then look down and realize that it might just be you...who's on fire.

Chapter 2: My First Dead Body

I have seen and handled a fair amount of dead bodies in my time, as this book and book 2 will later reveal. For better or worse, everyone remembers his or her first time. And, of course, I remember when I saw my first dead body. And I wasn't a cop. Growing up right there on the Jersey side of the Hudson River overlooking Manhattan, I can't say that I saw many people water-skiing up and down the Hudson. Ever. Small boats? Sure, a number of small boats can be witnessed, but the Hudson as a recreation "lake-like" body of water for water-skiing? That'd be a "No." But, my friend's Uncle Les would not let such common sense get in the way of fun on a hot summer Saturday afternoon.

Les decided to round up us young teenagers and take us out to the Hudson River right under the George Washington Bridge and do some water-skiing. Is there a city version of the word "redneck?" Or does redneck apply in urban areas? The plan was we needed one person steering the boat, one watching the skier, one skiing, and one up front ... looking for debris. This was about 1965-66? And the Hudson River was far from environmentally correct; and, in fact, the term "clean environment" wasn't even invented yet.

My turn on the skis came around. I dropped into the water, skis on, and took the reins between my legs awaiting the big pull. It was as I was bobbing in the water right under the mighty GW Bridge and waiting for Les to position the boat for a take-off, when we all seemed to spot something else bobbing around me.

"Looks like a fish or a dolphin," I heard Les say.

A dolphin? You mean like Flipper? I thought, here? New York City? The toxic water slopped in and out of my nose. Up the Hudson?

After closer examination, we discovered ... it was a dead guy. Not Flipper. Les coasted the boat back by me. They hauled me into the boat, and I got more of a bird's-eye view. Yup, it was a dead guy. Or was it a big rubber fake body? Les turned off for the Jersey coast. At the boat ramp, Les jumped out, ran up the ramp to a pay phone, and dropped a dime in it. We all followed to listen in. After all, who didn't want to hear a conversation with the Even half of one! He asked the operator for the police.

Les told the officer on the phone that we'd found a body and that we'd follow the body in his boat until a police boat could get there. dead guy was floating downstream and would be passing the Statue of Liberty and out into the Atlantic in a few hours or so.

"You kids stay here and wait for the police. I'm going to keep up with the body," Uncle Les ordered. He ran back to the boat and zoomed off. The dead off to find the body.

We saw a police boat go by us. It took about 30 minutes for the police car to arrive. The body hadn't floated all that far. We watched them net up the corpse and lift it into their boat. It was all black and bloated. Some kind of white van arrived, like a funeral van. The police boat and Les's boat returned to the ramp. Then I watched the police morgue workers prep, bag, lift, and toss the body into their station wagon. They bid us farewell, and that was the end of our group excitement for the day. We went home, but with a great story to tell. There was a dead body floating about 15 feet from me in the water!

My father read in the newspaper a few days later that the body we found came from a "dock incident" up river, a missing person case that smelled to him like union and mob work. Yes, probably like a "mafia" kind of dock incident.

The New Jersey side of the Hudson River, once a rathole of rotting shipyard docks, dangerous bars, and decaying houses, is now in the 21st century, a thriving new condo shoreline with expensive new restaurants and stores. But still, no one seems to go water-skiing out there, well, except maybe crazy Uncle Les if he is still around. When I see photos of the GW Bridge, I still picture my skinny self out in the middle of the Hudson trying to water-ski around a corpse.

We all get a glimpse of death when we are young, don't we? Relatives die. Relatives of friends die. We sometimes get that solemn peek at the lifeless. Or see them just before they die. Or see them actually die. I guess most kids and teens get dragged to a funeral. I know that some little kids have had to bend into the open coffin and kiss their relatives goodbye. Dear parents, this is like a Freddy Kruger nightmare. Forget this idea.

One afternoon, an old man down the street fell and skinned his brow while stepping up on his front porch. I saw some Cuban guys who lived next door run to him, lift him up, and carry him inside. The police and then an ambulance showed up the next morning. I wandered to the house to see what had happened. The old man had died in bed. He bled out through the night through that small eyebrow cut. I was fascinated by this. How could this happen? I had to learn more about this thing called death and the twisted ways it leaked or yanked the life out of each of us.

Chapter 3: And Dat's Da Punishment Arm Break

It was hard to live in northeastern New Jersey and not be exposed to the Mafia-like incidents all around you. As kids in the New York City Metro area, we used to see a particular guy in a raincoat and hat walking around the streets of our neighborhood a lot. He would use the pay telephone in Mike's Candy Store regularly, and one time we saw this guy pass Mike some cash. The word was the guy paid Mike a little "geetus" for the use of the pay phone inside his small store. The guy in the coat was placing bets.

Of course, anyone could use a public pay phone, but when you started giving the establishment owner a bribe or extra money? Then you hooked them into the enterprise, and they knew they could trust you more. Now you had something to lose, too. Skin in the game. Something to lose.

One day my dad saw this guy, and he said, "Son, you see that guy there? He takes gambling bets from people on the horses and sports. The guy behind him? Carries a baseball bat or a gun."

I looked behind him. There was no one! It took a minute for me to realize there was no guy actually "standing" right behind the bookie at the moment. My dad was warning me that this was a serious network of folks, as in the guys the bookie reported to. They busted up and killed people if they had to.

"Stay away from all those guys. Okay?"

Years later I learned that my dad had inside info on all this. My whispered family history disclosed that before World War II, my dad was also bookie in New York City. A rookie bookie, if you will. Trying it all out. He and his best friend ran book and had a wild, carousing, "zoot-suit" lifestyle as I was told. He was even married to a beautiful dark-haired girl before my mother, which was kept a big family secret until he was dead and I was well past 40. She died of some disease. As a child, I stumbled upon her picture tucked in one of my dad's old photo books. I didn't know her name, but she was indeed a raven-haired babe by 1930 Hollywood's standards.

But eventually his friend double-crossed the mob by skimming bookie money, and they killed him. My dad was loosely involved in this mess, and he fled the city and hid upstate for a while. Aimless after that, he eventually enlisted in the Army. As previously mentioned here, he did the full war years and was assigned to an infantry unit in Patton's command. He hit the beach on D-Day and invaded Germany. He survived all the way to Berlin. He turned out to be the "salt of the earth" of the "greatest generation," that other people talk about. When he returned five or six years later, whatever deadbeat bookie interest in him there had been had eroded away.

So he gave up that bookie life. But my Uncle Essy? Nope. Uncle Essy worked for a major manufacturing plant in a New England state. Essy ran the book for the plant as well as worked on the assembly line. There were a thousand or more employees, and many gambled. It was a great cash business for Essy. On weekends, he ran a popcorn stand in a park; and I can only guess he also ran a little book from the stand.

A big thing was playing "the number." It seemed like everyone bet a few bucks a week on the number. In different parts of the country, that magic number was derived from various sources. In our case, our local "number" was the last three numbers of the daily take at a certain horse racetrack. When the Daily News, or whatever newspaper, sports section reported the racetrack news, they also listed the total take of the day. THAT number. Everyone got the paper and first looked at this fine print figure.

Though my dad warned me about the bookie? At his factory job at the can company, he bet every day on this number. He won once or twice. He played the same number day after day after day.

Usually the local cops were in on this to some extent. They even got a piece of the action sometimes. Watch the movies "Serpico" or "Prince of the City" for a better idea on all this. I could tell you more stories on this subject, but they are not part of this story.

Strange sports things would happen like upsets and odd events, and Uncle Essy would get himself into trouble. Let's say a lot of people bet on a loser to win. They'd bet on an upset, slim odds to win, so the winnings would be big. Essy collected their money. But Essy, believing the oddsmakers and thinking those were sure losers, would at times never officially turn the money into the next higher level in the gambling chain of command. He was betting that the losers would lose, and he then could keep ALL that money for himself. Once in a while, the losers would win big; and Essy would have to come up with a fortune very quickly to pay off his customers. If his customers complained up the chain? The chain would suspect him of skimming all the time. You get the picture.

My grandmother lived upstairs from me in the old days, all of us crammed into one small house. (It was a Yankee thing.) I remember Essy's showing up in the middle of the night sometimes, begging her for money, for thousands even, to hold off this pending doom. I remember he hid out at our house for about a week once sleeping on the floor. This person, a guy with kids, a wife, and what would appear to be a normal life, was running from the mob. But we all knew back then the mob would not hurt any of us to get to him. That was not in their usual rules of engagement. Sure, accidents happen. Sure. They might beat Essy up and apologize to my grandmother afterward.

Of course, Essy had to collect a little money, too, from time to time. He knew ways to do it, too. On a New Year's Eve in the 1960s, there was party in the basement of our house. Uncle Essy, drunk with a bourbon in one hand and a cigar in the other, explained to me, a mere dumb kid and barely a teenager, about how to do a "punishment arm break." It went something like this, "Furst, ya gotta weaken the arm. Hit the arm muscle up here with a club," he pointed to his biceps, "or hit it wit ya forearm. Dis weakens his strength in his arm that protects the arm. Den you can break the arm back. Ya hold him face down on the floor. Use your knee against his elbow. Yank his wrist back with your two hands. Hard. Snap. Then? Always reach over to the other hand and break at least one finger. Two maybe. Den he has a big friggin' cast on his right arm and a cast on his left hand. He can't even wipe his own ass! Dat's punishment."

Yes. That's punishment. "The Sopranos" TV show was filmed all over my old neighborhoods for a reason. Many mobsters moved over the river from New York to Jersey just as seen on the TV show. Hudson County, New Jersey, was listed as one of the most corrupt counties in the United States in the 60s and 70s. The mayor of my city lived down the street from me; and he was killed, execution style, in his house.

My dad was right. Stay away from those guys. The "good" police even tried to. I will conceal the names for this one. One of my best friends while growing up was a kid I'll call William. William had an uncle who was a cop in Hudson County, New Jersey. He was a patrolman; and I'll call him Uncle Donald, and let's just leave it at that. We would be around those adults a lot for a variety of reasons, whether it was a family gathering, a visit, or just a home-grown construction project on someone's house in the neighborhood.

Donald was a good guy and while off duty, he ran a small construction and repair company with several other cops with whom he worked. They did small- to medium-sized jobs of all sorts. It was known to all of us that Donald was under great pressure to be "on the take" in some way. One way these cops on the take could peacefully coexist with the good cops was to somehow get them "in" on freebies. That way they couldn't talk or rat to the proper authorities about corruption because they, too, had their own misdeeds. Just like Mike's getting some geetus for letting someone use the phone in his store.

Uncle Donald refused those mob offers, as did many of his friends. But he told us some mornings about once every two months or so when he was off police duty and going to work on his small construction jobs, he would pull up to the location and discover a huge pile of building supplies: bags of cement, lumber, and tools. At first he didn't know what to do about it. There weren't any clues telling what supply store they had come from. If Donald wouldn't accept bribes, gifts, or the take, this was the way his comrades would include him into their system. He gave in and started using the materials to keep the peace and with the silent understanding within his agency that they were all inside a quiet conspiracy, that code of silence.

I started police work in the U.S. Army. Then in Texas. Say what you will about the bad arms of Texas law enforcement, the Cowboy Mafia, etcetera, those limbs would never reach the extent of the New York Metro area in the 60s. Though I did fear the evolution of the Central and South American drug cartels, sometimes I wondered what my life would have been like had I never left on that motorcycle back then? What if I'd applied to a Yankee Police Department for a job or to one of the county sheriff's offices surrounding New York City - known to be some of the most corrupt counties in the USA back then? What would have become of me?

Chapter 4: The First Guy I Knocked Out

I have arrested about 900 people in my 26 year career. That's not a lot. But more than a lot compared to most of officers who get admin-desk jobs after just a few years on the street. Career police officers don't arrest a lot of people in the end tally anyway because they seek promotion and get levels and steps away from the arrest action.

I never took a promotional test, and remained in line operations. I spent most of my time as a detective and had to first build the case, then arrest the bad guy. I remained in line operations. I never wanted to become a supervisor or climb the chain of command. While all my long-term friends were ensconced in dry, warm, day-job offices. Not me. I was manhandling knuckleheads long after most folks would have thrown in the towel.

Here's how I know about the some 900 number, which is also some police history. Since the Military Police Academy in the early 1970s, I was told to maintain pocket books of records. I, we, had these breast pocket-sized notebooks. I was instructed that these notebooks would possibly be needed in court someday, so all must be saved. They books include notes from squad meetings, BOLOs, crime scenes, and arrests way back to the 1970s. We were also warned that defense attorneys might examine these books if the court allowed them to, so we must keep all personal information out of them. "Just the facts," as Jack Webb would more or less say.

I had the name of the first soldier I ever arrested in that first book. It was a drug arrest. I kept this routine up, in one form or another, until I retired. And I kept really accurate, handwritten records until about 1992 or so, up until easily-accessible computers invaded the scene. Then my handwritten bookkeeping got a little sloppy, and the computers took over.

Those arrest numbers included when I was the official or primary arresting officer or when my partner was the official arresting officer, and I significantly helped. "Secondary," as some reports call it. Those figures are also included in my 900. As arrest profiles went, it was well known in the business that most arrested folks would come with you peaceably. The next biggest bunch would resist or run, but did not really try to out-and-out fight you. The next smaller bunch did out-and-out fight you; and finally, the smallest percentage tried to kill you. These generalities coincided with my experiences, too. A lot of readers and listeners are more interested in these lower-end, more violent stories. I understand that.

And also, for the record, I am not a tough guy. I know real tough guys, and I am not one. I am just a guy who knows a lot of tricks. Tricks from martial arts. I ... somehow managed to win out most of the time. I just do what I have to do. I do believe in cheating, setups, tricks, and gear to survive. But I also believe in fight training and conditioning. I've done boxing, kickboxing, and old school jujitsu to use some generic terms that everyone seems to know. Learning these things and the reality of fighting was an evolution I will describe in this book.

But I guess you could say the violent evolution started back in high school when I officially knew none of these moves.

The first guy I knocked out was in high school. Not really uncommon for many guys, but there is a teaching point to the story. As I have reported, I grew up in the west-side shadow of the Manhattan skyscrapers in a poor man's land of the Jersey Hudson River coast. The high school I attended had thousands of kids, and I was not a tough guy. I was actually a student with art as a major and bound for an art college.

By my senior year, I myself had been knocked out three times. Twice while playing baseball (Yes, baseball!) And once in an auto accident. Getting yourself knocked out takes quite a toll on the brain, as we have truly learned in recent years. They call it "accumulating damage." Sports was an early way to do this. Our NYC metro area was full of ballplayers and leagues. But if you played in the sandlot leagues, you were always playing unless it snowed. I first took a shot at being a catcher. But I became too lanky and skinny, 6 feet 4 inches. I wasn't really catcher material. Still, I tried.

One day as I leaned out to catch the ball, a long, tall hitter took a power swing at an outside pitch and spun completely around hitting the back of my head with his bat. Bingo. Starlight city. I woke up with a splash of jug water and then tried to count to 10 to see if I had brain damage. Then in another game, I tried to snare a ball from the outfield and tag out a runner charging in at me from third. It was a do-or-die catch, a pivot and a dive at the runner to tag him. I did, and his knee hit my face when I went airborne. He spun me completely around. Bingo. Starlight city again. Jug water. Counting. I eventually settled in at third base, which I loved.

Oh, the third? A car crashed into the back of my car knocking me out when my head bounced off of something. The steering wheel? I don't know. Probably.

Three for three. Woke up in the hospital. Since then I have been knocked out another one or so times. But I digress ... an obvious problem with my concentration, huh?

Senior year I was counting the last miserable days before escaping the utter waste of time civilization calls "high school." In our PT "gym" period or class in the spring, they pushed everyone, about 40 of us, outside to play baseball for 50 minutes. Well, it was some form of baseball. They never had enough gloves, and the few they had were old and stubby brown rags from the 1930s. Infielders got the gloves. And the ball was larger than a baseball and smaller than a softball. The gym teachers couldn't care less. They wandered inside the school and probably played poker as the "baseball" game just played itself out.

When the gym teachers disappeared, I did too. I wandered out to the outfield every day, jumped the fence, and walked down the hill to the candy store. Then just before the class was over, one of the "poker players" stuck his mug out the door and shouted, "Bring it in." I'd jump the fence and mill back in with the crowd.

Now we had thousands of kids in this school. And we had gangs, too; and this gym period was blessed with an interracial gang of goofballs led by a harnessing bully punk. What little I saw of the games before sneaking off the campus to the candy store down the street was that anytime Mister Punk came to bat and hit the ball, he would run the bases and generally mess up any of the poor teens who tried to throw him out at any base. He'd slap them around, shove them down, shake them, and make them drop the ball to the delight of his pack of sideline douche bags. Then trip them or toss them down in some sort of "schoolyard judo." Because of this, Mister Punk would always get a home run if he hit the ball. Whatever. I had a date with a Coca-Cola and some chips down the street; so like the gym teachers, I couldn't have cared less.

Well, that covert candy store mission I ran day after day got pretty boring, too. Loving third base and baseball as I did, I resigned myself to remaining on the field once in a while and became an infielder to kill the boredom. But the first day I was stuck playing shortstop, not third base. Mister Punk came up to bat, struck out, and sat down his first time at bat. His next time, he hit a ball into the outfield for a hit. Should have been a single; but as usual, Punk rounded first as the outfielder tossed me the ball at second. I caught it. He ran right at me yelling and cursing, and I pounded the glove and ball into his arm well before he touched second base. He was tagged out cold. Obvious. And I wasn't going to drop the ball.

"You're out!" the other infielders yelled in vindictive glee.

I routinely tossed the ball to the pitcher. This play was over. No time for pranks from Punk. Too late to slap me around and get me to drop the ball. Now, Mister Punk stopped a few feet after touching second base, turned, and marched up to me cursing. It was his regular showtime for his giggling goon squad, a show I'd seen and expected. His arms were flying. He got close. I punched him right straight in the face and knocked him out cold. He spiraled off his feet and hit the ground. All his punks ran out in shock. Not to get me, but to check on their hero. They carted him off the field.

When the gym teacher came out later to round us all up, he was told by a snitch that I had knocked out Mister Punk. The teacher said, "Good." There was none of this "zero tolerance for fighting" crap back then as there is today. Punks could get knocked out, and the world was a better place for it. But you know, those gym teachers should have supervised those games and never let those shenanigans go on in the first place. I was never bothered by that jerk after that day. Now, today, I guess you would have to worry about retribution and drive-by shootings if you did something like that. And for a time I was oblivious to the fact that word of the little knock-out incident got around the school.

Now the teaching moment. I'd never thrown such a real punch before, just ones in play and roughhousing like in the movies. I do not know why I punched him so quickly and so thoughtlessly. So instantly. He marched at me with his chin and face up and out. Barking with his shoulders back and his arms down. Totally stupid but ever so streetwise and quite common. Years later I learned that this very pose, the posturing of the jutted jaw, head, chest, and neck was so typical in many angry confrontations.

While this was unsafe, it somehow seemed a biological response for many jerks, didn't it? They first tried to scare you with face, words, and swelled chests. That was why so many shirts and jackets got removed before a fight. A little biological ritual. These antagonists often even strut up and bumped their target's chest with their chests, the classic, "chest bump."

A few of these instances happened to me early on; and I was lucky to survive them, which gave me a false sense of security that would catch up with me in the Army a few years later when I was pulverized a time or two.

Chapter 5: The First Time I was Shot At

I know what you must have thought—wow, that must have been some amazing police or military action. Ahhh, no ... not really....and here is a tale of stupidity for you.

Many moons ago, once upon a time, there was an amusement park on or about the Hudson River in New Jersey across the mystical, magical world called New York City. For one reason or another, the park was ripped down to make way for new and expensive real estate. The tear-down project took a very long time and was even suspended at times. It looked like the bizarre ruins in a science fiction movie with, you know ... clowns and rides intermixed with torn buildings, broken roads, and carnie huts. It was all a very weird landscape. And given its Stephen King nuance even though it was years before Stephen King became popular, we simply had to climb the fence and explore. What else could typical bored teenagers do?

Several of us who shall not be named (was I even there?) jumped the tall chain-link fence one night and looked over this macabre site. We kicked over stuff, examined stuff, and helped break more stuff like destroying a giant clown's head with two-by-fours. Hey! We were trying to help out! But at one end of the park was a long, broken-down, bashed-up wooden counter. We closed in on it to discover it was a carnival shooting gallery. There were the usual targets, but where were the shooting irons? To our delight and surprise, eight, count them, eight rifles were still screwed into podiums on the broken, collapsed counter! How could this be? The park had been closed for over a year and was currently abandoned. Surely those guns no longer worked. It seemed like a good idea at that point in time to further help the demolishing crews and rip out the .22 caliber rifles and take them. Surely, they were rendered useless and were pieces of junk? Because the wood was already bashed in and rotten, the removal was easy.

We carried the eight rifles, still attached to their swivel podiums, back to the perimeter over the fence and into my friend's car. Like mob henchmen and hoodlums, we drove across town with a trunk full of guns. Finally in one of the neighborhood basements, we examined what we thought were junk that we might hang on our bedroom walls like cowboys or "Natty Bumppo." We pried off the swivels and wiped the guns down. Over the next couple of days we worked on those simple 22 rifles. We were deer hunters and knew a little something about rifles.

Eventually, they seemed like they might actually work! After a few days, we took the rifles out to the Jersey swamp and test-fired them; and damned if six of the eight didn't work just fine! (That was why I have been vague with names and locations thus far, even though this happened about 45 years ago. The end fact was we had absconded with six working rifles from an abandoned amusement park!) As a result, no one wanted one of them for a wall souvenir as first planned. Even back then, guns and ammo were controlled items in the People's Republic of New Jersey. We sort of collectively kept them together in different basements.

One weekend we decided to go to the woods of western Jersey and shoot them. And that was where my actual story began. Drive west from New York City and through the parts of New Jersey, and you will find very pretty countryside. Then you are quickly in beautiful Pennsylvania. Somewhere in those wooded country parts, we parked; and six of us got out of the car. We started a walk into the woods and up some large hills. Each of us with a rifle, we started sort of hunting if you will, shooting the rifles at … various stuff. It was a winter day and cold, and scattered patches of snow covered the ground. At one point, the trail split and led off to two tall, medium-sized ridges with a small valley in between. Three of us went one way, and the other three went the other. Once atop these ridges, we could clearly see each other about 40 yards apart.

I was minding my own business enjoying the view of the rise and taking pot shots at the wildlife, rocks, branches, and whatever was at ground level.

Suddenly not far from me, the ground and snow erupted into a funnel! It coincided perfectly with a gunshot from the other ridge! What? I looked to my left, and there those three knuckleheads were standing on the other ridge laughing at me. One of them, I'll call him Johnny for now, was lowering his rifle from a shoulder position fresh from the shot. Okay! You want to play? I started half laughing also. I lifted my rifle and took aim about 8 feet from them and fired. They laughed and smiled and ran for some cover behind some rocks and trees. We followed suit. For about 10 minutes, we exchanged "near-fire," you know, like near-beer getting as close as we could without getting too close. Yelling and cussing at each other.

Somehow we called for a truce; and like six jerks,

we came down off the ridges laughing. What a great time, huh! What good, clean, American fun! We thought little of it. We hiked back to the car, climbed in, and drove back east toward civilization. On the way back, we passed a Jersey State Trooper squad car in a big hurry. There were some houses here and there back on that country road, and we wondered if some resident had called the cops over what had to have sounded like a firefight. A near firefight.

I know it's all a lot of fun until someone gets his or her eye shot out. And I know now that was utterly insane. And I know it broke every rule in the gun book. But we did what we did. I claim youth, ignorance, and stupidity. I'll bet there are many folks reading this who have done crazy things with firearms in their youth, and some even worse. I've been told a few.

So technically, this is the first time someone "shot at me."

Chapter 6: The Night I Killed Myself

The night I killed myself still lingers like a strong chemical stain in my brain. Ever have a serious dream? I mean a dream like an out-of-body experience? In triple Technicolor and high definition? One whipped up and cooked by your brain on such a cranky, vindictive night when it paints a palette of uncompromising, realistic, and emotional horror?

I was bound for many places on the bike. My plan was to rip about the USA and work here and there for food. Then eventually get space on a freighter in California for Australia. Was that even possible? I didn't know. You see, in the New York Daily News in the late 1960s, there were a series of fetching articles. The features displayed a bevy of long-haired beauties in bikinis on the Australian beaches. Often they looked longingly to sea, their hands shielding their eyes. The text of the articles reported a severe shortage of men down there, Down Under, you see; and those poor beauties were man-less! Man-less, I tell you!

So like the sirens in the tale of Odysseus, I could

hear them beckon to me. I was much more a lover than a fighter and knew how to do neither! But I was certainly willing to learn! And what better way than by helping those poor lonely beauties who were trolling and pacing the beaches at the very edge of their country, their existence all in skimpy bikinis and waiting for male companionship. The idea of golden beaches and babes of Australia was the end goal for the four-year plan. After that, I didn't know. What did Fletcher Christian do with his island beauties?

But instead I wound up in Texas trying to beat the second cold winter with only a motorcycle for transport. Little did I know it got cold in Texas, too. And then like a damn young fool ... I got married to boot. Who knew what I was thinking and what I was doing when I did that? But who knew such things about a damn fool? Worse, a young one. My Harley dreams suddenly became a "Hardly," and my bike was used to transport me back and forth to work at metal factories and not for heading down the highway. After about two years of a two-wheeler traveling dream, it all whittled down to that roller bed Shakespearean nightmare. Married and in poverty.

The theater nightmare unfolded one night in a cheap, two-room, shoe box apartment with a scrap of cheap furniture. Sheets for the old mattress would come with the next sorry paycheck. The old apartment complex supplied an air conditioning window unit to beat back the blistering Texas sun, and it rattled and dripped away as the sound track to my new life. My new trap. Each night grew tighter and emptier, and I finally fell deep asleep into a thrombosis hypnosis.

Then it happened. The two-room apartment changed dimension. I was awake, but I was not. It was here, but it was there. And someone or something was moving in the living room! As real as real can get, I whipped my bare dream feet from the dream bed to the dirty dream carpet. What? I listened again. There was someone in there. Someone with deep wolf breath right in there.

I stepped to the doorway and looked through the veil. There he was, a large man taller than me with a long dark jacket - hell, it was more like a cape. It had a huge collar turned straight up. He was looking about the living room with his back turned to me. I got up behind him, grabbed his shoulder, and turned him violently around ready to bark some threat.

But it was me! It was me in that cape! But, this version of me had a Dracula-like face, a monster's face. I, me, he sneered at me. A wicked smile. Big teeth. I froze like ice. Ice, I tell you. In his right hand was a large silver knife in an ice pick grip. He lifted it up. I couldn't move. He plunged it deep into my chest and into my heart like a hammer fist, like a sledgehammer.

They said you were not supposed to die in your dreams. The collective "they" in charge of the Nightmare Research Institute said that if you died in your dreams, you would die for real. Well, I fell back with that big-assed knife in my chest and hit the floor. That Dracula-thing that was another form of me just stared down at me. Grinning. I was dying. I was dead. Eye to eye with my own monster-self that smote me down good. Dead on the floor of a shit-hole apartment in a dried-up, no-where place in north Texas.

I woke up violently, kicking and gasping, atop a dirty mattress in that same shit-hole apartment in a dried-up, nowhere place in north Texas. My heart was out of control. I sat up like you see in the old B movies. Clutching my sucking chest wound, I ran to the doorway because it was all so real. I thought my monster was still in there. But he was gone; and there was no hole in my heart, just a helplessness in there. A breathlessness. A lifelessness.

I sucked in some air, still holding my chest and still holding the horror show in there and in my mind. I sat on the old junk couch in the dark. What was that all about? I was too young and stupid to know. And stupid is as stupid does. I wandered back into the bed of my own making, pondering the pseudoscience of dreams, the wonders of the universe, and the conspiracies of fate.

But I did feel or understand one thing way back then. A part of me died that night; I had killed off a part of myself. I came to myself with a big-assed knife and had done the nasty deed deep into my own heart. I did feel and understand that something had to seriously change.

Looking back years later, I better understood the big picture. I had killed off some kind of spirit in me that first took me away from New York City and onto the road west. The need to be different. To do bigger and better. I'd settled in too young. I'd cashed in all my radical chips and gotten married too young; and the cast of characters inside me didn't like it one bit, and they sent in Dracula to rough me up.

Dracula-Hock roughed the fuck out of me. After his vampire visit, I gravitated away from the metal yards and into college majoring in Police Science. I joined a security company and then joined the Army. AND, got a divorce. I never saw that Dracula-me again in my dreams, but I remember him vividly. I still see his face, still see his shiny knife, and still feel it pierce into my chest.

I suspect I might see this Dracula again the moment before I die. The Shakespearean chorus might send him back in to punish me for all my faults, failures, and misdeeds. There were a few. Life was a thin veil, and death was a silver knife.

Chapter 7: The First Time I Shot at Someone

I still teach now, for lack of a better word, "combative" skills to people, soldiers, and cops. I am not an incredibly famous person, but I am well known among what I affectionately call "a small disturbed crowd." I travel internationally to about 12 allied countries a year teaching hand, stick, knife, and gun material. In the last five years or so, I've noticed in my travels that an odd fascination has sprung up, almost a worship-like affection among my clients for bouncers or doormen. People with very few stamps on their "Man Passport," you might say, who'd worked as doormen (and some in quite calm places, I might add) were somehow viewed, at least by civilians, as master fighters and hypnotic gurus of psychology. Cops and soldiers didn't share that salivating awe.

One night while I was eating dinner with a group of citizens after a training session, a guy asked me, "So you have worked on the door (there's that magic phrase again)?" You must have some interesting stories?"

And the assembled masses all leaned in ears first.

Look. I have been shot at, have shot at people, and have caught serial killers and a hit man. I've put bad people in the hospital and some have put me in the hospital. I have policed streets in the Orient. I have arrested over a thousand people (some have tried to kill me) spanning three decades. I have assisted in the evacuation of Vietnam. I've organized security and stood watch for numerous stars, singers, and politicians the likes of Rudy Giuliana and Jimmy Carter. I was a private investigator for three years. There's more, and ... AND ... people want to hear some doorman or bouncer stories? What? Do you see what I mean about an unusual predilection about doormen?

My answer to the question is, "No, not really. It was such a long time ago." It was, after all, the first page and stamp in my passport. But if pressed, I could at least tell a few tales like the following one.

The first time I shot at something alive other than deer and some other Jersey critters was a crazy incident in the early 1970s. I was an armed, uniformed security guard for a firm in Texas; and a few nights a week, I rotated duties at different honkey-tonks and strip clubs on various seedy, low-rent strips and dark streets. We were the bouncers, but we were not called that. How did I get to this point? Shooting a .38 revolver at someone.

I was just a damn Yankee kid from New York, part biker dude back then and trying to get myself hired by a Texas police department. No chance in hell. I decided to go to college in the daytime and try my hand at security work at night. I foolishly thought that getting a college degree, taking karate, and doing some time in a security uniform would make me become totally irresistible to the local constabularies. Not!

Centennial Security hired me with no such requirements. I walked in; and within an hour, they gave me a few brown and tan uniforms and a big revolver. It was a very cheap revolver, and a cheap holster and thin belt came with it. Six .38-caliber bullets were in the gun, and there were six more bullets on the belt in the classic belt loop you never see anymore except maybe in old Westerns.

"Ever shoot a pistol before?" the manager asked me.

"Yes, I have," I answered, "but really not much at all." But I had.

"Good," he said as he handed me a big Smokey the Bear DI (drill instructor) brown hat. "Randy-Bob out front will give you your first assignment."

No guard school. No state certification. No gun training. Just a simple signed ID card as best I can recall. No training. Did I sit in on a one-hour training session watching a 16 mm film that explained my duties? I do seem to recall doing that somewhere but maybe not there for them, for I worked for a few of those guard companies. I could not swear which one. But no matter; I was to stand around, keep the peace, and make things secure wherever they sent me. I guess I'd learn on the job from the crème of the veteran guard crop I'd be working with? Well ... not!

At first I worked alone, wandering around a few factories in the middle of the night, some country clubs, and some Dallas-area power plants. I did some day gigs, too. Get this irony. I did my share of factory labor as a young man. I welded shopping carts and made aluminum windows and so forth, all at about $2.00 an hour. Hard, hot, and sweaty work, non-air-conditioned Texas labor. But as a security guard, I made $2.75 an hour and wound up watching factory workers make the same things I once labored to make; and I got 75 cents more an hour. Back then, that was a fair amount. True, watching workers work bored me to tears. But I found it ironic. I could make more "watching" work than "doing" work.

Then I worked some of the country Western bars on some nights during the week. It just depended on how, where, and when manpower was short and where the company needed me. At those dance and drinking halls, we had several armed guards working as was our standard procedure; and most of them did have experience in the ways and means of handling rowdy cowboys (and cowgirls). I did learn a thing or two from them, but those operations were nowhere near what you usually see today. Still, I had received no formal training as one might expect. And nothing with pistols. (That has changed now because armed guards must attend a week of state-certified training. And that is almost a bunch of nothing, too; but it's better than totally nothing.)

One night I was outside in the parking lot of one of the larger Dallas watering holes. Some of those places had acres of parking and a multitude of shenanigans going on. Sex, even rape in cars! Fights. Yelling. Auto burglaries. Wandering the lot was imperative.

I was a considerable distance from the front doors when suddenly a man burst out the entrance holding a knife in his hand. Hanging on to him was another fellow roaring and complaining. Yet another guy was behind them, and a blonde girl was behind all of them. All were trying to stop this guy, but he would not be stopped.

As he tried to shuck those people off of him, the blonde looked to me and yelled, "Stop him! Stop him. He's stabbed somebody! Stop him!"

In the lead, he freed himself and got to his car, an older dark sedan. I ran across the lot. He raced the engine and dropped that finned monster-mobile into reverse. The two guys after him had to do some fancy dodging to escape his backing up. The blonde screamed. He jammed it into first gear and was tossing gravel as he gassed it off the lot.

Well, in my own feeble young mind, I'd seen enough. Men in a chase. A screaming blonde. A reported knife attack. I pulled my pistol; and on the run with one hand extended, I fired once times at the car as it turned and raced away. It was about two lanes away amid catawampus parked cars, but I just knew I hit it. No glass exploded in a movie inferno, but I hit it.

We all ran inside the bar. Sure enough, there was a man inside stabbed and bleeding. I knew no first aid, but people were surrounding the man and treating him in some way that looked good to me. An ambulance and police arrived. The guy was whisked off to a hospital. Some patrol officers came around to talk to me. I told them I shot the car, and they asked, "Good. Do you know where?"

"Once in the rear, left side. Once in the back I think."

"Good. That will help us identify the car."

Then I returned to my very important "walking around." They said they would use the bullet hole to put the knifer's car at the crime scene to help support the case. They took my name. I never gave anyone a written statement. I never heard from them again. Did they catch the bad guy from that night? I didn't know.

But now here was the weird part. I thought it best to reload the pistol later that night. After all, young Matt Dillon here had burned a round in his six-gun! By myself in the parking lot under some lights on a wooden pole, I tried to open the revolver by pushing the cylinder thumb release forward on the side of the weapon. It would not move.

I let it be for the rest of the work shift, but when I got home that night, I set about the task of trying to reload the gun. In frustration, I even hit on that release a bit with a screwdriver and a hammer! I worked and worked on the gun. Nothing would release the cylinder.

I went to work the next few nights with five rounds in this pistol. Oh yeah, so stupid, I know. Sure, but I was just a really dumb kid and nothing more than an untrained security guard kid at that.

The third day I was off and free. I got up early and drove to the main office to see "Randy-Bob." I told him my pistol problem. He fooled with the mechanism and could not get the cylinder to come out either. He gave me another old pistol (none were new), but he opened the cylinder once to check on it. The newer gun had never been fired in training or at work.

I realized I had walked around for about five weeks or so with a pistol I could not reload and was too young and too dumb enough not to try it, clean it, shoot it, or really even know I should. That was the first and only time in my life that I had heard of someone not getting his or her revolver cylinder open and out. Years later, I had seen empty shells expand inside a cylinder that would not easily eject. That was in a police chase of an armed robber that led to his demise—but that's another story!

With this new revolver, I bought a box of bullets; and during one shift at a remote, half-built country club, I put 50 rounds through the gun out on an unfinished golf course. I then decided that I needed to shoot this replacement gun. I did at cans, boxes, and planks of wood, midnight shift when posted at a closed factory in Dallas. It worked and was an easy reload!

Soon after, on a red hot summer day in the early 1970s, I walked out of the Garland, Texas, Police Department, rejected yet again for a police job. I took a good look around at the world from those municipal porch steps.

In that world around me and beyond, no one wanted to hire some uneducated kid from Jersey on a motorcycle. I was one step short of being a vagrant.

Vietnam was cooling on the surface, but it was cooking into a bigger fiasco than anyone imagined at the time. Nixon brought to a public relations end what Eisenhower and Kennedy and the Dulles Brothers had started and what Johnson brewed up.

What was a foolish, immature, displaced, and rejected young Yankee biker dude to do in this broken world? No one wanted me. Well, one thing for sure, the Army wanted me. Yeah. The Army always wanted me. Even more than those Australian women ads in the New York Daily news.

Within a few months, I joined the U.S. Army where they taught me to operate, strip, and clean guns-specifically the .45 semi-auto pistol (once so flippantly called an automatic), a shotgun, and the M-16. And in the dark with blindfolds on ... and under a strict time clock with yelling instructors slamming sticks on our tables and swinging the sticks at us once in a while. I did learn how to "open up" and clean weapons; and I understood why I had to know.

I know that story is probably not as satisfying as a bouncer with his hands up de-escalating with NLP (Neural Linguistic Programming) versus an angry patron soused on beer being all mean and then ejecting him into the parking lot. You know, doormen are just like Batman.

(Several years later in Texas, I chased a murderer into some dark snowy woods, who had just seconds earlier shot a guy in the head with a shotgun. He had a getaway car hidden, and I suddenly saw red brake taillights come on. He took off and I shot the car twice. He sped away. An hour later, the murder scene was a major crime scene. Long story told elsewhere right here in this book, the detectives were excited that I had shot the car, for the same reason the Dallas police were. Evidence that the suspect's car was at the scene.

Chapter 8: Basic Soldiers and Cops

That first segment - part of my life ended when I joined the U.S. Army Military Police. If anything else interesting happened to me in those lost, wandering, pre-Army days, they won;t be included here.

I boarded that classic bus for Fort Polk, Louisiana, and Basic Training. I still had little personal purpose or mission except to live a life of surprise and excitement. You know, like you see in all the movies. It wasn't until a number of years later that I matured just enough to realize how important the military and policing was. I was a slow learner, but I got it now. The Army helped "square me away" and got me on a course. It was my real college, and I would forever be indebted to it even with all its faults.

In the beginning I wasn't a patriot. I wasn't motivated to save the world or help people. Fact was I was just a shallow, bored, and poor kid. I always felt a little guilty on Veteran's Day when vets were honored for their commitment and sacrifice. I was just a selfish kid back then when I joined.

The rest of my life has been a strange mixture of

military and police for a long time since, and it had all started with that session of basic training. In late 1973 I went off on a bus to U.S. Army Basic Training in Fort Polk, Louisiana or as it was called, "Little Vietnam," because of its weather and terrain. And I left home with just the few usual things: some clothes, some toiletries, and two thick paperback books. It was my plan to study those books like bibles over the upcoming difficult months.

One book was SOLDIER!, an autobiography by Lt. Colonel Anthony Herbert, a Korean and Vietnam War hero. It was mostly an action story, but it was a first-person account of his Army life; and this was meant to prep me for my time ahead in uniform.

The other book was called COP! (I think. Or COPS? Maybe. I was not sure.) It was hundreds of pages on the operation of the Boston Police Department, their big crimes, routine patrol, divisional structure, history, management, gear, and cars ... a complete dissection of the agency told in a narrative and not at all as boring as it sounded. It was alive and fascinating to me. Since my end-run goals were to join the Army, become an MP, and then become a cop in the civilian world.

This police book was meant to prep me for my time ahead in ... the next uniform. *Then Came Bronson* enlisted! Biker Bronson became a patrol officer. Biker Bronson became Dick Tracy. Sounded like a plan to me.

Somehow I finished both books in spare moments, on breaks, and during the rare downtimes of Basic. There was little free time. Sleep became a desperate commodity for me and others at Fort Polk. Toward the end, when there was some free time on Sundays? I slept.

They were tough on us back then. I was punched, pushed, slapped, shoved, and even kicked in the head once by drill instructors. I expected it. I wanted it. Hell, I was in the United States Army. It was the Vietnam-era training. Reading a few pages from those books was my reward in a very sparse and Spartan world.

I eventually lost both books. Years later I bought a used hardcover of SOLDIER! that I found in a used bookstore. It sits in my personal library now. My friend, David Hackworth, once the most decorated troop in the Army, told me once that he knew Herbert and knew he was a top-notch officer. The COP (or COPS) book remains unreplaced. If I could find it again, I would buy it, too, though Boston has had some 60 more years to evolve. It helped me grasp the big picture of how a big police department worked better than those dry police management courses I took in college. Together, those books helped shape my career for the next several decades. So, here's to you, Col. Herbert, and the Boston PD. I thank you, sirs.

So without further ado and rehashed details of the typical, old school basic training, let me tell you instead of a criminal tale or two in Army Basic Training.

Sergeant Bilking. Bilking. Did the word come from Sgt. Bilko? Or did they make a conman from the word bilking? "Bilking" was the colloquialism. I recall years later in the 2000s, I'd been following a criminal case in the U.S. Army about two drill instructors at Fort Sill, Oklahoma. It seemed that two DIs were illegally selling tobacco, soda, DVDs, CDs, and so forth to basic training recruits. On their shopping list also was "PT insurance;" that was, for a fee the DIs would guarantee the recruit passed the physical training final exam at the end of boot camp. One recruit paid $150 for his insurance. The charges included a threat of death if any of the recruits disclosed the operation.

This made me think back to Fort Polk those and other scams perpetrated in basic training through time. It made me think of my basic training and a certain Sgt. Bedock. He was a former state trooper who, rumor had it, was fired for a crime at his police agency and rejoined the Army. He was on the staff at Fort Polk, Louisiana.

At the time, I was a year or two older than most of the recruits and I that was why I was declared a platoon leader and then senior platoon leader. (That would be a peon in charge of other peons to make a DI's life even easier on the shitty mundane daily peon tasks done.) This guy Bedock was one of our main drill sergeants.

One day at an obstacle course, another DI from another company I'd seen around and who had no official contact with our unit, sort of wandered up to me and asked, "Is that Bedock over there?" as he pointed at him.

"Yes Drill Sergeant.

"Listen," he said in a whisper, "whatever you do, don't collect any money for him. Okay?" Then he wandered away. I thought that very strange.

A week later it made sense. The last week of basic training, Bedock called me into our company headquarters and said, "The night after graduation and before you all ship out the next morning, let's have a party. You go around and collect $5 or $10 from every soldier. Then give it to me, and I'll buy pizzas and beer."

Hmmm. That would be hundreds and hundreds of dollars. I was haunted by the collection warning and warned the other peon platoon leaders throughout the company with what I knew. I told them we would not collect money. If asked about it by Sgt. Bedock, just put the quest on me. Over the next few days, Bedock pushed me hard for the party money. I had become the number one trainee of the battalion of 1,100 men. He told me I didn't deserve it, and he wanted some other soldier to win. Then he would push for the money as though I should suddenly try to please him and get in his good graces. I told him I couldn't get the guys motivated to contribute. He grew angrier and angrier each time he asked. Then he finally gave up.

The last night, after graduation, at Polk was very relaxed, but we had a few small problems like theft and a fight or two. Bedock? He was not to be found! I asked Sgt. Macaskill where Bedock was, and Macaskill told me that Bedock had left on leave for a vacation. I think he left without about $500 extra spending money for his vacation. The snake, the son of a bitch. Who, on their last night in Fort Hell with tickets to leave out the next morning, would stop and complain about their $5 or $10 contribution for beer and pizza that didn't happen?

I, too, had never told anyone that because I seriously wanted the hell out of there the next morning myself. And ... with Vietnam flaring up and down at the time, I was afraid I might wake up one morning in a Southeast Asia foxhole and discover one Sgt. Bedock was my new NCO. Stuff like that happens in this man's Army. So there now, you see how these smaller extortions work so well?

Tigerland was the name of a U.S. Army training camp during the mid-1960s to early 1970s, located at Fort Polk, Louisiana as part of the U.S. Army Advanced Infantry Training Center.

These were the Fort Polk barracks.

Chapter 9: What to Wear? When?

This is an important lesson in life! We were about 4 or 5 weeks deep into US Army Basic Training, back in Ft Polk, LA in the early 1970s. "Little Vietnam" as they called it, and the drill sergeants, were starting to back off a bit from their constant, 24/7 abuse. We were in a formation in our company area, which was right across the street from a small PX, a laundry and a few things, like an old-fashioned, crappy, strip center. Restricted, we wouldn't dare go over there or leave the company area when on or off-duty.

The Drill Sergeant asked, "Any questions?" right before dismissing us one afternoon.

I raised my hand and asked, "When will we be old enough to cross the street?" And *everyone* laughed at my sarcastic ass, even the Drill Sergeant!

"We'll see," and he dismissed us.

My joke worked because within a few hours, the word was passed that we could indeed cross the street! Well! We did. The little store was worthless, but you could get a beer there, and a pretty piss-poor little pizza and a bag of chips. I and apparently quite a few others decided that we would deposit several sets of Army fatigues over there at the laundry and get them starched! Yeah! Be all looking like the "strack" (perfect) cadre walking around. Yessir! Be looking mighty fine for all those damn morning inspections too.

Within two days we got them back from the laundry.

Cost almost nothing. The following morning, we wore them, breaking that heavy, cardboard starch that only those of us in the "green machines your granddaddy called the service" would understand. Driving your foot through the cardboard leg of poster-board pants. OO-ahh. Draft dodgers have no idea what I am yakking about here.

And there we stood in morning formation. Hundreds of us in total, but only about 40 of us were starched up. Suddenly the drill sergeants, once friendly, but NEVER to be trusted, started walking the lines and picking some of us out!

"YOU!"
"YOU!"
"YOU!"

They started pulling troops from the lines! One even came by me, gave me a dirty sneer and called me a "YOU!" and he pulled me out too! What the…?

They put us in several, new lines away from the others. I took a good look around and we were all the guys who had our uniforms starched. That was the only common denominator I could spot. Maybe we were going to get a prize, you know? They marched us over to several of our nearby barracks. Now, these were old wooden barracks and being in the near swamp levels of Louisiana, the buildings were held up a couple of feet off the ground by support beams. And being swampy, the underneath's of which were also shady, wet, muddy and yucky. The "Hounds of the Baskerville Moors" of Polk quicksand!

They lined us up by these buildings, and then they ordered us face down on the ground, then they ordered us to low crawl up to…and then under those barracks, plum out the other side. All to the delight of the other soldiers watching with glee. WELL! I did what I was told, fearing worse on the other end! Why me, Lord? There are hairy spiders and poisonous snakes down here! Leeches and shit! Hells bells, they got gators in the Louisiana bayou! Lumpy mud and who knows what-all!

They lined us up and back again we were so ordered! Then back yet again. Then, they lined us up and the Drill Sergeants took a good look at us. One sarge, the most articulate at yelling in melodious cuss words and clever phrases of ridicule made a speech as only he could. It was full of cussing and yelling and stomping about and well, it was got-dam, beautiful, it was, you know, in that negative sort of way. I can't recall it word-for-word, so I will summarize it for you all here.

In so many words he explained that you cannot love your uniform too much, can't worry about it being too clean or kempt. He explained that we constantly clean and polish and brush our uniforms because we were supposed to get them dirty. Every day. All the time. That was our job to get dirty and clean them. Get dirty and clean them. You didn't love your country if you weren't getting dirty defending it. We were in the Army, all equally worthless, and if you worry about your clothes getting messed up or dirty, even for a second, you might hesitate to duck, dive or fight, and that might get you killed!

Actual Fort Polk photos of our basic training barracks. We are decked out in Class A Uniforms. No mud-messing up these uniforms!

So, he explained, in order for us starchie-low-lifes to get a proper day's training in, we first needed to be roughed up, and made to forget about how purty we looked. Then we fell in beside the other troops for the day's other fun and games of mental and physical abuse.

And we starchie-low-lifes spent the whole day in caked mud. From there after? They didn't care if you showed up in starched fatigues, because you've been read this riot act. It must happen every Basic cycle, huh? The message must be conveyed.

After that, we could go starched-up, but just don't get caught worrying about ruining your "look." Just dive into the mud hole when they say "jump!" Clothes *do* make the fighting man.

Movie critics once mentioned that there was a distinct difference between the James Bonds. Said one critic, "Sean Connery, when all dressed up, looked like he couldn't wait to get dirty. Roger Moore, when all dressed up, looked like he couldn't stand to get dirty."

What a great analogy. If my old Drill Sergeant had heard that line, he no doubt would have yelled that in my muddy face.

"Whooo are you, boy? Sean Connery or Roger Moore?"

"Sean Connery, Drill Sergeant!"

"Whhhooo? I can't hear you! You prissy little, misbegotten, piece of human excrement from some raggedy, house-mouse whore!"

"SEAN CONN…" …you know the routine.

It was a lesson I never did forget. And it has merit. It is inspirational and gets your head on straight as you step out the door to go to work. But the lesson doesn't always fit the organization. Even in the military.

Soon after Basic Training, after the military police academy, I was pulling garrison, (standard police patrol as I explained earlier) military police duty and in the day time we had to wear Class A uniforms which was worse than a thick suit and tie. Pistol belt outside the jacket, riding up your torso like a strait jacket. Those clod-hopper boots. Are you roller skating in a buffalo herd? The bloused pants with the special rubber-band-thingy on your calf. And heaven forbid you were caught without your big white hat on, even when driving in 100 degree weather (we had no air conditioners in the squad cars).

The whole thing was very uncomfortable and very restrictive. And you and yours were less inclined to get those Class A's dirty too, least of all run and jump a fence in pursuit of an AWOL, etc. I could read that mindset around me. But in the nighttime? Ahhhh…we wore fatigues and a ball cap. You could move freely and be lighter. Lean. Mean. Agile. Hostile. You notice the psychological difference. In many bases now, the MPs wear fatigues, day and night, all seasons. Smarter.

Speaking of Bond movies, Rozin Abbas from *Creative Ideas* reminds us that James Bond of the Flemming books famously distrusted any man with a Windsor knot tie. For him, it was too symmetrical, showing vanity and selfishness.

I, for one, hate bow ties. You'll never catch me in one. A bow tie is sissified little city-slicker apparatus that is a signal to be mugged, unless you are a bodyguard for Louis Farrakhan - in which case you have other psychological problems to consider.

I also remember a great line from the "Towering Inferno." Fire chief Steve McQueen was about to enter said towering inferno and was suiting up in his fire garb, circa 1970s. A helper complained that NFL players had better survival uniforms for what they did, than fireman had. McQueen said,

"That's because people don't pay to watch us play."

They don't, and it is up to us to do the best we can. Comfort and practicality are pretty important in your survival wardrobe continuum. I am in awe at what police officers wear today. All the gear, atop the vest too, for the working patrol officer.

When I started out in the early 70s, we had almost nothing on our gun belts. In Texas we had a revolver and some bullet loops. If we had a radio it went in one back pocket and a sap went in the other. A pair of cuffs hooked over the belt in the back. Bullet proof vests were about $10,000 each back then and we had none unless the Local Elks Club raised a fund for one at a time.

In my last few years back in patrol before I retired, Admin kept handing me more and more gear for my gun belt, and I turned it down if I could, opting for a lighter version of me. Some of these guys and gals today look like they think they'll be dropped into Cambodia for about a week. Especially SWAT teams, who often look like they're ready for a spacewalk on a hostile planet. Modern soldiers suffer the same, or actually worse, because they are indeed dropped into the "Cambodias" of the world for a week or way more.

Shoes are also important. The lighter the better if you are going to run, chase and jump, etc. In a worst-case scenario, survival experts suggest you wear good running shoes even when flying, since most crashes occur on or near the ground and you might have to flee fast from the crash.

If I were a police or military commander, one of my major concerns would be outfitting my troops for their maximum comfort, performance, and safety. Sometimes, as with the military the choices are mighty slim. Slim as in limited. I have come to believe that generally, if you are in the action-guy, or action-gal business, you should wear loose and durable, yet soft clothes, with good light shoes on your job (unless you are akin to a knight in shining armor doing specific tactical ops). But first, always answer the below questions as a guideline. The who, what, where, when, how and why Survival Wardrobe Continuum official checklist:

* Who are you to wear these clothes? Are they really needed and appropriate? REALLY?
* What are you doing while you are wearing these clothes, your mission, big mission and small? What do you wear when training? Do you train/work-

out in clothes and gear that you will be fighting in?
* Where are you wearing these clothes? Desert? Jungle? Alps? Office? Court -Tennis or trial?
* When are you wearing these clothes? Winter? Spring? Daytime? Night?
* How will you wear them? Too tight? Too loose? How well can you move within your clothes? How much do you weigh and how healthy are you anyway? Clothes "do make the man or lady?"

And one shouldn't care if one gets these clothes damaged or dirty, or my drill sergeant will come and getcha, and I swear...it won't be purty. No sir! Not purty at all! Go as light and fast as common sense allows.

A classic military police "guard mount" the gathering-inspection before old-school day shift patrol. Class A's. Evening and midnights in fatigues.

Epilogue to Basic Military Training and the Military Police Academy...

There was an adage in the military service, a story where a son asked his military dad if he, the dad, was a hero. The father replied, "No, son, but I served in the company of heroes."

Thinking back, I had served with heroes, especially in the early 1970s where so many people around me were both Korean War and Vietnam War vets. In my subsequent police work? Well, not so many heroes, I think. Not like those military war vets. I know that some nice folks would say, "Any cop is a hero. Any soldier is a hero."

But you know, I wasn't. No we all weren't.

Real heroes never admit they were heroes. That was-is part of being a real hero. Wasn't it? Isn't it? The real "Aw, shucks!" It was like a Zen riddle, huh? But I really liked that "company of heroes" observation.

Anyway, I did graduated my Basic Training class with the award of being number one out of the 1,100 men in our battalion. I did what everyone else did and somehow got that award. I never once came in "Number one" in an any category, just consistently high in all.

Biker Bronson Hock was a soldier. Then I was off to the military police academy...

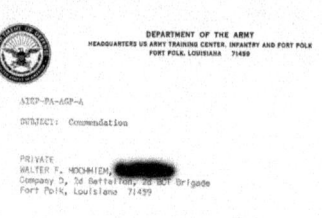

"The Rookie" TV show. Season 1 he was a rookie. Now into season 7 in 2024, he shouldn't be a rookie anymore?

Chapter 10: The First Days

Have you ever heard the true story about the rookie policeman (no, not me) who, on his first day, discovered his family followed him in their car to drive around and "watch him work?" How about the one where a training officer flipped the squad car keys to the rookie on his first day, and when slamming the car door behind him, the rookie caught and broke his thumb in the door? Off to the emergency room, NFG! Day One! Then there was the first-day rookie who shot the mirror in the men's room practicing his quick draw. (NFG. You know what that means? New Fucking Guy. Or at least it did many moons ago.)

Or, how about the very first night one of my friends started work in my old police department? Kind of a country boy from up north Texas way, he was hired into our bigger city, a place big, strange, and new to him. On his first night, he climbed into the passenger side of the squad car of an unfriendly, non-talkative, older, cranky, training officer. My friend was scared to death of him. His very job hinged on the eventual opinion and evaluation of this grunting, impatient, training officer. In the first 20 silent minutes, this vet spotted a drunk driver while trolling in our version of the unfriendly "projects."

The traffic stop was fast and furious as one might expect in the late 1960s, and the driver was quickly cuffed. Towing the suspect's car into the city pound was a time-consuming hassle. You, a partner, or another squad had to wait and meet the tow truck at the scene and then follow the wrecker to the pound. Then you had to unlock the pound and drop the car off. Then you had to deliver the car keys to the police station and fill out ... more paperwork about the car. Back in the 1960s and 1970s, we would often just drive the suspect's car ourselves right into the police department parking lot! That would save the drunk (or any suspect) some towing and pound fees, and we would use that as a bargaining chip to get suspects to cooperate with us. Talk, smile, and save impound fees! Of course, that whole policy has changed now. (I wouldn't be surprised if the cities today don't tune up and fix the cars they impounded. Like fixing inmate's teeth. Don't laugh; it is probably coming soon. Maybe in Berkley, California, first? It'll start with fixing the exhaust to "save the air." Next, increase fuel efficiency. Before you know it, a burglar will bond out and have a great getaway car waiting!)

Well, this cranky veteran officer was loading up his DWI suspect; and he decided that he was going to drive the suspect's vehicle and the suspect back to the station to save time. My rookie friend stood nearby, and the old vet suddenly tossed him the squad car keys with a command, "Here kid, follow us in."

Then the vet jumped in the drunk's car and drove off. Disappeared would be a better word. My rookie friend dashed to the squad car. His first assignment! Drive the police car to the station. He stuck the keys in the ignition, looked up ... and, and realized ... he was lost. He knew nothing of this new big city and couldn't even begin to find the police station. The training officer was gone.

So dressed in his uniform and driving a police car, he trolled the projects stopping and asking what few nightlifers he could spot, "Hey, can you tell me how to get to the police station?"

"Fuck you, smart-ass mother-fucker," was the high-percentage reply.

Eventually an old wino took pity on him and pointed him in the right direction. The old officer was so busy booking the drunk in jail that he barely noticed the long delay of his new young partner.

Those first days. They were tough. All eyes were upon you, both the eyeballs of the police officers and the usual glares and glances from the citizens. I remembered my first day back in 1973 in Oklahoma. There I was, all adorned in the day shift Class A Military Police uniform of white hat (worn absolutely all of the time), silver medals, training awards, a whistle on a chain, a shoulder-to-pistol lanyard, and a jet black night stick (all chips will be repaired with shoe polish!) In glistening boots, brass buttons, and a heavy pistol belt laden with an "antique" flap holster, handcuffs, and magazine case, I was given my very first police assignment. After six months of combat and police training, I was to place my stoic presence at an intersection and guide third-graders across a two-lane residential street at a school crossing. You see, the regular crossing guard was sick. Thrilling, wasn't it? Ohhh, but that was not all!

In a field nearby, two third-graders began fighting. In a flurry of school books and bags and little girls' impassioned pleas for help, it was here I began by first official police action. Feeling like a gawky idiot clutching my bouncing radio and pistol, I clamored and clanged my way to this miniature rumble; and with ropes and chains dangling and hooking little hands and feet, I managed to separate the ruffians. The fight had started over some horrible remark passed at recess. The boys went home, and I returned to my important post.

But those years in the military police were a roller coaster ride of experiences. So when I showed up as a rookie in Texas, I arrived with well-rounded experiences. But my first day, or should I say night, on the Texas police force wasn't without embarrassment. All eyes and preconceived opinions were once again on me. To make matters worse, I had been issued second-hand uniforms previously used by an officer who had obviously quit the department to join a circus freak show. The waist was too tight, the crotch was too low, and the legs were too long. With the promise of new ordered pants on the way, I reported for night shift duty taking short steps and bending down only long enough to pull my pants up from under my boot heels.

Just a few hours into my first shift, Sgt. Eric Jackson and I were assisting an injured person into Flow Hospital's Emergency Room when a wide back-porch step did me in. The stretch ripped the crotch of my pants from stem to stern. The band-aid the nurse offered me was not quite what the doctor ordered that time. I waddled back to the squad car clutching my crotch in a handful of material; and, I might add, all that was well before Michael Jackson and other crotch-clutching rappers were born. Ushered to the station for some delicate safety pin work, I was wisely assigned to the front desk and radio for the remainder of the first tour of duty, though sitting was somewhat uncomfortable on all those tension-loaded, pointy metals.

The very next night in the same week, in the same repaired and altered uniform, I arrested a murderer at the scene of his crime trying to remove the body! The "first-day blues" disappeared into the serious work I craved. Sometimes I loved it, and sometimes I hated it, but mostly loved it, but when you pinned that badge on the first day, you'd never be the same again.

Chapter 11: The First Time
I Was Officially Shot At

"Military police supervise or provide support to the battle field by conducting maneuver and mobility support (MMS), area security, internment resettlement operations, police intelligence operations, prisoner of war operations, civilian internee operations, law and order operations on the battlefield and support to the peacetime Army community through security of critical Army resources, crime prevention programs and preservation of law and order."

A few chapters back, I wrote about the crazy-weird first time I was shot at. For fun! And now I want to write about the first time I was shot at … officially, as in during work.

After graduating the U.S. Army Military Police Academy, I was labeled and stamped the old 95 Bravo MOS (nowadays called 31B) and shipped off to Oklahoma and into what they still call "Garrison Duty." There were two kinds of military police duty back then, Garrison Duty and Field Duty. Field duty was when you were attached to police units that were out in the field or you would follow those units around when they were in the field. Today, some call them Combat Military Police. Field Duty often included guard duties or what some now call Force Protection. Field Duty and Force Protection didn't interest me at all. I wanted Garrison Duty police work where I would be on a regular police force like working in any city. That was the difference between Garrison and Field Duties. What about military and civilian police work? Why let's ask Tom Cruise?

In the 2012 movie with a short Tom Cruise plays the famous, very tall Jack Reacher, and a city cop asks former military policeman/investigator Reacher this question, "So what is the difference between a city cop and a military cop?"

Reacher's (or Cruise's) answer went something like, "Oh the same, except every suspect ... is a trained killer."

Da-da-da-doooom. Yeah, right. That line was a real groaner. Especially for me, someone who had done both those jobs for real. Very dramatic. But, there are some similarities between the jobs (oh, like the boredom—which would not make for a cool line in a Cruise movie). Reacher's military police past was NOT like a Reacher book or movie or the very famous "NCIS" TV show.

Any decent-sized military base was just like any city. You name it: stores, malls, restaurants, schools, movie theaters, businesses, power plants, houses, apartments, and families. Then there were the military extras like barracks, ranges, tanks, and cannons.... Garrison duty was just like working at a police department in a medium- or large-sized city.

Upon my arrival, I started out in a patrol car with a training officer who was not much older than me, and about as dumb as I was. But this lasted a short time. Oh, maybe - like a week. This was not so uncommon in the

1970s. I very quickly found myself out on my own in a squad car patrolling a beat with all the aforementioned amenities. I was in a Class A pretty-boy uniform on day shift and OD fatigues on evenings and nights. I was officially "on the road." In fact, in the jargon of the day, a "road MP" meant you were a Garrison Duty cop working the streets (not deskbound). In the very beginning, that was all I wanted to be, just a road MP.

My patrol supervisor, a staff sergeant, was a cool guy in his late 40s, a Nam vet with a great attitude who we all knew was soon to cycle out for his next assignment overseas. One night we had a dangerous armed fugitive loose; and at the squad meeting, he really spoke frankly about taking the fugitive down without hesitation if we had to save our lives. Take no chances. I don't know, maybe because it was the very first time I had "that" speech for real. (And it was not a groaner!) But I vividly remember that night and his intensity. It was a quiet, intense speech I would hear again hundreds of times and make a few times myself. That speech. A speech that shaved off, that rasped off, a few layers of your "laid-back" and replaced it with a raw "get ready." That fugitive was eventually caught in Kansas.

Anyway, things like that made the Sarge A-okay with me and the troops. So when I heard him one night kind of lose his cool over the radio, I was really curious about why and what was going on? THAT speech!"

Late one night a common domestic disturbance call came over our car radios at a residence way out of my district. The Sarge intercepted the call and started issuing fervent commands over the airwaves. He sounded a bit rattled. It began to sound like a military assault rather than a two-officer domestic call. He even called me in.

"Car 11."

"Car 11, go ahead."

"Car 11, respond to the domestic. Park on the street. Remain outside until needed."

"Ten-four."

Okay. What's that all about? That was different, but then again it was all different for me - the rookie in his first month. I drove across the base and down the side street where a row of some 10 narrow, really old white houses were. They were all in a line like matchboxes, all on one side of the street with nothing across the street but a fenced-in, industrial-looking place. The street was dark. Depressing government housing to live in. Each house had a small front porch in the center of the house front. In my memory, there were at least four or five patrol cars parked on the sidewalk curb out front. A lot of cars. I was in about the fifth car there. I came from the farthest distance, so I pulled up last.

I parked and got out. All of the MPs present were still on the street side of their cars. The Sarge was shouting to a man. I could see a white male standing on the small front porch with his arms down at his sides. I was off to his left and at about 4 o'clock and a good maybe 40 feet away. I remember his visage on the porch, a bright white light right over his head. His face in stark white and black shadows. T-shirt and pants. Silent. No one approached him as yet?

I started to decipher what the Sarge was yelling when … that guy lifted his right arm up straight. There was a pistol in it! He started shooting at us. His arms swung the wide span of our cars as he fired away. I dropped down and fumbled open the flap holster of my .45. But it didn't take long; and for the first time in my law enforcement career, I drew out my pistol. With those explosions, I also dropped down behind my car. Everyone else did, too, that I could see. Nowhere in my training was it ever mentioned about using parts of a car as a shield against gunfire. The tires. The engine block. Ricochets, etcetera. But then again these were stout cars of yesteryear metal. Old 1970's AMC Matadors.

One of my vivid memories was the metallic sounds of the bullets smashing into our cars. Thumping also described it. My car! In split seconds he emptied his magazine just as I peeked over my car at him while getting up to take a shot. No one else had shot yet either! Why? Everyone else was so much closer than me. I could see he dropped his gun arm back down to his side; and the Sarge rushed him, gun out and yelling he would kill the man. Other MPs rushed him. The man stood still like a statue. By the time I got around my car and halfway to the house, the man was cuffed. He was yanked off the porch. Another MP held the suspect's pistol in his hand.

Then a woman and three small kids barged out of the door. The woman cried and embraced the Sarge. The kids were crying. My friend who had parked right in front of the house said the kids were crying in the front room while the man stood on the porch. And the wife was at the door inside until he started shooting!

In a quick sit-rep, no car windows were blown out. Not every car was hit. None of us were shot. Any other rounds the man fired must have landed in the industrial place across the street. Nobody died. It was another good day.

It was apparent the Sarge was very familiar with the "situation" at the house. Another MP told me they'd been dispatched there several times in the last few months; and this showdown was really brewing, which was why the Sarge reacted to the call as he did. The man was arrested by the district officer who cuffed him, and I returned to my district. Not even a witness statement was needed. Just one report by the arresting officer covered the whole story.

At the end of the tour, we turned our car keys over to the next shift with a new story. "You see that hole?" At the station, the Sarge collected our final reports from the night and thanked those of us who were at the shooting for responding "so well" to this domestic incident. He thanked us for not shooting at the suspect right away. He told us that the old wooden house had been full of people, the kids and the mom; and if we had all lit up the man and the house with .45 ammo, we could have hit the family inside. And the fact that he took a little time to "debrief us" was another lesson in professionalism for me. He even patted me on the back as we all split up to leave.

Pat on the back? Hell, I was 40 feet away, and the whole thing was over in about three seconds. I hadn't done anything at all. But it was still a moment I would never forget. Multiple first impressions, really. The way the Sarge deployed us. And his forethought in worrying about the family inside the thin wooden walls of the house. I mean, I never thought about such a thing. Oh, well, they barked the four basic gun safety rules at us, the 3rd Law being, "Always be sure of your target and what is behind it!"

Suddenly that rule had real, physical teeth. Flesh. Real meaning. Oh! Is THAT what it meant? The Sarge knew the wife and kids were right there behind the target. And who thought about the "suicide by cop" syndrome back in the 1970s?

So in the first month on the job, I'd pulled my gun to shoot someone; and I was shot at. Was that the life I had chosen? The career? The expectations? The reality? Yes and no, but I reckoned so.

No real regrets, except that I did regret that I could not remember the Sarge's name. I didn't know back then that such remembrances were important later in life, if only for yourself. Within a few weeks, he was whisked off to his next assignment. He was a cool guy all right. And the next guy was okay, too, but I don't remember his name either.

But wait, that story wasn't over yet; and I had learned the BIGGEST lesson....

Payday was a big day at a military base, and back then it was all paychecks and cash and carry. The banks went wild with walk-in and drive-thru business. Being the rookie, the lowest of low on the totem pole, I was assigned to direct traffic at one of the banks. I was stoically positioned up on a painted podium in the middle of four lanes of traffic, Class As WITH white gloves, white hat, and the mighty whistle, working the cars in and out and to and fro. I knew little of this process, too, but it was not brain surgery; and I picked it up quickly. TWEET! Oh, and I did hate it, too.

There were many people and cars crisscrossing everywhere around me. I saw a staff sergeant in his Class As with a big smile leave the bank and walk across the street right by me. WHAT? It was the guy who shot at us. That was the guy! Right there! He didn't recognize me or even look at me. I have to admit I was shocked. How could a guy shoot at MPs and then three or four weeks later be bouncing around the post, smiling, and as free as a bird? That was another big first lesson for me.

The criminal justice system, whether military or civilian, was a strange, dysfunctional, and bizarre place full of imperfect and often incompetent people. Yes. I was now one of them. And the view from atop my little painted podium that day and for the rest of my life ... was not always a pleasant one.

Chapter 12: Seven Men Down

How many handcuffs should you carry? Usually you are first issued but one shiny pair; and, in a pinch, you can hook up two bad guys with one pair. In the olden days, it was up to you to obtain a second or more pairs of cuffs. And sometimes when suspects are so broad (muscular or fat) and you can't get their hands together close enough to handcuff them, you can use your second pair as a link between the two pair. Two on one. But you quickly learn that one or even two pairs of cuffs are often not enough.

Today you can load up on the light, small, plastic thin strips called "flex-cuffs" or "plastic cuffs." You can buy a hundred of them in a bag and shove them under your front seat. But way back when, when I started, we didn't know about how common phone and electric wire cable ties could be used this way. I got wind of this idea back in the late 1970s and would get batches from phone company repairmen. Before then, we did what we could with what we had, and at times we could count on backup officers showing up with more metal cuffs. Old or new times, though, the bigger question looms-how many people can you arrest by yourself?

How about old Sgt. York? In WW I, York captured a German officer at gunpoint and ordered the Germans still fighting to surrender. York and just a few others ended up arresting 132 prisoners of war and marching them back to headquarters. York became a national hero and was awarded the Medal of Honor. But if you watch the Gary Cooper movie as I did as a kid, it seems York did this great feat all alone! Alone! One hundred 30-two POWs. York did not have 132 pairs of handcuffs either.

Solo police arrest two suspects with some frequency or sometimes more suspects. Police survival stats say that about 40 percent of the time when fighting, officers deal with two or more suspects. Then three suspects about 30 percent of the time. Then four? Five? On down the line. None are good odds when you are the lone ranger. How about the unlucky number seven? That is my highest single arrest number in one situation; and like Roger Maris and Bobby Bonds, that seven comes with an asterisk (and that asterisk is named Willie Morman).

I have been on raids and task forces through the years where we arrested quite a number of people at one time and place. But the most people I have ever arrested in one incident by myself were seven; and it happened in the first few months of my very first year of police work. It was a felony traffic stop of a car with seven armed robbers in a four-door sedan. It was back in the "big-boat" era of large cars from the 60s and 70s.

"There is no such thing as a routine traffic stop," they say. Traffic stops are risky and, like domestic disturbances, are responsible for many officer injuries and deaths. Back in the old days, a Seven-Step Traffic Violator Contact Program was very popular around the USA and was taught to most officers coast to coast. It was a system I was taught in the Military Police Academy and again later in the Texas Police Academy. It is still in use in many places today. The training manual reads:

Officers will follow the Seven-Step Violator Interview unless circumstances exist that make the use extraneous or non-applicable. The steps will be used in the following order:

1. Greeting and identification of the agency;
2. Statement of violation committed;
3. Identification of driver and check of conditions of violator and vehicle;
4. Statement of action to be taken;
5. Take action stated;
6. Explain what violator must do; and
7. Leave.

We once had an old Texas police chief named Wayne Autry, an ex-Texas Highway Patrolman from the 1960s, who, when faced with one of our officers screwing up in a traffic stop, would lecture us all with his baritone, gravel voice, "If these guys would only follow the Seven-Step Violator Contact steps, none of these problems would happen."

Spoken like a true highway patrolman. His voice was easily imitated by several mimics in our agency; and if you had a problem or received a citizen complaint on a traffic stop, you would likely hear several comic versions of this advice and ass chewing teasing you. And then eventually you would hear the serious riff from the man himself back in his brick office down the hall, all in the form of a scary counseling session.

So, the Seven-Step pointers were top on our list for the, let's not call it routine but rather, "common" traffic stop; and most times this procedure was true to the cause, unless of course the vehicle occupants were very suspicious and/or known to be involved in crimes. In such cases, other strategic steps were required. "Known" being the key word here. The typical problem was and still is that officers start the classic Seven-Step protocol, but with dangerous people they didn't know were dangerous! And then after about Step 3, the Seven Steps would turn into an infinite number of other, bad-step possibilities. That's polite society talk for the traffic stop would "go to hell."

In preparation for these various, go-to-hell "Car War's" moments, one such lengthy training session every cadet had to experience hands-on was the multiple-opponent felony traffic stop. In our Texas Police Academy, they even used blank firing guns in this training, which was my first exposure to such training. Be it the military police school or the Texas police school, while we were taught the Seven Steps we were also taught how to handle felony traffic stops versus one-on-up-to-multiple offenders. We were taught how to stop a felony vehicle and tactically remove all the occupants from the car and stretch them out on the road aided by our angry, impatient voices and pointed guns. While they always told you to wait for backup, it would depend on who you were, where you were, and what was happening. Sometimes you just couldn't wait for backup. This is not just a problem in Alaska. This can be a problem in the metro Omaha, Nebraska, area or just about any police beat at certain times.

In all those felony stop training sessions, there were only two or at worst maybe three bad guys in the suspect training cars. But in the real world, it is not uncommon to have four people in a car and maybe sometimes even five. But not seven! Not like the number I faced down one night. Still, these hands-on, back-lot training courses for both a common traffic stop and multiple-felon traffic stops were instrumental for me to stay alive on many a night and remain alive this aforementioned night when I, Mister

Hotshot Rookie, corralled the Unlucky 7.

Our traffic-stop and Car War's training would include various live-fire setups, which was my first introduction to shooting in, out, around, from, and at cars. This type of "advanced training" was in-service conducted at our assignment locations.

Today I use simulated ammo to have interactive gunfights in this type of setup, like in my Walmart Madness Scenario. Back then, we didn't have any substantial simulated ammo methods to shoot at each other. You are not really learning how to gunfight unless moving and thinking people are shooting back at you. The range is very limited.

But back to these seven arrests. It all started at about 2:30 p.m. on the evening shift. They called it "Guard Mount." And no, it's not the latest Brazilian Jujitsu move. It's an age-old military term that means "to go on duty as a guard or sentinel." Most platoons did not have a guard mount, but our new rule-happy 2nd Luey, a certain Lt. Crell, liked to push his power around; and he instituted the optional mount for our everyday lifestyle. We had to arrive early at the MP company barracks or in the police station parking lot for his little game session of lineup and questions. He made us amass in a line, the "Full Mounty" if you will, in an inspection formation. For us it wasn't just a mere roll-call head count; it was truly an inspection, followed minutes later by a sit-down regular patrol shift briefing.

Today these inspection/guard mounts still do exist and not just in the military, but also in some police agencies. Police work has always been declared as "quasi-military"; and some, not all, city, state, county, and federal agencies have them daily or with some regularity like once a month or on special events.

I've never been one for rules, or rulers for that matter, especially pain-in-the-ass ones; but in an effort to dodge fines and imprisonment problems, I can clean up pretty well. Buttons all brassy, shiny belt buckle, and shoes-a-shining each day. Before I rolled out of my POV (privately own vehicle) in the parking lot to attend guard mount, I'd spray my boots with a false, temporary "plastic" shine spray you could buy at the PX. Eventually this would crack into white lines like a drunken spider web. But it would get me through inspection.

On line while at the position of attention or maybe even parade rest until the lieutenant got right in front of you whereupon you would snap smartly to attention, Lt. Crell gave us each the evil eye and often asked a question about some kind of Army thing he thought we should know. It might be a question from a future sergeant's exam or the serial number of our .45 handgun. How many trucks were there on the base (that's a trick question)? How much wood could a woodchuck "chuck" if a woodchuck could chuck wood? We were supposed to know all by heart and verse. He had a little crony at his heel, usually a buck sergeant, to keep track of our "demerits"—a list of screw-ups in his little black notebook that he would someday use against you when you'd ask for a vacation day to visit your dying mother or to justify your mediocre evaluations. (Actually, I liked Crell. He was a pretty good guy all-in-all, and you have to understand some of these officers often have absolutely nothing else to do with themselves but bust balls. And I was a soldier in the United States Army! And I retain my God-given rights to bitch and moan about the service in general! It is just what we do.)

Crell was always obsessed about the length of the corners of my moustache. If I grimaced a bit at this point, I could maintain a slightly longer "stache." But he would always look at my boots and say, "Hochheim, I know what you are doing with your boots and that cheap spray. It looks good for five minutes, and then you pay the price to clean it all off later. You are not fooling anyone but yourself."

"Yes, sir," I would reply. Keep it simple, or the banter would continue.

But we all knew that no matter how hard it got, Crell couldn't jack around with us for too long because we had to beat feet over to the squad room and get that briefing started so we could relieve the other shift, that day-shift lieutenant, and deploy on time. So the dentist always had a short drill. You cannot delay the out-going, older lieutenant with shenanigans from the incoming younger lieutenant.

This Saturday afternoon there was a bit more primadonna and showboat ball-busting in play because among us in the line were several visiting, U.S. Army Military Police Reserves. They were fulfilling their weekend warrior duty. Lt. Crell played Patton on them a little extra, freeing us regulars from his normal scrutiny. After railing on the poor Reserves, Crell dismissed us; and we got inside the PD and downstairs for our squad meeting. The patrol sergeant was already there at the podium and waiting. We started right up with his news: "Since 1100 hours this morning, there's been a series of armed robberies. The victims have all been married couples up in the parks, lakes, and rec centers of the north side. The couples were all officers and their spouses. They were all roughed up or beaten. Two of the suspects brandished knives. The suspects are five or more black males, short hair, in civvies, but probably military."

The suspect vehicle was a 1960's four-door Ford Galaxy. They even had a partial plate, but no state was known. (This was a prehistoric age in policing. Researching partial license plates was done by a hand search of handwritten paper files in many places.) Our base had way more people and cars than a large American city, and researching license plates like this was a major undertaking. Our one National Crime Information Center's (NCIC) so-called "computer-machine" back then was a huge metallic device about the size of a giant church organ in a Flash Gordon movie. It was like a primitive ticker tape and unable to play the modern search games for people and license plates. The Sarge reported other daily business and then issued our patrol district assignments. He also had to assign the weekend Reservists to officers.

"Pvt. Willie Morman? You ride with Hock." Willie looked the room over for me and I flashed a pointy finger up to let him find me.

Then we all disbursed ... dismounted ... infiltrated, whatever ... we left and stood in the police station parking lot as the day-shift officers drove in. We took over their squad cars and traded smack talk or anything we needed to know. Each shift you needed to check the car for dings and dents and check the shotgun, which I did with such extra care under the curious and thirsty eyes of Willie Morman.

Morman and I climbed into our car, and he immediately started calling me "Specialist," which I immediately nixed.

"Hey man, just Hock."

Within the first 20 minutes on patrol, I got the full intel dump on the life and times of Willie Morman. Twenty-four years old. High school grad. He was a shoe salesman from Ft. Worth, Texas. Married with two kids, he joined the Army Reserves for all the good intentions and the college benefits. He had graduated the Ft. McClellan military police school, which frankly had already become a joke to us when compared to the older hard-core

Fort Gordon police school I attended. Of course, every vet cop, soldier, and ice cream salesman has this "older-was-better" attitude. But Ft. McClellan was like an experimental school "campus" with a lot of new ideas like dorms and mostly video-style or TV instruction. That's right! You watched TV for your lessons. In fact, the McClellan approach was eventually dropped. Today, the MPs attend Ft. Leonard Wood, Missouri, a beautiful and professional facility. A showcase of modern police training. And, yes ... probably some of those guys are watching computer screens for some of their lessons.

Morman was quick to warn me that he had seen no action in his short weekend reserve stints, which often consisted of classroom training, coffee, doughnuts, and volleyball for PT. He was nervous and had a nervous giggle. I confessed that I, too, was fairly new at all this and had only seen some "police action" here and there. I reminded him that our base was no national crime capital, which seemed to calm his nerves. But I just couldn't stop thinking about catching that Ford Galaxy crime wave full of armed robbers.

The southwest corner of our patrol district had thousands of soldiers housed in it, and I drove to its massive parking lots trying to spot the car and partial plates while Morman talked and giggled. I looked at parked car after car after car. But late that afternoon, unknown to me, the Galaxy crime wave was actually still busy up north roughing up and robbing one more couple.

We stopped at several of the artillery-unit mess halls, all giant operations, for some coffee. As long as we brought our own cups with us and went through their back doors, the mess sergeants didn't care if we MPs passed through and raided their back-kitchen coffee urns. I became a black coffee drinker in those days, forgoing the civilized luxuries of sugar and milk or cream just to get something hot to drink and stay warm and awake. In the 70s, a "Latte" was the name of a topless dancer. Willie Morman didn't have a cup; so we got a thick paper one at a coffee vending machine, the kind with the poker hands printed on it so he could keep reusing it through the shift until it turned into mush.

We had a few forgettable calls, but my mind was still preoccupied on the Ford Galaxy of robbers. Night fell. A chill blew in from the flat west lands. I circled the southwest parking lots on my high-percentage bet that these units were the possible places such a group might come from.

About 9:30 p.m., I turned down the far west road of the area bordering the parking lots. Those roads were quite wide as they sometimes handled tank traffic. (Did I tell you one of the "parking" lots had about 50 tanks in it? Hell, it was the military! You had to park those babies somewhere.) In the distance I saw some headlights of a single car approaching. I U-turned so that it would pass us and be in our same direction of travel.

The car approached in my rearview mirror. Big. Wide. Dark. Closer. A Galaxy! It was crammed full of silhouettes. It slowly passed us on the left. The license plate matched the partial plate we had. I got behind them.

"That's them!" I warned Willie Morman. He was about to become my asterisk.

I picked up the radio and reported in telling the dispatcher I was following the suspect vehicle. She ordered several units my way, but they were afar. Did I mention that our base covered 93,000 acres? Most of that turf was wide-open country, ranges, and reserves with unmanned open gates, too. We were driving south on a road that would soon lead to this open wildness and remote gates on the west side. I envisioned a chase and even an escape out one of those far west gates. It had happened before.

Or a game of hide-and-seek down dirt roads and hills? Couldn't wait around for that.

"We're gonna stop them here," I warned the excited Willie. No time to explain why. I threw the switch for the red lights. "Put a bullet in the chamber." (You see, we could not carry our .45s "cocked and locked," that is, with a bullet in the chamber. Doing so was a hanging offense.) Willie took out his pistol and gingerly racked the slide.

"This is a guns-out deal all the way, podnah," I told him because, you know, I'm not sure he understood what was happening.

The car stopped. I stopped. There we sat stopped. We knew. They knew. They knew we knew. And so on.

I opened my car door and pulled and racked the round in my pistol. Willie mimicked me and opened his side door. I put a left foot on the street. He put a right foot on the street. I twisted the mounted spotlight so as to beam into their car and bounce on their mirrors. There were a lot of people in the car. A lot. With the mike in my left hand, I told the dispatcher where we stopped. The full license plate. How many folks I guessed were in the car. I hung that mike up and got the loudspeaker mike unhooked from another small box under the dash. I turned that on.

"Driver!" I ordered over the speaker. "Turn off your car!"

Nothing.

"Turn it off!" My mike boomed from a speaker atop the car roof.

Then the big rumbling engine stopped. Silence. The last bit of smoke left the exhaust with the night wind.

"Roll down your windows. Everyone in the car! Roll down your windows!"

Nothing. But it was hard to see from where I was. I

stepped out stretching that coiled mike cord into a straight cable line. Willie got out, too. Two windows rolled down on my side.

"Driver! Throw your keys out the window. Now!"

The keys hit the street! I took a deep breath. The backup cars were still far way. We couldn't just sit there. I imaged four men with guns suddenly kicking open their doors and charging us while firing. A really worst-case scenario! Or, what if they all bolted off in different directions. Also unacceptable. What if he disconnected the starter key from the chain and threw all the other keys out the window?

"Stick your hands out the windows. I want to see hands AND arms!"

Nothing. And only the four door-bound people could stick their hands out anyway. I looked at Willie Morman. He was standing by the open door of our open car. His gun was half up and half down.

"Willie," I whispered. "Move up by our headlight up there and get a good two-handed grip."

He did, but I had no confidence in him. I was alone here. I could have had a manikin propped up over there.

"Stick your arms out now! Or this is gonna get REAL ugly!" If you've ever done this kind of thing or are even just reading this now, you know this kind of showdown smack talk is much like a giant bluff. But the bluff often works. Eight hands and forearms thrust out the four windows!

"Any of you all have guns or knives throw them out now! Now is the time. Throw them out now because I will kill you later if you don't." Nothing. Oh, well. Nice try with that.

"Driver, step out of the car! Get out and put your hands up behind your head."

He did! He was a tall, thin black male. Young. In

his twenties.

"Don't look at me! Face the other way and walk backward to me."

He did.

"Stop! Get down on your knees. Keep your hands on your head. If you fuck this up, I will kill you. Anyone else gets out of the car unless I tell them to, I will shoot them down." Another bluff.

I left the squad car's side. Willie did, too. Ordinarily, one partner would cuff as the other did the "voice-over" and the backup pistol-aiming routine; but one look at Willie, and I thought better of this scheme. Willie was standing with his pistol in a two-handed grip all right, but his pistol was actually shaking; and his face looked like he'd seen two Godzillas having rough sex.

I knew I was a lone ranger on this. If Willie would just stand there with his gun up, he might help scare them into our handcuffs. Handcuffs! Oh, yeah! Handcuffs! I suddenly needed a lot more handcuffs.

"Willie, toss me your cuffs," I whispered.

Willie pulled his cuffs from his Sam Brown and flipped them over the hood.

"Any more?" I asked as I caught them and draped them over my belt. He shook his head no.

I backed up, opened the back door, opened my suitcase on the back seat, and got my other set of cuffs. Just great! I got about a hundred guys in that car up there and three sets of cuffs. Great! I still envisioned everyone bailing out of the car at once for who knows what? Shooting! Mass escape? Mass attack?

With my pistol aimed into their back car window, I walked up to the kneeling man; and I cuffed the right hand of the kneeling driver, swung his arm down, and cuffed the left hand and pushed him down on his chest. I barely touched around the small of his back where his hands now were for any weapons. Well, this whole thing was wheels-off anyway. I backed up a bit.

"Here's the deal," I shouted. "This ain't no traffic stop for speeding. We know you sons-a-bitches have been robbing people all over the post all day long. You are all under arrest for armed robbery. I am going to bring you out of the car and spread you out on the street one at a time. I will shoot and kill any one of you who fucks this up."

Not exactly the Seven-Step Violator protocol speech. Technically you shouldn't curse, and you should never talk about killing. But remember this was also the 70s. My voice was angry, and frankly I was pissed at all of them and myself for being put in this awkward position. But you know what? Barney-Fife timid doesn't exactly elicit control over a pack of felons. Crazy and angry does, and I was a little bit of both. They call it "command presence" in the badge business.

I brought out the driver's-side back-seat man ordering the door shut behind him and the next inside man's arms stuck out the window. Walked him back. Hands on head. I ordered him to his knees. I put my second pair of handcuffs on his wrists. Touched around that small of the back for obvious weapons. Then he went down on his chest.

Then the next guy from the front seat. Must have been in the middle? Same process. Last set of cuffs. Where are those backup vehicles? I decided I just couldn't leave those dark figures in that car. They could have any number of weapons just sitting in there waiting and making up plans. They had to all come out where I could see them. Cuffs or no cuffs. Spread-eagle.

I ordered the passenger-side guys out one at a time. Hands on their heads and walking backward, they passed in front of Willie and in between the back of their car and the front of ours. Willie was still doing a good job as a statue holding up a gun. I ordered each one facedown, legs spread, arms spread, and palms up. I now had three cuffed guys on the street and two more guys un-cuffed prone on the street. And wait ... there were still people in this car? How? This was like the old college telephone booth crammed with people.

"I will shoot off the first fucking thing that moves!" I told the guys on the ground with a growl. "Finger? Foot? Knee cap? Twitch? Don't matter. I will shoot it off." I couldn't and wouldn't, but what did they know?

And I heard distant sirens! Help was closing in on us.

"You, in the car! Stick your hands out the driver's-side windows! Now!" I shouted.

Hands appeared from both the front window and the rear window. Jeez. Seven people! I ordered the front-seat guy out of the car. Hands up! Face away! Walk backward! Stop! Lie down. And then finally the seventh stepped through the routine. Now all we had to do was wait.

Our patrol sergeant finally screeched up in his car and bailed out with a shotgun. Apparently, the Sarge threw me his only pair of handcuffs. Now that's four cuffed. Three still not cuffed with their arms spread wide and palms up. But the Sarge with a shotgun walked their perimeter and enforced their stillness and surrender. I was damn glad to have him there. Willie Morman still stood by my right front quarter panel.

Then the next squad car came. This one with two men. I asked them to cuff the rest, and they had enough cuffs. Then another MP car rolled up. We started searching the suspects. No weapons on any of them!

Then a CID sedan showed up. Two agents. And they looked relieved. They were the investigators working all day interviewing victims and witnesses and doing a little searching for the suspects, too. Our arrests enabled them to close out a very ugly, high-pressure affair before the Monday morning bigwigs came in. One of them nodded at me as he passed. They started flashlighting the interior of the car as we lifted suspects up off the asphalt. Willie Morman spoke right up to the agents.

"They threw something out over there." Willie's flashlight beam guided them to the spot. That was news to me. The agents found one switchblade knife and a plastic bag of drugs in the roadside grass. Good eye there, Willie!

The agents ordered a tow truck to seize the Galaxy. I recall that once the car was impounded, the agents found more stashed knives and more drugs. The patrol sergeant arranged for all of the prisoners to be transported to the station. We only had a small holding cell at the station, but there was a minimum-security prison on base where bulk arrests such as these were detained. Those details were above my meager pay grade. And CID had to interrogate all of them anyway. My work here was done, well, except for the paperwork.

And that was the single largest group I corralled for arrest. Yes, Willie Morman was there. The asterisk. But I felt very much alone until the others showed up. The next day I drove to a downtown Army Surplus store and bought eight more pairs of handcuffs and tossed them in my cheap, imitation-leather work briefcase. Ten pairs of cuffs sounded like a whole lot when they only issued you one pair! The old school rule was "One is none. Two are one." I guess "Ten or more were SNAFU."

Within a few years, the word spread that common telephone company plastic wire "gatherers" made for great field handcuffs. We could even wrap several strands inside our hat brims. You just needed scissors in the jail to cut them off.

Soon police supply companies made more expensive, "tactical" ones for sale. Next, some were made in "staged," double-looped positions ready to apply and pull tight on the wrists. A small industry developed from simple plastic wire ties.

The common traffic stop and the Seven-Step Violator program can go straight to hell and fast. It helps to know trouble from the get-go, such as with this case to know that your vehicle has bad guys in it.

My next biggest "catch?" Well, there have been a couple of sixes; but one set of six will always stand out. Years later, a Texas Highway Patrolman and I arrested six armed robbers of a clothing store. I got the robbery-in-progress call, and I chased these jokers north from the scene; and this lone Texas State Trooper stationed up north stood in the middle of the interstate highway waiting for them and me to show up. And I mean right on the white lines between the Interstate lanes with his shotgun up ready to shoot the windshield and kill all of the bad guys inside. The Trooper would indeed shoot, and the bad guys knew they would die. Simple gun math.

So they stopped stone-still right there on the highway just a few feet in front of him from my angle. (I was moving off to the side when I spotted that scatter gun.). I thought they would run him down! But they didn't! Whew-boy! What a sight. Then he and I got them all out of the car and cuffed them. The Oklahoma Troopers were no doubt lining up on the border salivating with their Tommy Guns at the ready. In those days if you were chasing a felon and approaching the border and heard the OHP was setup? Best lie back a bit when you drew close or else be hit by some random .45 rounds. But that's another story or two for another time.

After that evening shift, I never saw Willie again; but he now had him a real-deal police story to tell. Beats the hell out of volleyball for PT. Everybody working from CID, MPI, and patrol eventually showed up on the scene that night. Everyone but 2nd Lt. Crell, who was probably real busy back at his office making up tomorrow's ball-buster Trivial Pursuit Army questions for the next guard mount. After all, tomorrow was another day! And another blast of plastic spray on the ol' boots of life.

Chapter 13: Car 54. Car 54. Be on the Lookout for ... a Tornado

"The TV news said a tornado has touched down here!" My late wife Jane reported as she burst into my office just a few years ago. (2010s)

"Right here! I don't hear any warning sirens," I replied, looking around for my boots. A tornado watch was when one might happen. A warning was when one had been sighted. There were supposed to be sirens!

In my boots and pants, well-heeled but not socially acceptable, I stepped out into my Texas backyard for my own sighting. Sure enough the city's tornado-warning sirens wailed away albeit from afar and not loud enough by far, especially for my half-blown ears. But Jane hadn't heard them either. The sky looked bad but not that bad. Not bad like some; I've seen *really* bad skies before. It had been raining all evening but not that much. I walked through the house and out the front door. Same personal weather report out front. I stood out in the street. Alone, which I thought was odd because none of the neighbors were out investigating those unfriendly skies.

There was indeed that odd vacuum-like feeling I'd felt before. You could feel it in your ears beyond any sound. The rain fizzled to a mist. Some of the clouds were low and started rolling by like in a sci-fi movie. A little wind but mostly stillness. It felt like a tornado brewing, a feeling I'd experienced near ground zero several times. I walked back in the house looking for Jane to give her a more localized weather report. Couldn't find her. I walked into the long bedroom closet, and she was on the floor in the corner clutching an unhappy cat and surrounded by bed blankets and comforters.

"Taking this a bit seriously, ain't cha?" I commented.

"Hock, the warning sirens went off!"

"Well, don't ya care to rescue me, too?"

"I have already warned you, and I knew you would wander off."

And I wandered off again. Way too interesting outside to miss.

The word "tornado" was an altered form of the Spanish word "tornado," which meant "thunderstorm"; but many folks also called them twisters and cyclones. Climatologists, when they weren't preoccupied screaming chicken-little that my toaster oven was destroying the known universe, said that tornados could form and drop to the earth almost anywhere. The textbooks said that, "Although tornadoes have been observed on every continent except Antarctica, most occur in the United States. They also commonly occur in southern Canada, south-central and eastern Asia, east-central South America, Southern Africa, northwestern and southeast Europe, western and southeastern Australia, and New Zealand."

And a whole lot of them landed in Texas. I've seen them from a nice distance in Texas and Oklahoma. A nice distance. No handshake. No thanks.

Growing up in the New York City area I had never seen one, though I'd heard of some landing thereabouts. My earliest memories of storms on the upper east coast as a kid were scarce. In a duplex, apartment building near the Hudson River when my mother heard some thunder, she freaked out. She snatched me up, me a toddler, and a blanket and a flashlight and ran for the kitchen table. Under I went. She threw the blanket over the table like a tent and climbed in. With each flash of lightning or rumble of thunder, she would scream out loud....

"Sweet Jesus, Joseph, and Mary, mother of God, save us!" or words to that effect as a good Catholic girl might petition. Sometimes she would try to read me a book to calm me down. I sat there dumbfounded looking at her, as the storms never phased me. It was hard to finish off a page while listening to her pleas to heaven.

When I got to Texas in the early 1970s, I learned a fool could go stir-crazy worrying about tornados. They visited us Texans a lot. And Okie land too. And during the last decade, they seemed to be hitting all over central and south USA. Tornado-alley they called it. Today we have those storm-chaser cable TV shows camping out in Texas and Oklahoma where vans built like tanks and full of Starship Enterprise gear roam our countrysides on the rabid hunt for a whiff or a glimpse of a tornado.

"PLEASE," they begged for one! "DAMN," they cussed if they missed one. When they did see one, they screamed and hollered as if they'd won the Super Bowl.

I watch the TV news these days, and the modern weathermen can actually tell you at what moment rain will hit on exactly what street in town. Name that street! That is amazing. To me that might just be information overload unless you were the Wicked Witch of the West and melted on contact with water. She needed to know that precise stuff. Did you? Years back, it rained on you when it rained on you. Give or take a few minutes?

I can't document what kind of tornado-detection devices we had years back, like in the 1970s when I first had to worry about the weather, professionally speaking that is. We had some kind of Cold War radar alerts I guess. "Duck and cover!" Back then I was part of the sophisticated detection system of the day. That system being my simple eyes, my simple ears, and my slick raincoat. Boots on the ground. And a radio to scream in.

When I was stationed in Oklahoma as a Military Policeman in the 70s, my first real contact with tornadoes and public safety began. If our old-school weather radar reported an encroaching storm, say from the west side of our enormous base and surrounding shooting ranges and preserves, the Head Shed (powers that be, and I add, safe, secure, dry powers that they were) dispatched us to the high grounds west of the populated areas to look out for these pending tornadoes. In short, yours truly was the tornado watch and tornado warning. And unlike Prometheus, I was not chained to a rock in case the wind kicked up.

For those around the world who didn't know or hadn't seen it, the vastness of the south and central west half of the USA really began in the middle of Texas, Oklahoma, and Nebraska and ran flat out to the Rocky Mountains. Travel way south, and it ran almost out to Los Angeles and the Pacific Ocean. And there was a beauty and majesty to the land, a special vista that was a unique sight. In southwestern Oklahoma, some folks called it the "Big Pasture" or the "Badlands." You couldn't see much at night; but when lightning storms flowed in and cast sudden white light across the plains, there was a natural genius and wonder about it all that defied description.

And those lightning storms got crazy! Like on Mars! Or at least a movie about Mars. I have seen a few of those nights, and they remained etched in my feeble brain. Out there on those oh-dark-30 nights ordered to the boonies to spy on invading tornados was where I caught my first glimpses of those mighty storms. They were electrified into my vision by bolts of white lightning. I have even seen one tornado peeling across the ground during a sunset. Most of the time I stayed inside my squad car as tons of heavy rain pelted down and the old, extra-heavy car rocked with the wind. One night I even nosed my car into the wind hoping I wouldn't flip over! Visibility ended at the windshield like a dirty fish tank. But I still recalled those magic times when the wind and the rain were afar, and I stood outside my prowl car dry as a bone with binoculars and watched the sheer, almighty chaos of it all.

One such evening I was sent to the northeast side of our post for storm-watch duty at sunset. A truly horrendous sky was forming above us. It looked like Michelangelo's Sistine Chapel meets the Big Bang Theory, all on LSD with a Hendrix sound track. Right above me were miles of deep, multi-colored thick clouds swapping lightning bolts as they swirled. This sky scared the hell out of me like I was a caveman in Papua, New Guinea. The air around me stood bone still. Then, a breath-taking vacuum sucked through. I watched this abomination of nature inch by overhead. It passed me. Passed over us and the whole fort. I wondered about the ranches, farms, and the cities further east. Would they be so lucky? There was so much empty land out there. Would it, could it just touch down over some sagebrush valley? Or the next city east? But we at least escaped the threat. Those of us on watchdog duty checked in that it had passed.

Later that night it hit the city of Duncan ripping the city completely apart. My God, it killed so many. A week later I drove through Duncan like a sick rubbernecker, but I just had to see. It looked like an A-Bomb had touched down. A part of the city had spun like a top and turned into flying splinters that killed like giant darts. About 25 years later, I returned to Duncan while working interstate drug rings. It had all been rebuilt.

We'd had various, very serious storms through Texas when I'd been on duty as a patrolman or a detective pitching in to help out in weather emergencies. And some tornadoes came and went, but that one Duncan twister brewing over my head that night was as close as I have come to a big, bad mega doozy. When it sucked the wind from your lungs, that was close, bubba. Scary. Unforgettable. Doomsday.

Back to 2008, 30 years later with Jane and the cat smartly in the closet, I walked back outside to see the skies again. The half-muted sirens still sounded. Most folks collected their cats, dogs, snakes or whatever, kids, and grandma's valuable antique clock and took to the padded corners of their closets as I was once again apparently alone on the street, mesmerized and looking up.

Deep down, I guessed I understood when storm chasers whooped and hollered when they saw a twister. It was the goddamned magic of just being there and seeing it, a piece of brilliant creation and murderous destruction at work, all at once. Otherwise, I guessed you'd have had to be a damn fool to stand outside in a tornado warning. But then? I guessed I'd been that kind of damn fool my whole life.

Chapter 14: The Tale of Two Quonset Huts

It was the best of times; it was the worst of times. Icy South Korea in the 1970s. Cold enough to freeze your eyeballs. Looking back, it was actually my worst of times. Best because I was young and stupid. Worst because I was where I was and was another faceless victim of a primitive Pentagon binary computer shipping live warm bodies all over the world. I didn't want to leave my investigator job back in the States; but my computer number came up at the Pentagon, as they say. In fact, if you ask people in personnel, your career in the military to *some* extent is calculated the moment you enlist. Little did we know?

And this tale began on such a bitter cold night in the People's Republic of South Korea. I was minding my own business in my cinder block hooch down in the village. I was trying to stay warm with some contraband Johnny Walker Red, a local woman, and that damn too-small Kimchi cook stove. It was like a small version of a foreign jail cell, except for the lady of course. A small black and white TV pulled some historical Korean soap opera through its tin-foil-enhanced antenna. I was reading a book. Somewhere, some MPs were in a Swiss Chalet right now. Or on a beach in Panama. Or....

Someone fervently banged on my door.

"What?"

"Hock, it's Kevin."

"Wha...." I opened the door. Toe-curling COLD invaded the hooch! In a single-room hooch if you open the door once, it will take 15 minutes to reheat the place up again. Damn Kimchi stoves.

"They beat up Slayton!" Kevin said as he stepped in.

"Who?"

"Some jerks from the missile unit ...," and he proceeded to rattle off a few names. Yup. They were a couple of punks and some country boys who wanted to be like city punks. Jerks.

Slayton was a young kid from Midwest USA, a new dog handler, and this ice-chip hell-hole was his first military police assignment. Bad luck for him, too. Bad draw of the cards. Like I said. Unlucky in cards. His first night in-country and off duty, and he treks through the snow and the killer wind-chill factor to a local bar; and the new MP kid gets all beaten up. "Hey, let's beat up that new MP kid!"

"The guys (MPs) were meeting up in our Quonset hut. Most were drunk, and they were thinking about finding those punks and kicking their asses."

Some of the guys would include the new MP Sergeant Hattie, too! He pulled the cork a bit but was trying to fill the boots of our last team leader, Thomas Gaston, which was quite a chore to fill. Hattie was a good guy, though, and he was trying. I did not know Slayton at all, but the idea that some missile boys could just beat up some new MP for fun was not good for the company business.

At such times, one would think that one could fall back on good Army discipline and the chain of command meting out harsh punishments for the rule of law. But it was a bit of the Wild West where we were back then, way west of Camp Red Cloud and way north of Yongsan headquarters in Seoul. Usually, Admins did not like crimes reported to headquarters; and most local "events" (crimes) were kept local. That meant little to no in-company punishments. Kick a guy's teeth in? Send the victim to the dentist in Yongsan and confine the kicker to his room for two weeks when off duty. Confined to quarters. Or restrict him to base. Etcetera. No need to write a bunch of reports that will run flags up the chain to Red Cloud and Seoul.

No justice? No peace! At least there would be no peace for me that night. I told Kevin to wait as I got dressed. What was going on in the MP Quonset hut? Within minutes we left my hooch huddled over and chins down to battle the Siberian cold front, and we crunched our way up the icy dirt road to the Army base. We waved to the Korean KATUSA gate guards and climbed the hill to the MP Quonset hut, the first of two huts I would be visiting that night. The first hut was a visit. The second hut was more like a brawl or invasion.

This half-circle metal hut had a series of single- and double-occupancy rooms, but the front had a bit of an open bay area. That is where I found some agitated and angry off-duty MPs. Seven of them. They were pacing, shouting, and drinking. Someone handed me and Kevin each a beer. Young Slayton made eight, seated on a chair and quiet with a busted-up face. One black eye was closing up pretty good. He had a rag with ice wrapped up in it pressed against it.

Sgt. Hattie was sipping whiskey with a dour expression. He, too, was quiet as the others suggested we march on down to wherever the bullies were and kick their asses up and down the rice patty. I saw that Hattie was drunk.

"Find out where they are," Hattie finally spoke up. Which was clear code that we were indeed going to march on down to them and kick their asses up and down a rice patty.

So I was standing there in the bay, and I knew this was wrong. Wrong as the day was long. But you just had to be there right on the scene back then. Time and time again whenever there was a fight or a problem, whether it involved an MP being injured or not, nothing happened to the attacker. Nothing really. Some in-company finger wagging. Nobody cared. It was covered up. Not that long ago, I had broken a Sergeant's pinky finger after he jumped me and was strangling me. Nothing happened to the Sergeant who attacked me. Nothing happened to me either for breaking his finger. It was just all nicely covered over. The Captain gave us both dirty looks and a good finger wagging. No derogatory reports to HQ for an unblemished record and career. It was very complicated, though. Military life was ... complicated.

I've seen a rapist get confined to quarters for two weeks until it was all smoothed over with the locals. Hell, they were still sneak-shooting each other up on the DMZ a few miles north. What happened in oblivion stayed in oblivion. I was living in this state of oblivion. And, hell, I mean ... it was not like we were gonna hang somebody from a tree, just gonna beat some people up.

The beer and whiskey flowed. The cusses—they did, too. Until one of the guys burst into the hut with a message.

"They're all back in their Quonset hut."
"Let's go!" Sgt. Hattie said.

Off we went to Quonset hut number two. It was the best of times. It was the worst of times.

It was a scattered march over to that Quonset hut perched on a frozen hillside, and we all got quiet as we approached. I could hear rock music pouring out from it into the night. That ... that breed of heavy music crap was played by men with womanly, blow-dried long hair and wearing skin-tight leotards all singing in screeching high voices like scared women. Later to be AC/DC shit. Shit I don't much like.

Hattie shoved the door open, and we all piled in. But there was yet another doorway to a room from whence all the commotion came. Hattie pushed that open, too, and we all poured through this bottleneck. It was a big room with a lot of double bunks, desks, chairs, and stuff. About eight guys were spread out all over the room. Two or three were smoking dope. Sitting around and stretched out.

SURPRISE! They knew. They knew we knew. We all knew why we were there.

One stood up and immediately mouthed off to Hattie. Words I couldn't hear over the AC/DC Highway to Hell music, but I guessed the gist. And Hattie shoved him back. Another guy got up and went after Hattie, and the whole thing went to hell right there. Asses and elbows with that damn heavy metal for a backdrop.

I threw a few punches, mainly body blows in that mess, hitting torsos and arms. Took a few glanced, gawky shots off the shoulder, was tackled and bear hugged into a metal double bed, and that didn't go far. I had an arm free and beat the guy on his back with punches and hammer fists and got out of that one. It was all a crazy mess of shouting and movement.

The guy who first rushed Hattie came at me, and I hit him somewhere in the face with my left fist. He fell back on a bed in a bunk. He was down and done. ANNNND ... so was my left hand. I helped some of our guys two on one, but I knew my left hand just wasn't working too well.

Then it was over. Within seconds? About a half a minute. Some furniture was busted up and knocked around. We had surprised them and jacked them all up. Even young Slayton got in a few revenge licks. WHAT a sad introduction to police work, I thought. Sad. But he stood there chin up. Chest out. No worse for the wear. I also saw one of their guys standing in the corner. He never once got involved. He watched the whole thing, but he had a very serious expression on his face. Probably the smartest guy in the room.

Out of breath, Hattie spoke up, "You all leave us alone! You hear!"

Another sergeant with us had the wherewithal to add, "You were all up here smoking dope and shit. You're lucky we don't bust the lot of you!"

Good point on many levels, if you get my meaning. Those joints had disappeared in the fray anyway, probably into a few digestive tracks, but a quick toss of the room would probably find a stash and who knew what all else. I think the rocket jockeys got that message.

We left. Everyone was pretty quiet assessing in their minds what had just happened, as we crossed the frozen ground back to hut number one. None of us seemed hurt much. We all had jackets on for a little padding, but there were a few bloody lips. No doubt a few shiners would brew up overnight to match Slayton's. Me, I never got hit in the face one time; but my left hand felt real funny in that painful, swollen sort of way.

We stepped into the MP hut and talked up a postgame smack. Instead of drinking the cold beer, a few held the cans to their faces. I knew I had to leave. I stepped outside with that same yucky feeling after a weird, off-the-charts deal like this. Body chemicals I guess. My fingers were swelling, and my ring finger was really hurting. This ring had to go. Had to. Feeling like a lone target of possible third-string revenge, I left the huts the back way and walked down the stairs of the hills to the front gate keeping an eye over my shoulder on the missile-men Quonset hut area. Bye to the gate guards. Down the dirt road back to my warm, quiet hooch where I should have stayed anyway.

Once inside, I told my … what do you call her … "girlfriend" that I needed to saw the ring off my finger. Bad. Fast. She got up, got dressed, and guided me though the apartment "hooch" buildings to a local "papa-san." I knew this guy. He sat me down in a torch-lit, greasy work room. He took out a thin metal saw, and I lay my hand on an iron work bench. He began the gingerly task of cutting off the ring from my purple finger without splitting said finger. Very unpleasant, but swelling pain outranks being skittish. (I once took a power drill and drilled a hole in my big toe's toenail to relieve a pressure buildup from a barefoot karate school accident. Like I said, pain outweighs skittish.)

Finally he sliced that thing open and pried the ring apart. Whew. And not a moment too soon. Ice. Ice was next on the list and easy to find. I kept a plastic ice cube container on the windowsill of my hooch. Put water in. Set it on the ledge and let the Siberian cold front do the work. Kept all kinds of cold food there. Beer and Dr. Peppers. I went to bed with an ice pack on my left hand. Jesus, what a stupid night.

You worry a bit about the next morning. Showing up to a shit-storm over something you did last night. I walked through the camp's gates, past security, and into the MPs' headquarters. Nothing brewing. Sgt. Hattie emerged from the headquarters building. He did tell the company XO that a collective "we" went to investigate a report of one of our MP's being assaulted. He told me he said, "During this inquiry, a fight ensued with drunken members of the missile battalion. The incident involved minor drug possession we observed upon our arrival."

Hattie said the XO's head was spinning with assault, drunks, and drug charges possibly hitting the Captain and on up; and he asked Hattie the classic question we heard all the time, "Can we handle it here at a company level?"

Hattie told him, "It has all been handled, sir, as far as we are concerned."

"Well, case closed then. Carry on."

Thank you very much, Lieutenant.

My hand got better in about a week. I must have hit that guy on the forehead. It was a natural reaction to duck like that when a punch came. Yeah, that was a wedding ring. That marriage was shot anyway. A stupid folly by two stupid, too-young people. That was another story, and it was not worth telling because most people have had one of those in their past. You wanna hear another "Dear John" story? Nahhh, I thought so.

It was the best of times; it was the worst of times. But it wasn't over yet. The very next night, two other missile men came banging on my hooch door … that third-string revenge thing. And somebody lost his two front teeth! That was the little epilogue to that small tale of small people with small minds and their small problems in a small base in a small Asian village. It was about two nights later after this fiasco; and the swelling in my hand was going down. "Boomer T." Belton, another MP from Texas, was down in my hooch for a visit. The night of our gang fight was Boomer's night off; and, oh, how he deeply regretted missing the scrap at the Quonset hut. He was off in another village somewhere. Boomer was a high school football state champ, an aggressive, full-contact lover, and always up for any confrontation. Here's what I meant by that statement....

One Sunday afternoon weeks before, Boomer T. and

I were walking a bit of a beat on duty minding our own business; and some off-duty soldiers were sitting in chairs outside their place, drinking, and soaking in the sun. It seemed a very calm setting. Boomer was talking to me about something. Suddenly we heard a muttering from them. The classic "anti-cop" muttering of the 70s....

"Pigs."

Before the letter "s" of pigs could split the air, Boomer T. spun, sprang, and charged them. The dash was about 15 feet. Of course, we couldn't tell who actually muttered the word; but that didn't stop ol' Boomer. He grabbed the closest one by the throat tipping the chair back.

"PIG?" Boomer T. growled. "Pig! Who called me a pig? WHO! Come on, who?"

Those three guys were completely overwhelmed. I was still standing pretty much where I was before I heard the word! Man! That lit up Boomer T. like an M-80! I had to follow him in.

"Huh? Who?" he demanded. The three just gasped and mumbled in shock. One jumped back into the hallway behind them.

"Yeah, ya all are pussies. Pussies!" Boomer T. let the guy go. He strutted off like a banty rooster; and Boomer T. said one more thing over his shoulder to them, "Don't be callin' me no pig."

Boomer T. had a … short fuse.

So back to us in my lukewarm hooch drinking hooch. Boomer T. was always ready to go-go-go, and he regretted missing our little unofficial trip the night before. Boomer T. was decked out in jeans, boots, and a starched cowboy shirt with some extra manly Western jewelry. I'd swear in my memory he often wore cufflinks, but I can't say now for sure. He was out for a night on the town.

What a little town we had. Me? I was in my Mickey Mouse pajamas and my Ho Chi Minh flip flops. I wasn't going nowhere. Hell, there was a line of detective TV shows that night on the one GI-television channel. Barnaby Jones. Cannon. Followed by The FBI with Efrem Zimbalist Jr. himself. A Quinn Martin Production roll call heaven. If I could just get enough tin foil on the left antenna of my coveted TV, I had a bird's-eye view of prime time, deductive entertainment.

But there came a thunderous, angry knock on my front door with a shout. Boomer got up, walked over, and opened the door. It was one of those missile boys from the night before. He looked all tanked up on the local juju mix and was posturing for a fight I guess, and he knew where I lived. Right beside him was a young redheaded, freckle-faced kid who was all grins and "aw-shucks" the first few months he was in-country. But he, too, was a missile-man and started hanging out with the group of wannabe tough guys. He took on their bad habits.

"What chu want?" Boomer cried out, striking that banty-rooster pose. He marched forward, and these two creeps backed out onto the open patio area of the hooch right beside the chicken pens. I jumped up, peeled off my pajama bottoms, and was slipping on my pants as I stumbled.

The door knocker was affected by Boomer's instant aggression; but the redhead, also drunk, had to show some colors and mouthed off. He started waving a hand, sneered, and took a step toward Boomer T. A mistake. I barely got my zipper zipped when ... boom went Boomer T.!

Boomer laid him out! I mean one punch to the jaw. This kid went airborne like a stiff corpse, and let me tell you that I saw his two front teeth fly right out of his mouth into the air. Right out. He landed on his back, and then his two teeth landed and bounced on the cement. He was out cold. Boomer stood there with his fist cocked and an angry sneer.

"YOU want some? You want more?" Boomer shouted to the second guy. "COOOOME ON!"

That freaked out the door knocker. I think he actually whimpered. He gathered up his limp, redheaded friend. Some other residents started opening their doors. Our company commander secretly lived with a local woman down in the corner hooch, and even he cracked open his front door to see the ruckus. I watched him … wondering … then he ducked his head right back in.

"I see nothing! I know nothing!" Like Sgt. Schultz.

I saw you again, Romeo, I thought to myself. I'd seen the CO in and out of that hooch countless times. I saw him there shacked up this very night, too, him all married-up back home in the States as he was, should this little tooth fairy story become a problem tomorrow morning. Of course, it didn't.

The two guys left the complex. Boomer T. came back in smiling. Then happily went out for his night on the town. I could easily predict how all that would go. I wrestled with the tin foil on my antenna. It's hell seeing three ghost images of Efrem Zimbalist Jr.

That was the end of that mess. The feud, or whatever it was, was over for a while. The only long-term victim of this sordid business was the poor redheaded kid who walked around with a gap in his teeth until he left country. He might even still be toothless today.

That feud was over, but I would learn through the years that any fight you're in, shooting or otherwise, may well have much longer ramifications, least of all criminal charges. But a stewing feud. I've worked cases where tens of years later, some guy would get drunk, get in his car, drive over to another's house, and fight or shoot some guy he scrapped with decades ago. Sometimes he would bring his friends. You never know. You just never know. Your past doesn't always lie out cold on the cement and stay there. It limps up and groans and festers behind you. Somebody's revenge. Somewhere back there, always behind you.

Yes. A Tale of Two Quonset Huts. Back then it was the best of times because I was young and stupid. It was the worst of times because … jeez ... what a mess, huh? What a lousy place.

Me and Dennis Deitz in the little MP HQ

Typical village view right outside our northwest base corner. Of interest behind them is the first valley the Red Guard crossed in the Korean War two decades earlier.

Chapter 15: My Longest, Worst Fight

J. W. Ducks ripped the car door right off the Korean taxi cab. J. W. was mad. Madman mad! We were surprised when we heard about it the next day. Well, I wasn't too surprised about the strength part; because I knew J. W. could rip a door off a small Asian car. Ducks and I had been defensive linemen on our Army football team. He and I had chased quarterbacks together. No, this wasn't Army/Navy college-level football. It was more like the football in the original "MASH" movie. Each company in the battalion had a team, per the Colonel, and it was all taken very seriously by command staff.

Ducks was a big, stout, black guy from Alabama, the head mail clerk of the Army unit I was attached to as a Military Policeman. We were all stationed in the village on the north end of South Korea in a country place where Americans crossed each day off a calendar much like a prison inmate in hopes of doing their tours and returning back to the promised land of American women, bottled beer (not cans), and football games that didn't come six days later on some kind of old-school video tape/film. Some called it "Asia 1970s."

Joseph W. Ducks was "Xing" off the days on a calendar in his mailroom and going back home soon! His days were numbered. He was "short" on Korea as they say. And just when he should have started packing things up, whistling and smiling, he started messing up. Now, J. W. always hit the bottle hard ... whiskey. Everybody liked Ducks. Who doesn't like the main "Santa Claus-boss" mail-call guy? They liked him unless ... he'd badly bruised his brain with a bottle of whiskey. Whiskey made him testy. And I had been able to talk him down a few times when he got confrontational out in the village or on the base. So had others. But this cab door thing was a surprise as he'd grown testy enough to start dismantling a taxi with his bare hands. As the cab driver screamed, J. W.'s friends pulled him away from the cab and hauled him back to his room.

The next morning, our MP office received a complaint from the driver. I stepped outside to see the irate driver with his four-door sedan - now with three doors - parked outside the main gate. He was yelling and waving his hands in the air as a KATUSA translator explained the problem to us. Several MP NCOs and unit artillery officers converged. A donation was immediately collected; and we all orchestrated a repair of the cab just so there wouldn't be any legal problems delaying Ducks' departure. But back in the MP office, we all concluded that Ducks didn't want to go back to his Sweet Home Alabama. The Xs on his calendar were not heading toward his bliss but his depression. A pact was made by all of us to try and keep Ducks out of trouble and homeward-bound sans a trip to the Korean or Federal jail. Just three weeks! SON! Did I eventually blow that!

Later that afternoon, J. W. returned in a deuce-and-a-half truck with the daily mail run from Yongsan. Once inside headquarters, the XO (That's executive officer for you draft dodgers out there.) explained what deal we had done with the cab driver. The mail clerks watching this said J. W. was touched and almost cried. In the afternoon, he waved to me as he walked by knowing I had kicked in 30 bucks to the repair job. I waved back. I really liked Ducks, but a day or so later he got back on the whiskey again hard ... and changed. And I tried to kill him with my bare hands.

The one Army AM radio station reported another Siberian Cold Front blowing in, which always frosted the mind into experiencing a cold front like no other. Siberia was once the Gulag, the purgatory, the solitary-confinement camp-land for all bad Russians. Now it was capital of Russia's oil and gas industry. Oil rig or slave camp, cold is cold; and if you whistle while you work too long up there, you imagine a long, thin pencil of ice quickly appearing before your lips. Johnny Carson once said that far north Bangor, Maine, was so cold.... "How cold was it?" .... "I once saw a dog frozen to a fire hydrant."

But there was no Carson "The Tonight Show", no dogs, or even fire hydrants as I was walking a beat down through the village just south of the DMZ and northeast of Incheon Bay. The dogs here were served medium rare for dinner, "Gaegogi" they called it; and there were no underground pipes for any water except the paved parts of downtown Main Street. Nothing but the threat of that cold front looming from the great Red commie north. At times like these I thought about the Korean War, the sheer winter of it all, and what a miserable experience it must have been to slug it out in this weather.

Our foot patrols were usually kept just to the main areas where GIs either lived, shopped, or frequented, which was a turf redefined and reneged on at times by the local Korean village police. Many times we were even barred! Local politics! But we were always supposed to patrol the "general" grounds all around the base for a variety of security reasons. I guess that's what they now call "force protection." Once, my MP K-9 buddies found a hidden North Korean weapons cache buried on the hillside for a future "re-load/re-arm" attack. A dog smelled it all!

There was one paved main downtown village street. And to the right a typical village cop we dealt with, problem-solving the comings and goings of soldiers living and visiting the local population. For the most part, I always liked those guys. The girl with me? Don't even ask....

Ordinarily, hardly anything much at all happened. Pretty boring things. But on this dark and frozen night, I made a turn down a courtyard of small apartments—what the indigs (locals) call "hooches" and wandered through the maze of alleys behind the infamous "Ventura Club." Ventura was one of the many hangouts and bars in the village where a troop could sit and listen to KC and the Sunshine Band, drink opium-laced wine, buy raw street drugs, feel up floozies, and get rolled by local "slickyboy" thugs on the walk back to base. Fun night. The walkways and hallways of the hooch mini-complexes were cement and/or cinder block walls with dwelling doors every eight feet or so. Once in a while the walkways would open to some courtyards that housed small chicken pens, outdoor bathrooms, or hand well-water pumps. All kinds of people lived there. A Captain kept a prized hooker there. So did a corporal; "pussy" sometimes being the great equalizer. Among them were factory workers, farmers, and families.

One night I heard something funny down one alleyway, a whimpering of some kind, and took a turn to find the shadowy source. Two people. One big. One small.

The sounds came from a small Korean girl. But she couldn't make too much noise because J. W. Ducks had his huge hands on her neck and was choking the life out of her!

"JOE!" I shouted and sprinted toward them. Fresh off the "let's save Joe Ducks" parade, I was incredulous and confused. I latched onto one of Ducks' arms and yanked it free of the teenager. He leered at me with the bug-eyed face of a wild lunatic. The girl was still powerless under Joe's one hand.

I yelled his name again and punched the inside of his arm knocking his last grip away. The girl gagged and bolted from us, but she fell clutching her throat and remaining at the turn of the alley.

Joe pretended I wasn't there. "Come here, you fucking bitch!" he yelled to her. When I got in his path, he tried to shove me aside; and the old football-style grappling that we had done in practice ironically returned to us.

We struggled all the while with me telling him, "Quit, man, quit! Quit!" I was still in reasoning mode.

Joe finally reasoned that I was there to stay. Unlike the offensive lineman he'd blasted past before, he was grabbing, gripping, and clawing at me; and I battered it aside.

Then he stepped back. "Okay, you mother-fucker, okay!" he growled, swelling up his chest and winging out his arms wide, all the usual animal-about-to-fight signs. Something commonly done "for show," for the "look at how big I am" message. It was a biological thing.

Well, sir, we had us a fight right there. We hit like Sumo wrestlers do and bashed into the wall sideways with Joe still trying mostly to get around me. He bounced off the wall lunging for the girl, who crawled off and screamed. I clasped onto his leg and scaled up his back until he lost his balance, and we crashed again into the opposite wall. I got up and tried to talk more sense into him and position myself between him and the girl. We stared at each other for a second; and I felt that in the dark recesses of his whiskey-addled brain (and he stunk of it), he recognized me as his friend. And I still didn't want to really hurt ol' Joe.

And for exactly that reason, that became the longest and worst fight I had ever had. Just a few years before, I had been a student of Kenpo Karate. I was taught the skill and had decided all my future confrontations were going to be fast and effective. None of this wrestling around crap! Just serious, quick business. But in that alley, I made the mistake of not wanting to be too "serious" with Joe. And so, it lingered on into that mess....

He rushed me swinging his fists; and I caught several glancing blows, one to my face. But I caught his left arm above his elbow forcing him across the alley to an already-familiar wall. He hit face first. I pulled down hard on his arm while struggling for a behind-the-back arm hold. But Joe was a bull. With his free hand, he grabbed my belt. We grappled along the wall exchanging wild punches until he fell into several large, empty kimchi jars. I fell on top of him. By this time, some of the hooches were showing signs of life. Lights coming on. Doors were opening. The locals chattering.

Joe and I wrestled around in the smashed rubble. His fingernails had slit my gum, and I was bleeding from my mouth and nose. My breath was short, and I was hot. Joe's fingers were in my eyes as he pushed my face away. My "good ol' Joe" attitude was slowly leaving. I punched him in the face a real brain-shaking hit. I stood up, feeling confident I could shove him down if he tried to stand among the shattered jar pieces.

"Stay down!" I ordered. I still had my .45 in the

flap holster on my belt but was not going to pull it. I just knew not to "gun-bluff" Joe as it would work at him, and I did not want to shoot ol' Joe Ducks! Plus, I could just predict we would start fighting over that gun. I wore gloves and had several layers of clothes on under my flight jacket, and all this cement and cinder block crashing and scraping had not reached skin level yet. Other than a little blood and swelling, some pain, I was … doing okay so far. But so was Joe-Joe under his many layers.

He collected his senses, ignored my commands, and started climbing out of the clutter. The athletic bastard took all my shoves and still came up to his feet thrashing his arms at mine. His head was about stomach high on me, and he charged. Even with my back-peddling to try a head shot ... something ... he tackled me right down and was damn near running right over the top of me with those heavy old Army boots coming down hard. He essentially ran right over me like a freight train. Even stepping right on my head and really twisting the hell out of my ear!

He was back and bound for the girl, who by this time was accompanied by her sister who must have responded to the shouting. Joe got to both of them. I was almost flat out wondering if my ear was still attached to his boot sole. Or had it relocated to the top of my head ... or maybe in orbit as I felt like I was in orbit. The girls screamed. He was hurting both of them.

Ducks had the girl by the throat again and was thrashing away at her sister. I guess he was dead set on strangling that girl to death. The sister screeched Korean curses. I reluctantly staggered to my feet, limped over, reached out, and grabbed the back of Joe's jacket collar; and then I kicked down very, very hard on the back of his right calf.

A textbook move. Why is it textbook? It works. I pulled back as hard as I could; and Joe was going down but pulling the girl with him. He also reached out and hung onto my sleeve on the way down, and we all three ended up in a tangled pile. She crawled away; and Joe and I wound up wrestling and punching at each other with most of the blows landing on multiple layers of clothes.

We actually used our own forward momentum against each other to get back up on our feet. I'd thought I'd belted in some really good head shots. I had practiced and worked out for years at this point, but they were just not working. My gloves? His drugs and drink? I just couldn't get to his jaw and neck because of his big winter jacket, flannel shirt, and sweatshirt—and whatever the hell else he was wearing. It was like we were both fighting each other in football uniforms.

We crashed into and knocked open a hooch door falling right on top of two Korean couples' playing cards on their floor. They shrieked, and deservedly so, as two giant Americans exploded in. As the couples scrambled free from the fracas, Ducks started beating down on my head and shoulders. My boots were slipping on the linoleum and just couldn't get a grip to escape. Their neighbors outside, and now some Americans, rushed to the doorway to see the rest of the show.

There was a small stove in the middle of the floor with a metal tube chimney that ran up to the ceiling and then to a window. We slipped, skidded, and scrambled near to the stove; and with a knee up and pivot I threw Ducks into the whole hot thing, and he demolished the entire rig. A huge round piece of bright, glowing red coal, the size of a coffee can, hit the floor; black smoke hit the air as the chimney collapsed over us and, well, the whole room was a freakin' mess. "Sorry, folks, just

Americans passing through!"

Joe seemed stunned and tried to get up in slow motion, so I reached back and swung at his face but missed. As if off balance for a second, he fell again. His arm landed on the coal. The Korean who lived there had a fire poker of some kind and tried to retrieve the rolling, red-hot coal from the floor; but Joe snatched the poker from his hands and sneered at me. He got to his knee, and I could tell by his face he was ready to whip me good with that metal poker. Okay, that was a new ball game. Football was over, my friend. That old flap on my holster did not slow me down. I pulled my .45 out as Joe reared back that poker.

"Don't even think about it!" I barked. I was ready to shoot that fucker dead right there. Mother-fucker! Right there! Nothing else had worked! And that metal poker in his hand was now his season ticket to a bullet.

Looking at the business end of my .45, Joe froze. Suddenly we both realized just how completely out of breath we were. Getting my handcuffs on this big bastard was my next plan. How would that go? There was a greater commotion outside; and suddenly Joe's section chief, a respected, well-liked warrant officer, appeared in the doorway with another NCO. I later learned the duo had been drinking in the Ventura Club and had been summoned to the scene by the frantic locals.

"J. W., what are you doing?" the warrant officer asked, looking at the two of us. Him with a poker. Me with a pistol.

It was as though Ducks suddenly snapped back into sanity. "Man, oh, man," Joe said, shaking his head. He sat on a nearby chair arm sucking air. He laid the poker on the chair. I holstered my gun. My vibes told me the struggle was over. Wrong again, Sherlock.

The Korean, whose hooch we wrecked, yelled for

us to get out. Sorry, we Americans are occupying this foreign soil a little longer. You will return to your card game when we're good and ready. And worse now, the girl and her sister were there. Plus some older folks that appeared to be their relatives.

Joe started talking some gibberish about the Korean girl. Pointing at her. I saw that her clothing was torn. Her face was bleeding. Even the protective sister was banged up. I slowly began to realize that I had probably interrupted a rape. The warrant officer stood beside Ducks, almost coddling him, rubbing his shoulder, saying "Come on, J. W., come on. Let's go back to the base, J. W. Come on ... come on." The officer knew to get Ducks off the scene before the Korean police got there. Notoriously inept and slow, that was not a usual problem; but it was a problem in such a case as a rape.

Joe pulled away from those good intentions and the officer's friendly hand. The sister began shouting. The man who owned the hooch continued his broken English chant for us to leave. The family shouted in Korean, shaking their fists at Ducks.

The angry, staccato chorus of voices ticked him off again. He shot up to his feet.

"Shut up! Shut the fuck up!" he shouted back.

The wide, bugged-out eyes were back. The back spread wide again. The raised arms. The demon eyes. He shoved the warrant officer off. He shoved away the NCO. He charged at the original girl yet again!

You know, sometimes I try to recall exactly what kind of instinctive, chemical "burn" I felt at that moment. What was it? Where did it come from? That raw emotion of murder? Of death? I knew my face must have contorted. I lost all feeling in my body and in my thoughts. I was going to kill Joe Ducks. And in my gut, I knew deep down my gun just wouldn't do. Wouldn't do it justice. It wouldn't be satisfying enough. Those were not thoughts, just emotions that took over my head and chest. At that point, Ducks was just seven or eight feet from me; but I bolted for him like I was starting a 100-yard footrace. Joe became my demon quarterback, and he was going to hell. Not even Siberia was far enough away.

I crashed into his side at a hundred miles an hour. We went airborne into some furniture; then he landed chest down on the hard stone floor with me square on top of him. He tried to get up, but I aimed and belted him about five hard shots in the side of his face. His head bounced off the stone floor. Hitting him anywhere else was padded. His neck was smothered in clothes. Killing Joe Ducks was all about the head now. Somehow, somewhere in this roughhouse struggle, I lost both my gloves off my hands. I buried both my hands deep into his thick afro. I somehow remember the feel on my fingers. I began lifting and banging his skull on the stone floor. Oh, I figured 30 or 40 good smashes might do it up real good. Everlasting good.

The spark of resistance left him. Suddenly I was yanked off Ducks. Airborne! The warrant officer had one of my arms and the NCO had the other. Hell, I think even the little Korean homeowner had a piece of me. I was airlifted across the room. Ducks was out cold and was drooling, and bleeding. I craned my neck to see his carcass, to see him dead. You have to see....

"Hock! Hock, he is out cold," the warrant officer's voice began to metastasize in my brain. I calmed myself down. With this release of tension, they let go of me. I walked back across the room, lifted his limp arms behind him, and cuffed them. The warrant officer and I pulled Ducks into a chair. Looked him over. His spark was coming back as he mumbled. We each grabbed an arm.

He barely resisted us as we pulled him from the hooch, down the courtyard, and down the long dirt road through the village. Then after several stops to collect his balance, we hauled him back to the base. At that point, I was so maddened and determined, I could have dragged him all the way back to the States.

It was our practice to put detainees in the lobby of the headquarters building. You see, we were so far away from major posts that we had no official jail and no holding facilities. We had to requisition a police jeep from Kenpo, wait for it, and take him in. It was not uncommon for everyday disruptors, assaulters, or drunk and problem children to be "sent to their rooms" so to speak. In the barracks, some commander imposed watch or control. Then his fate was left for the company captain in the morning. More often than not, news of these events never reached battalion headquarters at Camp Red Cloud; and no small scale, non-court-martial punishment was doled out. It was handled "in house." But not this time. As we passed our MP office, I shouted in for an order of an MP vehicle to come and pick Ducks up.

The officer said, "No, no, Hock, we can handle this here."

I ignored him. A police jeep was going to carry J. W. Ducks away to jail, or I was. We continued across the grounds and into the HQ building. I sat him in a chair in the orderly room. Ducks sat with his head hung low. The room stayed quiet. An MP Sergeant joined us. Twenty or more minutes later, the transport jeep arrived. I filled out some brief paperwork with charges on disorderly conduct and aggravated assault. Something like that; I can't remember. They carted a quiet, solemn J. W. Ducks away. I stepped outside and watched them go down the dirt road and then turn right on the paved streets of the downtown village.

Back inside HQ, I went into the bathroom and looked in the mirror. Dried blood on my face. I could almost chip it off at that point. My cold face was just swollen and numb. I found my ear was still where it was supposed to be, just a different color. The swelling in some of my fingers ached. Motion was limited. Where in hell were my gloves?

That sure was ugly. Having to fight a friend. The broken furniture, kimchi jars, stoves, pipes, hot coals, pokers, guns, flips, punches, kicks, and a damsel in distress; yup, that was one fight to remember, I thought, as I hit the dirt road on foot. The Siberian cold front was just now really blowing in. I tell ya it seemed like the wind chill could freeze the water in your eyes. I still had to collect some witness names down in the village. That poor girl's name for sure. And I still had another hour or two before the shift ended ... still time for one more turn through town.

This arrest? It was a screw-up on my part. That encounter lasted too long, so much longer than it should because I had violated the impersonal, "get-it-over-quick" rule. Since I knew Ducks? I let the fight last too long. I also believe he felt the same toward me. This delay was an unprofessional screw-up, which resulted in more injuries, more damage, and even worse, my own personal descent into madness. Temporary insanity you might say. Losing it. That was the first time in my life, as well as the last time, that I felt that exact extreme primitive, animalistic feeling.

I have taught in my classes and seminars for many years now the idea that inside each of us was a Wolf-Man, a Dr. Jekyll to your Mister or Missus Hyde, a beast we might need someday to call upon to stay alive and survive. It is biological. He was that growl in your chest. Locate it and feed it just enough to keep it alive.

It will keep you alive. And in the meantime, better learn how to keep it in its damn cage.

Oh, did Joe fly home to Alabama a few weeks later? Yes, he did. The Army has a certain way of handling these things.

Chapter 16: Me and the ROK Marines

The textbook manuals will define the ROK Marines as: "The Republic of Korea Marine Corps, also known as the ROK Marine Corps, or the ROK Marines, is the marine corps of South Korea. The ROKMC is a branch of the Republic of Korea Navy responsible for amphibious operations, and also functions as a rapid reaction force and a strategic reserve."

"Korean soldiers were highly motivated. Because of their own struggle with Stalinist North Korea, they hated communists. They were also tough. Each man was trained in the art of tae kwon do, with 30 minutes' practice forming an integral part of morning physical training. They were also subjected to harsh discipline. Time magazine reported in 1966, "Captured Vietcong orders now stipulate that contact with the Koreans is to be avoided at all costs—unless a Vietcong victory is 100 percent certain." – National Interest Magazine

1975. The first days of the first week I was in country, up north in South Korea, HQ asked me to deliver some papers to Camp Red Cloud. They gave me our intrepid KATUSA – Mister Lee as a driver, and together in an old, open US Army jeep we made the long drive east. Once at the base, Mister Lee took us to the Red Cloud headquarters. On the open grounds outside stood a formation of Korean soldiers and a sergeant yelling and beating the holy hell out of a soldier. The troop stood as best he could, arms down and at a wobbly attention. Finally. the blows knocked him off right off his feet. Down, he was kicked.

"What's going on over there?" I asked Mister Lee.

"Ohhh, ROK Marines. Dey crazy. Dat Marine fucky up somehow." Mister Lee said.

And that was my first introduction to the ROK Marines, other than having some of them, along with South Vietnamese Army combat vets, teach a few courses in basic training. Upon my return to our little crappy forward operating base, (FOB) as I was a "cherry" (new) I quickly learned that we also had ROK Marines stationed right with us too!

We, me, the MPs there were to do police work and help provide force protection for this FOB, but the grunt work of guarding was done by KATUSA (Korean Augmentation To the United States Army, a branch of the Republic of Korea Army that consists of Korean drafted personnel who are augmented to the Eighth United States Army), K-9s (dogs), MPs and ROK Marines. One big happy (?) family.

Missile jockeys operated on top of a mountain inside our camp and from that elevation, with binoculars one could see into North Korea and at times watch their knuckleheads doing PT or snaking around over there.

"The beatings will continue until morale improves!" And I continued to see periodic ROK beatings in their morning formations. We never knew what they did wrong, but they must have "fucky-ied up" in some way.

The ROK officers and NCOs spoke some English but the typical ROK Marine did not. So while we saw them a lot, and they ate in our mess hall, we never got to know them beyond the occasional smile, a wave, and a thumbs up.

Me on a foot patrol. Part of the MP job was to patrol an area surrounding the camp, being so close to the DMZ

Part of our job description was "force protection' to also patrol the outside of the base, check the perimeters, etc. and the ROK Marines did that routinely. We MPs did on are own. We not have to go on every run with them, but we were supposed to go with some regularity, and keep abreast of the breastworks, so, with some regularity, we went.

On one trip, they found a cache of buried weapons, hidden by stupid commie sympathizers for North Koreans to sneak in and dig up. (I think a K9 smelled it out, as I recall). The commies were always sneaking in, or building tunnels under the DMZ, etc. Those days, the 60s and 70s were considered very dangerous times in Korea.

(Years earlier, the NKs perpetrated North Korea attempted assassination, "The Blue House Raid," also known in South Korea as the "January 21 Incident." It was just one raid launched by North Korean commandos to assassinate the President of South Korea, Park Chung-hee, in his residence at the Blue House. President Park was unharmed.)

Taking us out, taking our missiles out, or sneaking past us to go south was always a problem. We sat in the valley first invaded by the Red Guard back in the 1950s. One part of my MP job I discovered was to run an M-60 machine gun team on the northwest peak of the camp that touched that very valley. (In the MPs, when the feces hits the oscillated blades, we are all infantry. Which is why we received all the infantry training.)

On one of these walk-arounds, the ROK Marine Sergeant (also named Lee) mentioned to me that old classic observation, usually attributed to the Japanese,

"America will never be invaded," he said.

"It won't, you think?" I said.

"No, too many guns."

Some of these inspections were run in the dark, a.m. hours. Just cuz. Just cuz they could and really they should. The boogie-men come out at night. And as we passed a few guard posts, Sgt. Lee would stop us at a distance and stealthfully get near the post. He would at times catch the ROK Marine there asleep and steal something from them, sometimes their M-16s!

The next morning the ROK Marine would be chastised and then beaten in the formation. I often wondered what these Marines thought when they woke up and saw their M-16 WAS GONE!

In 1976, in a routine mutual agreement, the DMZ, 38th Parallel often gets trimmed and cleaned. This escalated into the beating death of several US Army officers. And touched a war...

Chapter 17:
This is War! T.C. Gaston's Follow Me Order

On a mountain top, five decades ago, on a foot patrol in the way north half of South Korea, I stalled for moment and looked at the vast landscape before me, which even revealed southern parts of the "Hermit Kingdom" North Korea. As part of our "force protection' assignment, we had to patrol the areas in and around our Army base for...problems. My military police sergeant, the one and only Thomas Gaston asked,

"Whatcha doing, Hochheim?"

"Just lookin' at the scenery, Sarge," I answered.

"Yea well...ya can't fuck the scenery, Hochheim. Let's go," he said.

One of my personal heroes is T.C. Gaston. He was kid from the projects of Washington D.C. He joined the Army and was a decorated Korean AND Vietnam war vet and my MP Sergeant in South Korea.

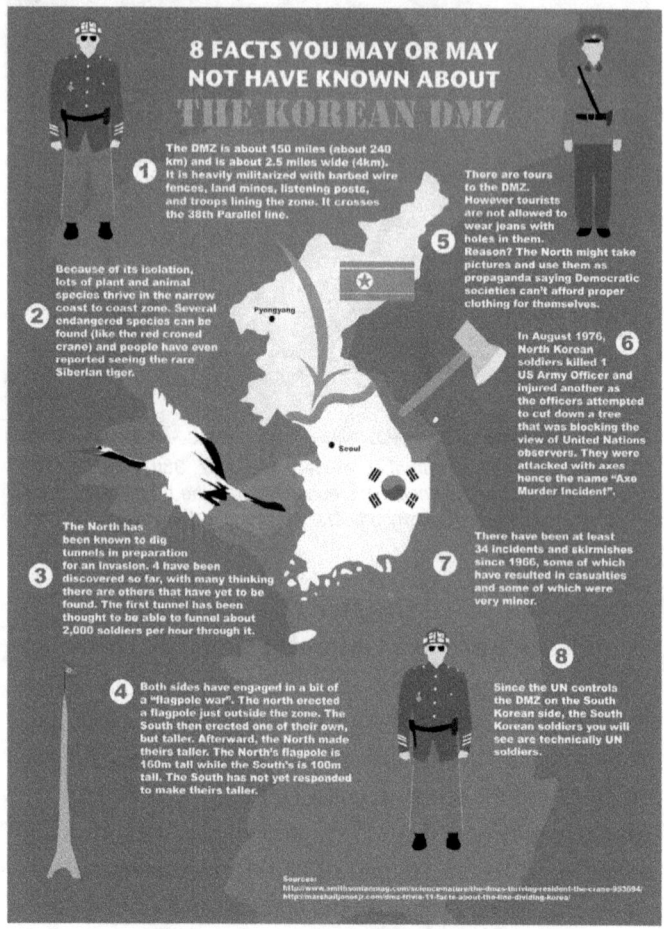

In the 1970s, we were all stuck in a crappy Army base just south of the DMZ on the west side of South Korea. As mentioned in the prior chapter, we did the usual policing and force protection along with the ROK (Republic of South Korea) Marines and overseeing the KATUSA security (Koreans Augmented to the USA). Gaston never went to college but he was one of the smartest guys I've ever met.

For the "great unwashed" here is a DMZ rundown.

"The Demilitarized Zone (DMZ) was established in 1953 as part of the Korean Armistice Agreement between the United Nations, North Korea, and China to end the Korean War. It's in essence a 'line in the sand' that extends the entire 160 mile width of the Korean peninsula. At some major points it is 2.5 miles wide." - Time Magazine

Sgt. Gaston - If you could imagine a black Clark Gable in mannerisms and speech with a wicked sense of humor and real understanding of human nature. Through the years some of you have heard me talk about and write about him. My recollections are of his fighting and uncanny way with dealing with all kinds of people (he had most of the officers afraid of him). I could tell many Gaston stories but briefly, here's one of my favorites:

In the 1970s, and I hear tell in the 2010s too, there was constant trouble at the DMZ, and we had various levels of alerts, but one morning the war sirens went off. When this special baby sounded off, we appeared ASAP, even if in our skivvies, civies, Mickey Mouse pajamas or Ho Chi Minh flip flops. You got there.

In this ragtag formation a LT told us, "I don't know anything about this yet, but we now are at war. Somethings happened. We are at war."

Everyone was quickly released to scatter off to their

attack positions and jobs. A few of the guys, some were missile tech guys that were only in the Army to eventually go to college were actually sobbing. For me, I had this sick sense of being at the really wrong place at the really wrong time, but I was in for it. There. Not up for it, there. It's an "oh-shit moment."

The MPs met at our little station house and were given the force protection assignments. My job was to oversee a 50 caliber machine gun team on the north west corner of the camp. It faced north and overlooked the valley/rice paddies that the Red Guard first invaded in the 1950s. It was a breathtaking valley I had walked over and jogged on and now it was a ticking time bomb.

We each had an M-16 and a .45 pistol. Big problem, while we MPs had ammo for our .45s, and while some of our guard staff had some M-16 ammo, we and no one else had any ammunition for the M-16s or the 50 cals! I learned later that through history, in places like Pearl Harbor and other small and big disasters, the ammo was locked up and no one either sent ammo release orders, or they forgot too up and down the chain of command…I don't know…but locked-up ammo has been a problem throughout modern military times.

Gaston, now suddenly in full charge of force protection, walked in the shack having just supervised a bunch of stuff outside. Several of us said,

"Sarge, we have no ammo!"

He was aghast, "WHAT?" So far, he'd only had his pistol belt with mags. He disappeared and marched across the chaotic grounds of the base. He commandeered an open-backed duce and a half (a big old Army truck) jumped in the bed and standing up in the open back, ordered the driver up a long steep hill to the ammo dump. In his force protection role, he had keys to everything, include the ammo dump. They returned within minutes, him standing behind the cab of the open truck with bandoleers of ammo hanging over his shoulders.

At the main grounds he shouted out to all, "Ammo! Ammo!" and desperate men ran to the truck where he dispensed the ammunition to the troops.

A Captain and the LT ran out of HQ and the CO said, "SGT Gaston! No one authorized that ammo release from the dump!"

Gaston gave him a dirty sneer, ignored him and continued distributing the ammo. They could not say much. I mean, how could they? Gaston whistled us over, and we got our ammo too.

This little base has several operational assignments. One was to missile the holy fuck out of North Korean planes and bomb a few sites over the DMZ before we were over run. We were not meant to "stay." To "defend." Just hang on till the damage was done, then "retreat" the best way to Seoul. Mucho miles away in a combat situation.

Gaston was in full combat infantry mode, once back in the shack. He looked pissed. He looked concentrated. He looked at all of us and said, "When they shoot off all their missiles this place is empty. Worthless. We'll work out way back to Youngsan ." He looked into each of our eyes. "When we go, you don't follow these officers and these college boys, you follow me! You got that? You follow me, because I am a combat muther-fucker, and I'll get you there alive."

I'd follow that son-of-bitch anywhere. I still get goosebumps when I think about that speech. I guess ya had to be there.

We remained on war status for several days. Intense at first because we heard nothing but the classic "rumors of war." The GI radio and one TV station told us nothing.

The people in the village played out their lives. We sat and stared at that valley and the skies. The thought always does occurs to you in these times, "We didn't make enough sandbags!"

Then it downgraded after a few days, day by day. There were numerous alerts while I was there but none as big and serious as that one. It was all over a multiple killing incident at the DMZ that is too long and distracting to explain here.

This is a small story. I could tell many stories about Gaston. Police stories too. Like the time he knocked out a knife attacker with one punch. Or, when he played on the unit football team, damn near 60 years old, playing tackle with us kids. On the way to the games in one of the deuce-and-a-half trucks, he'd have a pack of gum, 10 pieces and give nine of them away to us nearby. I noticed small stuff like that. Or the time…well…DON'T get me started.

Gaston retired right after that tour and returned to his life in the Washington DC projects. I was on a security detail on a small mountain that overlooked the base below and I saw him get into a KATUSA jeep for last ride to Youngsan . I watched the jeep for as long as I could from up there. I never saw him again. None of us heard from him again. He carved an ever-lasting impression on my life, as a cop, a soldier and person.

I can still picture him on the back of that deuce and-a half, ammo hanging off of him, and see him handing out ammo from the back of that truck to the troops.

Chapter 18: The Knights. The Duel. The Fair Lady. The First Murderer I Caught in Texas

The first murderer I caught in Texas was an interesting case. I think this was the first one there, but it might have been the second. I can't remember for sure. If you are indeed used to that kind of thing, it was typical of murders in many ways; if you are not and new to it all, it was shocking. But all murders have many intriguing, classical aspects in the timeless, human drama and trauma of life and death.

After years in patrol and an investigator in the US Army, I was no "first rodeo' guy. In my first few months on patrol in Texas in the 1970s, I was riding shotgun with Officer Ron Atkins. About 4 a.m. one night, we got a call from an angry neighbor in what we once called "shacktown," the projects, or the "poor" part of our city … you get the nickname; you get the very sad picture. The neighbor reported men fighting in the house next door. I later heard the original call on tape: "They's fightin' something horrible next door. "They's young, drinkin' people, and I don't know what all is goin' on over there. They's yellin.' They's screamin' something horrible. I can't get a nod of sleep!"

On this street, the walls of those single-story, old, small, wooden houses were very thin; and noise would carry. I reported "10-4" to the dispatcher, and Ron headed that way. As we got close to the block, Ron turned out the headlights to approach the house as quietly as possible. Classic patrol tactics. Then, as now, we boys and girls in blue would get ambushed in route to disturbances with some frequency. Lights out. Never park right in front. All that tactical stuff.

It was pretty chilly as I recall, and it surprised us both to see a nearly naked man alone and busy in motion in front of our target house. He was a tall, thin, black male dressed only in cut-off jeans. We coasted closer and watched him. Ron finally decided we needed to see what was going on; and he pulled on the headlights, high beams, and our takedown lights, powerful light bar beams from our car roof that really turned darkness bright like a movie set.

WELL! This young man was busy working at the trunk of his car. The trunk was open, and he was wrestling with … a lifeless body. The body was as long and lanky as he was; and as quickly as he would shove an arm into the trunk, a leg would roll out and vice versa. The man was covered in swirling blood stains, that is, blood painted in circles and swirls on his skin. In my business, that generally means people were bleeding and fighting.

He froze in the bath of those bright lights. I can still see that picture in my mind today. He was half crouched over, eyes wide. Incredulous and shocked. There was no way he could identify who we were behind our bright lights.

I turned to Ron and said calmly, "I guess we got a murder?"

"Yeah," Ron, too, said calmly.

I sprang out of the car and pulled my Colt Python .357 magnum and pointed at the man. "Police! Hands up!"

He stood straight up and shoved his hands up high.

Ron and I approached from opposite flanks and handcuffed the man. Ron knew him immediately, "Terry, what is going on?" he asked.

"Ohhhh, MANNN! This mother-fucker tried to kill me."

Terry was indeed cut by a knife and had multiple slashes. I looked in the open trunk with the help of my Maglite flashlight – the large black male in the trunk was also cut up. He, too, was naked except for cut-off blue jeans. I felt for a pulse. None. It was more than obvious that Terry had put the body in the car planning to dispose of it later. Terry tried a few real Swiss-cheese excuses as Ron walked him back to our squad car and used the hand mike to call for an ambulance, a Sergeant, and for CID. He sat Terry on the ground and started to talk with him and inspect his wounds.

Curious, I walked into the house with my gun up and out. The house was partially furnished and, where so, it was with very old and pitted junk. All made worse, if possible, by the signs of a struggle. The living room was an upturned mess; and where it connected to a dining room, a cheap table and chairs were tossed away and turned upside down. There was an ancient carpet on the floor, and it was covered in a giant bloodstain. And atop this ritual, wet, red site? Two big kitchen knives. I imagined two 6 feet 2 inches lean black guys in matching cut-off jean shorts, no less, ducking, stabbing, and slashing. And yelling loud enough to wake the neighbors.

I saw a dim yellow light on down a short hall; and gun barrel first, I made my way into the room. On an old bed lay a white girl about 20 years old, later I discovered quite drunk, and with long blonde hair. Her shoulders were bare. She clutched a soiled and crusty sheet up to her chin.

"They were fighting over me," was all she said to me. That pretty much told me a lot.

"Get dressed," I told her. A duel. A duel for the "fair" lady.

She did, and I guided her out to the front of the house. By now, ambulances and supervisors were arriving. With my arms folded and the two of us leaning against a car on the street, I got a preliminary tale from the girl.

The sad story went that the girl was from out of state and attended one of the two big, local universities we had. She met Terry somehow (as Terry was hardly college material) and began this...this so-called affair. Terry then shared his best friend with her, but the sharing became too tense and complicated. Call it love? Territory? Honor, I guess? Call it what you will. And so, Sir Terry and this Sir Friend had to duel it out with kitchen knives over the fair lady in the dingy little dungeon of the castle. Murder ensued.

In the end, it was another torrid love story in the near-naked city of cut-offs, a mythic melodrama as old as the knights of yore. The duel of edged-weapons, as if told by Shakespeare himself. In the end of the courtroom case months later, the third act you might say, the prosecution could not prove who was defending himself against whom? And Terry Raygins received about a six-year sentence. He was out on the street in two and a half years on parole.

Terry was the first murderer I caught in Texas, that I can remember (after 50 years). I got to know Terry as the years went on. He stayed out of major trouble after that. These fair damsels can make you do crazy things.

Post Script: And through the years, I also got to know most all of the Raygins family. All was not well at Raygins' family castle either. They had a huge family and were a colorful bunch of troublemakers and sad sacks. Poppa Raygins was a hard-working factory man whose feisty wife had tossed him out of the house one winter. Tossed him out … to the garage, that is. Daddy Raygins lived in the unattached, dilapidated garage at the end of the driveway for several years. No heat, no air. We used to drive by and look down the driveway and see ol' man Raygins watching TV in his garage, or showering in boxer shorts by the yard hose, cooking on a hot plate, and sleeping on an old couch. If he sneaked into the house, his wife would beat him and toss him out. A time or two, I had an occasion to walk up the drive and talk to him, because? Because that is what good patrol officers do. They know the people of their beats.

One day Daddy Raygins decided his hot plate was not enough. He needed an electric stove in his garage. With a stove he could cook better than on the hot plate, and he could also leave the oven door open and heat the place in the winter. He bought a used kitchen stove from Ray Blevin's Used and Repaired Used Appliances. He cleared a space in his cluttered garage, plugged it in, turned it on, touched the metal contraption and electrocuted himself. Fried stone dead. His crispy self lain in the garage a few days until someone eventually saw him, found him and called us. Kilt by a stove he was.

His wife said, "Good riddance to that old bastard."

Sometimes, life ain't so pretty in the various Camelots we find for ourselves. Things can get mighty rotten in Denmark. Sometimes.

Chapter 19: How to Be Sued for $1.75 Million

The names have been changed here to prevent another lawsuit. Lord knows I don't know where I might come up with another million! That's right! Me! Sued for a Cool One! Here's how the front page of our local Sunday newspaper read back in 1980:

MAN FILES SUIT AGAINST CITY POLICEMAN

A Texas man, alleging false arrest for rape and murder, has filed a $1.75 million federal lawsuit that claims his civil rights were violated by the city and police detective W. Hochheim. The complaint filed July 16 by Joe Dips seeks $500,000 for damage to Dips' reputation and credit rating, $250,000 damages for "undue humiliation, shame, embarrassment, and fright," and $1.75 million in punitive damages from Hochheim.

The plaintiff is represented by attorney Roofus Rehabber. In the complaint, Joe Dips claims he was arrested without a warrant and without probable cause on _____, 1978, in the Wagon's West Ballroom by Detective Hochheim. The plaintiff was told by Hochheim that he was under arrest for rape and murder, handcuffed, taken to the police department, and jailed, the petition says.

The city is named as a defendant on grounds that since the detective acted under city authority and followed city policy in making the arrest, the city has failed to "properly train" the defendant in the legalities of making an arrest. Attorney Rehabber said the plaintiff was apparently mistaken for a suspect sought by police in the September 11, 1980, abduction, rape, and murder of an 18-year-old Texas waitress. The woman was assaulted, strangled, and left for dead in the woods near Hickory Creek Road according to the County Sheriff's office offense reports.

Investigators later identified as a suspect in the attack a man who was also wanted for murder of a female in Arkansas. That suspect was later arrested in Syracuse, New York, the paper further reported.

Yep. Yes, sir. There I was cruising down the old interstate burdened with one of those pesky unsolved murder cases. I needed a suspect, so I coasted into a bar parking lot, two-step-waltzed on in, and looked the crowd over for a prime one.

"Well, there's Joe Dips over there," I said to myself. Never have liked him. Why, I shuffled on over there, arrested that sucker, slapped cuffs on him, and yanked him out for rape and murder. Case closed, by God ... sure!

What more can I say other than the plaintiff's case was the sheerest of horse manure in the deepest sense. Yes, he was the wrong man, completely wrong. But you know, I didn't arrest him! I didn't even find him that night; another officer did. And this other officer didn't put him in jail either. So in an ironic twist, Plaintiff Dips and Attorney Rehabber were doing to me what they were accusing me of doing to Dips, picking on the wrong man!

My end of the ugly deal? $1.75 million dollars. This was the first time I was sued in my young life; so you know, I took it a bit personal. EVERYONE in our city got to read in the popular Sunday paper what an untrained boob-screw-up I was. But internally, our city PD from the Chief on down knew the knuckleheads at the County Sheriff's Office were really responsible. Several, including our Chief Hugh Lynch, knew Joe Dips was a local alcoholic dip-wad; and unesteemed Attorney Rehabber was just out from another trip from the rehab house.

Murder, bad cops, dopers, and drunks. And little ol' me in the middle. Here's the truth. Yes, in the fall of 1978, a woman was indeed missing from a local city hotel, taken out to the country, raped, strangled, and left for dead on a Texas county road. The criminal incident started inside the city limits yet ended up out in the county, making jurisdiction for the case a minor legal question but not a real problem. Since the abduction started within the city, it could've been a city case. It ended outside the city limits, so it could've been a county case. Either agency could effectively be the "case agent" for the crime. The County Sheriff's Office was called first and took charge. The actual acts of rape and attempted strangulation did occur out in the county. Detective Deputy Buckhead, under the loose supervision of a Detective Sgt. Wronghead, took over.

Buckhead had virtually no investigative experience. Wronghead was well known in investigative circles for deciding on a suspect in cases way too early; then he stuck with that wrong suspect stubbornly even well after evidence proved otherwise. Thus, the nickname. You see, Detective Wronghead often went "with his gut" too early and often had to vomit out his theory too late. He was kind of your worst nightmare to an innocent citizen who fell under the scope of an investigation. He got a gut feeling on you? You couple a jerk like that with an overzealous prosecutor; and your worst nightmare materializes into a hellish reality, and you're now in a Hitchcock movie. Both these knuckleheads slither around in our criminal justice system. I knew them. I'd seen them work. The next time you moan or make fun of a twitchy, angry criminal defense attorney? God actually made them for a real reason.

Me at the time of the crime? I was just a dumb kid in a patrol car. That's correct; I wasn't a detective then. Despite that fact, the lawsuit and newspaper made it sound like I worked the whole case and arrested the wrong man. In fact, I was working patrol shift the night of the original crime; and I recall all the County Sheriff's radio traffic when the girl was found.

The country Western bar where the suspect first met the victim was attached to a highway hotel. The hotel clerk at the hotel turned out to be a key witness, a lady named J. L. Tyler. At the desk, an Arkansas traveling salesman named Rory Clinton checked into the hotel with her. Tyler later saw Clinton and the ill-fated victim leave the club together. They walked through the lobby, happy, hugging, and drunk. Clinton returned alone through the lobby according to the clerk and then checked out early the next morning. Somewhere in the county woods, the woman lay raped and near death.

She was found alive. Within a day, Clinton had developed as a main suspect. BUT! There was a small problem. The man who checked into the hotel as Clinton was not Clinton. The real Rory Clinton was already dead himself! Clinton, the real traveling salesman, had been killed a day earlier in another state. When Buckhead put Clinton's name into the police NCIC system, authorities from Arkansas called. "We have him. His body, that is. He is dead."

Even rookie Buckhead deduced that the Arkansas murder suspect was probably the same one as his Texas rape and attempted murder suspect. The murderer probably used Clinton's identification and checkbook to check into our Texas hotel. The villain became "suspect unknown."

For those of you keeping a chronological checklist on all this? I am still a dumb kid in a patrol car driving around for all of this. My biggest concern in life back then was dodging spit from handcuffed drunks and where I might find the largest pool of available, wanton females. Discos or country bars? Ladies' night or discount drinks? Decisions. Decisions.

But anyway. I digress. We were told all these developments in a midnight-shift patrol briefing in the week that followed the crime. If my memory serves me well, Detective Wronghead himself came to the city squad room and explained that the suspect could be a city resident. Huh? The salesman was murdered in Arkansas. Yet Wronghead got it in his head that the killer-rapist was from our city. You know, he had a gut feeling.

A few nights later, a hysterical J. L. Tyler, key witness and hotel clerk, called the Sheriff's Office from the hotel bar. She was off duty and hanging out in the bar. She breathlessly reported to the dispatcher that this ... this "Rory Clinton feller," the one she'd checked in last week ... the rapist and killer ... was right then and there back inside the country Western bar. She said she was sitting at a table in the bar with friends watching him. The bar was very crowded. She was frightened to death that he might recognize her and "silence" her, too.

Now, get ready for a series of "called-fors."

The County dispatcher called for Detective Buckhead.

Buckhead called for Wronghead.

They would be late, so they called for backup.

Since the bar was in the city, the county dispatcher called for city police backup.

Beat cop and city officer James Brighten called for his backup, which was me.

Me? I had no one called for, as I was at the dirt, dog-scratch level of this totem pole.

No city detectives were called for because everyone assumed county detectives were in route to work their own case. So I was off to help catch a rapist and a murderer. And honestly, there was nothing more I would rather do. For me, there was no greater thrill or pastime than catching real, hard-core criminals. None. I still miss it every day to this day. As a last string, backup officer, I arrived in the bar parking lot rather late. That country and Western bar was popular, and it was packed as usual. Parked cars all over the lot and in the open field next door and even up on the service road.

I expected to see County Detective Buckhead or Wronghead or both! But instead, I saw a regular uniformed county deputy patrolman huddled with our city patrolman Brighton by the front of the establishment.

I joined them and listened in. Sadly, it appeared that the County Deputy was just "as in the dark" about all this as we were. He had no insider information and no support suggestions. We were to find and "catch" this bad guy. He thought we would be in charge. We thought he would be in charge.

Since I knew the witness, J. L. Tyler, just from patrol contacts, I entered the club first and started a hunt for her. I tried to smile and talk to patrons as though I was making a common and routine "bar check." I spotted her nervously perched at a table. I returned to the club door and told one of the bouncers to walk over to her, tell her to wait one minute, and then walk to the front door and meet us. That was done.

Within minutes, Tyler was outside talking to us. She was gasping. She told us where this suspect was seated, what he looked like, and how he was dressed.

"That man is him. I know it. I know it! I can't believe he came back!" she said.

Okay! We sent her to wait in the hotel office across the parking lot. Once we found our man, we would stand him in the lot outside an office window and talk to him under some lights. She would have to peer out the lobby window and look at him again. We needed her to identify him again for us in isolation and under the lot lights.

Brighten, the Deputy, and yours truly entered the loud, smoky club and spread out. Our killer was not where Tyler said he was! So we started searching. Mine was futile. Then suddenly I couldn't even see the deputy and Brighten. So I made for the front door, and a bouncer gave me the "thumb-this-way" message. My guys were outside and with the suspect out in the parking lot. I found out later that Brighten had spied him in the club and, fearing violence against himself and customers, approached him from behind, grabbed a wrist, identified himself, and ordered him outside. No handcuffs.

By now, you have guessed this mystery man in the club was Joe Dips. He looked VERY familiar to me because he was something of a regular.

"Is HE the killer?" I asked myself. I walked into the office and entered to find Tyler.

"Is that him?" I asked her.

"THAT is him," she said, peering out the window curtains. "Oh, my God!"

I returned to the group and gave the deputy and Brighten the nod of approval.

Brighten explained to Dips that he had been identified as a murder suspect.

Dips declared, "Murderer! Rapist! Is that what you want? Whew! Well, I know I didn't do that; I thought you were here to arrest me for hitting my wife. I just left her back at the house." This is the kind of cat we were dealing with. His ID showed him to be a local with a city address.

The deputy sat in his car and called his dispatcher and then walked back up to us. "Buckhead said to arrest him. There is an Arkansas 'John Doe murder arrest warrant for him."

Well, not him-him. Not Joe Dips directly, just someone who raped someone else and used someone else's ID to check into a hotel. But we "on the ground" were to decide who John Doe was. We? Or the county detectives working the case?

"Okay," we said and started moving Dips to the deputy's car.

"Ahh, no, no! Since this is within the city, Buckhead said you have to arrest him."

"WE do?" Brighten said.

Ahhh, the old arrest paperwork dodge. The city jail versus the county jail? Damn it, well, he did have us on some kind of technicality. We were in the city. But why not just take this county suspect to the county jail. And where were Buckhead and Wronghead anyway? Didn't they want him at the county to interrogate him? Well, I guess he had to be arrested somewhere. You just couldn't tell a traveling rapist-murderer to be in the office Monday morning for a chat, huh?

"This is a big mistake. I didn't kill anyone," Dips said calmly. "Y'all are crazy, man."

"Will Buckhead and Wronghead meet us at the city jail?" Brighten asked. "And straighten all this out?"

"Oh, yeah, yeah, sure thing," the deputy said. And

he got the hell out of there in a few seconds leaving us in the lot with Dips. We watched his taillights. He damn near burned rubber.

Dips consented to go to our city police station where the matter could be sorted out by the crackerjack county detective team. He got into the front seat of Brighten's car, without cuffs I might add, and rode to the station where some kind of a decision would be made. Witness J. L. Tyler followed in her car back a ways, presumably to give a written statement on her identification. The deputy left, presumably to our station for more follow-up? I was left standing in the parking lot with nothing to do. I just resumed my normal patrol duties.

I didn't find him. Didn't touch him. Didn't handcuff him. Didn't arrest him. Didn't transport him ... and I got sued for $1.75 million? Why? The saga continues....

What I did for the next two hours or so is a blank. Routine patrol? I do know I was getting curious about how this whole Dips thing was going. I made my way to the police station. It was then about 3 a.m. I wandered through headquarters and did not see the county deputy nor either of the two county detectives. Brighten was back out on patrol.

What I did see was our Patrol Lt. Russell Trapp in one of the offices talking with an unhandcuffed Joe Dips. I asked the front desk officer what was going on with Dips.

"No one from the county showed up," he told me.

"No one? Did Brighten book Dips in for murder?"

"Nope. Trapp wouldn't let him. Trapp doesn't think Dips is the killer. He talked with that hotel clerk, and Trapp thinks it is mistaken identity. He pushed it. He sat Dips in a hallway while Tyler studied him. She changed her mind and said he was too short to be the suspect. We can't reach the county detectives."

"Can't reach them?" How typical that was.

"Well, I think Trapp is right. Something ain't right about this deal," I said.

This meant the county left us out to dry on this flaky ID connection to the Arkansas murder case. Within the next hour, Trapp let Dips go. Trapp felt Dips was a local and would be around for further questioning. Gutsy, but something wasn't right. Basically, the crackerjack county detective team of Buckhead and Wronghead let a midnight-shift patrol supervisor for another agency make major decisions on their murder case, an attempted-murder case, and a rape case.

Lt. Trapp got Dips a ride back to his house. I do have a memory of eventually seeing Detective Wronghead talking to Lt. Trapp some hours later, about 6 a.m. near dawn. Trapp was explaining that he could not hold Dips, especially after Tyler recanted her ever-so-positive identification. Wronghead did show up.

I heard nothing about this particular case for years. But, I'm told that County Detective Buckhead was fired shortly thereafter for hanging out at the local truck stop too much while on duty. Yeah, that was his death knell. There had to be more to that story. Someone even suggested he was at the truck stop that very night when he should have been down at our station house working on this crime.

Before the million-dollar lawsuit, within the next few years or so, I had a few run-ins with Joe Dips and Attorney Rehabber; some were violent and involved threats. In the following two years or so, my last two in patrol before I became a detective, I did see Joe Dips around town. He got arrested a few times for public drunkenness and for assaulting his wife, but not by me. In the personalities one meets in life? Color Dips an unshaven, uneducated, stinky, dirt bag none of us would miss.

While in the patrol division, I arrested Attorney Rehabber twice and was involved in arresting him at least once with another officer for a total of three encounters. One cold winter night, I was patrolling another bar parking lot and spotted him beating a woman. They were arguing, and he was pulling and pushing her and slapping her around. He froze when he saw my squad car stop. He growled at me and shouted something. No doubt a challenging curse, but I couldn't hear him. He flung the woman aside and marched to my car as I got out of it. He was talking smack the whole way. He was a big, bulky guy and wore many layers of clothing and an overcoat. I got his arm and dumped him over my car hood and cuffed him. His drunken march ended with me marching him into a jail cell. He was drunk as a skunk.

About a year later, I arrested Rehabber again, this time for DWI. As he sat on the booking room bench, a pee stain down his pant-leg, he sneered at me, "I am going to get you, you know. I am an attorney."

"Yeah, yeah, yeah." But I guess he did try something years later.

After I became a detective, I was involved in a few high-profile crimes that got a lot of media coverage and subsequent name recognition. Rumors at the courthouse had it that Rehabber and Dips, over umpteen midnight whiskeys in some bar, decided they should sue someone for that old "false arrest"; and the only name the both of them could remember...was mine.

Thus, the lawsuit and defamation in the newspaper. But the case was quickly dismissed after the first round of legal depositions, in which I made a small, unprofessional, immature scene. Our city attorney tried to calm me down, but it was more than evident these two knuckleheads sued the wrong person, the wrong officers, and the wrong agency. My redemption was a small paragraph on Page Nine.

The cast of dubious characters evolved through time:
- Rehabber went in and out of a few rehabs. I think he may be dead by now.
- Detective Wronghead bounced around a few agencies.
- Detective Buckhead is collecting shopping carts in supermarket parking lots.
- Officer Brighten is still a dedicated, good officer.

Joe Dips, you ask? In about 1981, ol' Joe's mother died. She left him a lot of money. A lot. He bought a small metal-shop factory he once worked in. He hired a few new employees, and one of them was a serial killer. "Rodeo Bob." I got after Bob; and he fled Texas and then resurfaced when I tracked him down to San Diego, California, where he had a refrigerator full of carved-off human faces in Tupperware containers. Nice hobby. Rodeo Bob, the serial killer is another story in book 2, the detective part of these memoirs.

Chapter 20: The Bouncer Jump

Rookie and even veteran officers! Take heed in this next short essay, and lesson. In the 1970s I was quite dumb, shallow and short-sighted. Probably really selfish, but many of us were, at 25 years old or so. Some weren't, sure, but, I was not put together that well.

It was Saturday night; and I went to work like I did every night back then, motivated to "get into some shit." Stir things up and make arrests. Chase. Shoot. Fight. Whatever. That was my mission.

The shift started at 3 p.m., and it was nearly 9 p.m. And for a Saturday night, nothing much was going on. Dull as a stump. I recall that I was exceptionally frustrated that night at the lack of activity. I was working a southwest side district, which included one of the major universities in the whole state of Texas. With all the related bars and hangouts, surely, surely somebody was fucking up somewhere; and all I had to do was find him or her. Hunt. Hunt. And hunt.

I turned down a street with a row of night clubs, and there was a popular hot spot of hard rock and druggies down that way. The door of this outfit suddenly burst open, and four bouncers were fighting with one guy in the middle in a cluster-ruckus. Delight! I floored the gas pedal down the street, jammed on the brakes of the car with a screech, and bailed. The ejected patron was a white male in the middle, and I leapt over the two bouncers on my side of the melee and flat-out attacked the guy.

But I really screwed up. By the time I opened the car door, the fight? It was really over, and I saw this; but I was already supercharged and well on my way. The four bouncers quickly ignored the patron and essentially rescued that customer ... from me. Imagine that karma.

"Hock! Hock!" they yelled to me, trying to calm me down. We all knew each other from many prior disturbance calls. They shouted for me to stop. "It's over." Things like that. Eight hands and arms gripped me and hauled me back. With their extra grips, I finally got a grip on myself. The once-rowdy customer, his pale white jaw dropped low and eyes wide, backed away; then he turned and scattered down a side street.

"Damn, Hock!" they muttered at the scene I'd created. I looked them over. They were no angels themselves. Redneck bouncers in a hippy bar; and if you know your Texas history, that's like matter and anti-matter in the same hot tub. They all had their share of overkill in bar enforcement through the years. They just didn't like wrestling with the cops, too.

I didn't say anything to any of them. I was wrong and should have been plain embarrassed. I straightened out my uniform and ran my hands back through my thick, long Johnny Cash hairdo. There, good as new! But the slobber from my mouth and my racing pulse could not be so thusly organized with a few magic hand passes. Orderly on the outside, but all kinds of disorderly on the inside.

I returned to the squad car and drove off without a word. WHAT had just happened? I lost it, man, that's what. I tried to catch my breath, snorting in the car. I knew that fight was well over before I charged them, yet

I was there to fight. I was going to fight the guy and fight the bouncers. The fight switch was thrown. I pulled over in a corner parking lot and sat mind-numb, watching the traffic on a major avenue run by.

That was not what I was supposed to do. That was not right. What was I? I understood my immature frustration. I understood the wrong. I really did want to be ... that whole professional thing. That modern professional in uniform. The better side of me ordered that this could not happen again. But it did happen again. Worse and even more dangerous a time or two. But I will never forget that night decades ago. I grew up a bit that night. Just a notch, though. Just not enough yet.

Chapter 21: Me and the Lone Ranger

When I was a kid in the 1950s, the Lone Ranger was on prime time television. And along with many Westerns like the Cisco Kid and Hopalong Cassidy, children of all ages were mesmerized by the black and white box in their living rooms. The first years of my life, I grew up in a tenement-style, claptrap apartment in Union City, New Jersey, in the New York Metro area. When it burned down one Christmas, taking with the fire my Zorro and Lone Ranger gun sets. Masks, capes, everything ... GONE!--that, of course, deeply scarred me for life I guess.

Anyway, a big highlight for me was going to Madison Square Garden in NYC to a "cowboy show"; and appearing was the Lone Ranger and Tonto shootin' blanks and riding in circles, doin' horse tricks, and whatever they did at these things. Wow! Then my dad took me a couple of times to the Macy's Thanksgiving Day Parades. From my superior vantage point atop his shoulders, I saw ALL the Western stars ride by on horseback. Bonanza guys, Paladin, Josh Randel, all of them. Even Matt Dillon. Of course, the Lone Ranger and his faithful sidekick Tonto trotted by.

"Who was that masked man?"

Then they left. Because, well ... their work there was done.

When I talk about being a bodyguard and doing security work for famous folks, I usually never mention the ones I did as a police patrolman or detective. I was assigned those jobs; it was not like in the latter years as a private investigator when I had to hunt and get selected for such work. As a cop, I was assigned to people like Coretta King, various Dallas Cowboys' players, and even attached to the Secret Service with Bush #1, etcetera. And, yes, even the Lone Ranger.

In 1980, a huge new shopping mall was built in our city in Texas; and the grand opening was a big event. The company hired stars to come. Let's see if I can name them. From Star Wars, Billy D. Williams who played Lando Calrissian in "Return of the Jedi?" Phyllis George who was Miss America in 1971. Ahhh ... two other famous dudes and then, Clayton Moore as The Lone Ranger.

As fate would have it, I was assigned to Clayton Moore. Now Clayton thought he was the Lone Ranger. He never appeared in public without that mask. When MGM made a new Lone Ranger movie (a bomb) about that time, they sued Clayton to get him to remove the mask for good. They wanted their new star in the new Ranger movie to be the only famous Lone Ranger. That was sure a lowdown move, wasn't it?

But Clayton bought a pair of big curved dark sunglasses and wore them everywhere, the kind people wear these days when they have cataract surgery. Clayton's mask-like eyewear let him thumb his nose in the face of MGM. I imagine they cussed their specific "mask" verbiage in that court settlement.

The "mask" lawsuit put ol' Clayton back in the news

instead of banishing him. The Texas Rangers ball team felt sorry for him and hired him as kind of a mascot. He would ride out on horseback at the seventh-inning stretch; the park was bathed in his theme song of heroic trumpets, and it would whip me and the crowd into a complete frenzy!

So back at the mall grand opening, he was very popular. Clayton was decked out in the blue suit and legendary gun belt, hat, and mandatory sunglasses. He sat at a table and signed autographs and walked the mall shaking hands and talking.

At the first break we wandered back into the mall offices. He took his hat and gun belt off and hung the black leather, double-six-gun rig on the back of a chair. I stood before the belt and its silver bullets and was transformed into a kid again. It glistened before me like Christmas morning.

"The last time I saw you was in Madison Square Garden in the 50s," I told him.

"Yes," he said, "Tonto and I were there in 1957 for the rodeo show."

Therein lay his obsessive commitment to the character. He didn't say "Jay" or "Jay Silverheels" and I; he had to say, "Tonto and I."

Anyway, the day was a blast and a blast from the past. Thrilling days of yesteryear. The Lone Ranger is still on TV somewhere in the world. There were 221 television episodes. Clayton Moore died in 1999. I can only guess ... his work here was finally done.

Hi-yo, Bubba. Hi-yo.

(More bodyguard stories in Book 2 of this two-part book series.)

Chapter 22: Some Gunplay and Some Fisticuffs! Night of the Mad "Pay-tre-ons"

Country and Disco; Rednecks and Hippies. Back then when I first patrolled the streets in the 1970s, be it in the Army or out, I ... profiled ... or rather nicknamed the guys I would see roaming the bars and restaurants at night. When the dancing parlors shut down each night, waves of "Country and Disco" folks would gravitate into the 24-hour diners. Some gravitated into our jails. It didn't take long to realize you were more likely to have trouble with a guy dressed in black with a felt cowboy hat than one duded up like a hair-sprayed member of the Bee Gees. Profiles in wardrobes.

Some of the bouncers in the country and Western clubs were rough and rowdy people, and I have written some of their stories before. Like them or not, we got to and had to work with them; and they were indeed the first line of eyes and ears for a lot of stuff. They tipped us off, they pulled us out of scrapes, and they watched our backs. We watched theirs. When I was a detective later on, they helped clear some cases, even murders, for me.

One night at the Duster's Club, two bouncers I'll just call Ralph and Randy were whistled over by a barkeep pointing to a loud patron who was starting trouble. As they approached the disturbance, the patron turned, yelled, and held them at bay with an open palm.

"You stay outta this!" the man screamed.

Ralph thought the man was drugged more than he was drunk.

"Say, padnah," Randy said, "come on, we just need you to leave, hear?"

"Fuck you, skunk!" the man declared, "I ain't cha padnah!"

With that, the man pulled a big revolver from under his jacket and pointed it at them and shoved it straight out at arm's length. Randy and Ralph ducked and backed away, and the customers nearby shrieked and ran. But overall, this place was noisy and big; and the shock wave didn't rumble through the whole crowd. The rest of the place just two-stepped right on by. Kind of like life, really, when you think about it.

The man charged the bouncers swearing he would kill them. The barkeep called the police. And that would be me. I was about two miles away.

"Pay-tre-ron at the Duster with a pistol," the dispatcher told me on the car radio. This dispatcher, not a mental giant, always mispronounced the word "patron," calling them "pay-tre-ons," like they were some kind of an alien race. Our running joke for night shift when this dispatcher was on duty was, "wonder if we'll be invaded by the Pay-tre-ons tonight?"

"Ten-four," I said; and, of course, there was no backup available. Everyone was busy with his or her own Saturday-night alien invasions.

As I pulled up into the Duster parking lot, to my surprise, I saw Randy and Ralph kneeling beside some parked cars in the parking lot. They were peeking over the trunks and hoods to the north to a cheap motel beside the nightclub. They ran to a wall and motioned me over.

"He's in there!" Randy told me as I walked up to

them. He pointed to the motel. I stared, ducking down, too, because ... I can take a hint.

"Who?" I asked. "The guy with the gun? I thought he was in the Duster."

"He ran out the door and across the lot. Ralph and I follered behind him. Come here," Randy said, and brought me to the corner of the motel. "He is in that room."

"He's madder than hell. He is on drugs," Ralph said. "I swear he was gonna kill us. He's got a big-assed revolver. He pointed it at us and at half a dozen people in the bar."

He singled out the room window for me; and I could see a light was on inside, and there was a lot of movement inside. The curtain was partially open. I worked my way around the corner while staring at the room window for any action. And then I slipped down the motel's south wall and up the west wall until I was right beside this window.

This was an old-fashioned, cinder block-constructed motel. Each room had a horizontal window with a sliding glass, windowpane, and a curtain. The window was partially open. No screen on the window. I peered inside.

An angry man was pacing the small room from the bathroom door to the front door. He was quietly cursing to himself, clenching his fists, and waving his arms. On the corner of the dresser by the front door was the "big-assed revolver." I pulled out my .357 Python, my own big-assed gun, in case he decided to continue his angry walk out the door holding that damn thing.

I stepped back and saw Randy and Ralph looking at me from across the parking lot. The loud and busy interstate highway ran behind them. I made a big circling motion with my hand and then pointed to a spot on the far side of the door, a signal for them to go up the service road and down the far side of the motel. I was all alone here and needed their help. (That was back in the day before God made SWAT. You know that type of thing could become a full-fledged parade today. In those days, we had to handle stuff ourselves.) But if my quick plan would work, I needed them; and they were itching to help.

I watched the man pace. When Randy and Ralph got into position on the far side of the door, I got into mine. At a moment when the man was near the bathroom door and far from his gun, I reached into the partially open window, hooked the curtain, and pointed my Python at him.

"Police! Freeze!" I barked. Which he did. His eyes cut to his pistol.

"No! Don't even think about it."

Outside, Ralph tried to open the door; but it was locked.

"You will walk over to the door with your hands up. You will unlock the door," I told him in the most menacing voice I could muster. "If you touch that pistol, I will cut you in half."

He understood that and marched over to the door. As he got close to his gun, I inched my pistol in just a bit more for a better angle. Yes, I would have cut him in half. He unlocked the door.

As soon as the knob jiggled, Ralph and Randy barged in with quite a double tackle on that guy right onto the bed. I thought the bed would collapse, but it didn't. They immediately proceeded to pommel and beat the tar out of him. I stepped around the wall into the room and stuck his pistol into my belt line. I took a quick peek into the bathroom for anyone else. Accomplices. Beaten-up girlfriend. Dead guys. Yeah, no telling. But it was empty that time. Meanwhile, the beating on the bed continued.

"Okay, okay, okay," I said, trying to tone those guys down just enough to get a space to handcuff the guy. The suspect was busted up a bit by now; but way back then, which I still affectionately refer to as "the good ol' days," the jailers accepted and booked-in near-dead prisoners and never so much as offered an aspirin to them. Today they get new teeth, a manicure, and a scholarship.

Off to jail. Detectives on Monday morning would work the rest of this. Get statements. The guy, a Texan but an out-of-towner, had no prior criminal history. I charged him with possession of a firearm in a bar, which was a felony then, and for the assault of pointing that pistol at Randy and Ralph. Why'd he do it? Hell if I know. I just did my part of the job. As usual, I never saw nor heard from that suspect again. He must have plea-bargained himself a deal.

Yup, I never saw him again. Just a whole lot of folks like him. The world was full of those damn "Paytre-ons." It was an invasion. The truth was out there.

Chapter 23: Harvey, Give Me the Shotgun

"Harvey ... give me the shotgun."

That was the time when cops usually got killed, I reminded myself, looking at an angry Harvey Wilson with a 12-gauge pump aimed at me. But I thought since I knew him, I could talk him down ... I thought....

The first time I met Harvey Wilson, he was drunk riding a horse. Not too unusual since, after all, it was Texas. It was a bitter cold winter night, about 2 a.m. back in the 1970s; and Garry Burns and I were on patrol when we spotted Harvey slumped over the saddle. Harvey had a barn on the back of his one-acre lot with a house in the city limits, and apparently this horse didn't know the way home to the barn. Or it was on a walk, and Harvey was just there bouncing along for the ride. We coasted up beside the horse and rider.

"Harvey!" Garry shouted.

No answer.

I pulled up far enough ahead that we both could get out.

The old horse walked up to us. We grabbed the reins and stopped the gelding.

"WHAT?" Harvey snapped awake when the horse stopped. "What!" and then started kicking at us. Harvey was a hard-working stout black man in his late 50s at the time, living alone in a neighborhood of welfare cases, drug addicts, screw-ups, and fuck-offs. Harvey was a little rowdy and tended to "pull the cork"; but despite the whiskey, he was always at work the next day. That night he fussed and kicked at us enough that Garry decided Harvey needed to spend four hours in our urine- and puke-stained, stinking drunk tank.

We hauled him off the horse and cuffed him in a frisky little wrestling match, all under the big eyes of his calm horse. I put Harvey in the front seat; back then in the pre-cage days, that was where we transported prisoners so we could watch them as we drove. Garry got in the driver's seat, and I climbed up into the saddle. I rode the horse to the city animal pound while the dispatcher paged out the on-call animal pound worker to meet me there.

Not six months later and alone this time, I repeated the whole affair again with a smashed and frisky Harvey and his horse. If you looked at Harvey's file, you'd find multiple drunk-in-public arrests. Still, he never seemed to hold a grudge and always held down a job. On weekends you'd drive by his small wooden house; and he would be painting, or cementing, or fixing something. Salt of the Earth. Every once in a while when I was on Saturday or Sunday day shift, I would pull over and get out to talk with him for a few minutes.

"Whatca' doing, Harvey?"

"Ohh ... oh, fixin' to clean out my septic tank lines," he would say softly and breathlessly and rest on a shovel and tell me the symptoms and cure for his latest housing ailment.

Then a fairly new red Camaro started appearing; it was parked on the street outside Harvey's house. One day I saw a very attractive black girl, say in her late twenties or early 30s, pulling up in it and walking into Harvey's house with her arms full of shopping bags. She entered without knocking. The car remained night after night. I asked Marvin Hayes, a retired postal worker and neighbor down the street, about this mystery car and curvy girl.

"Harvey's got him a girlfriend. YaHeah! And I means to say girl! Young! She's a sweet young thing, too. From Dallas. I don't know how they met. And I don't know how he keeps her. But he bought her dat dere car, you know?"

"NO!" I declared. "The Camaro!"

"Yes, he did. Bought her dat car and, and jewelry, and, and I don't know what all. YaHeah! I hopes he knows what he is doin. Cause you know, this kind of business don't end well."

I ran the license plate of the car in the hopes of getting her name and seeing if she had a criminal history. The plate was still registered to a car dealership in Dallas. Back then it used to take a while, maybe even a few weeks, to catch registrations up on NCIC.

In our squad meetings, the Sergeant read us the daily blotter each day, the list and quick summary of the events since we left the day before. Over a period of three weeks, there were several domestic disturbance calls at Harvey Wilson's house. There was already trouble in paradise. I never caught a single one of those calls at Harvey's house until one Saturday afternoon.

Neighbors reported another fight. When I pulled up, that girl was almost through packing her Camaro. She looked up and smirked at me and continued yelling over her shoulder at Harvey, who was up the small hill of his front yard and by his front porch. When I climbed the small incline, I got my first look at Harvey. He was holding a pump shotgun at port arms. His eyes were red and wet, and the veins and muscles in his neck bulged. I knew if I drew my pistol, that action could be a catalyst for him to react and shoot me or her or both. I could just tell. And that is how many, if not most, cops are killed in domestics.

"I'll kill her!" he yelled.

"Harvey. Put down the gun. You can't kill anybody," I said.

"BITCH! I'll kill you, BITCH!" he yelled. He was barely paying attention to me and watching her pick up her suitcases from the lawn.

"I bought that car!" he said.

"It is in my name, mutha-fucka!" she yelled.

He pointed his gun at her. My thumb undid the snap of my holster, and I grabbed a handful of my pistol handle. I did not draw the gun yet.

"Harvey. Harvey. Harvey," I repeated calmly. "You can't kill her. You can't kill her over a car. You know that. Give it up man. You can't be doing that. Put the barrel down. Let her go. You shoot her, and your life is over. She ain't worth it!" I inched closer and closer, and he got madder and madder. He was losing it. He waved the gun over to me, inches from lifting the stock to his cheek and shooting.

He glared and gritted his teeth, and I could see his fingers moving in waves on the gun. The barrel wandered from me to the girl, to no one, and back again. I got close enough to lunge out and grab the weapon with both my hands and pulled the barrel up and the stock down. With a motion not unlike rowing a single oar of a canoe, I ripped and rolled the gun from his grip.

The girl slammed the car door and burned rubber down the street. Harvey's little temporary paradise … was gone.

I ran the pump up and down, which spit out the shells across the manicured lawn. When it was empty, I laid it against a porch railing. Harvey sat on the stairs of the porch. I sat down next to him. Marvin had witnessed the whole thing from next door and walked over. He was probably the one who called us.

"Man! Fuck!" Harvey said. "Did I get fucked?"

"She was no good," Marvin said. And I agreed. We sat there on the steps for about 10 minutes talking. My backup squad car drove up and stopped. I waved him off, signaling it was all over and everything was okay.

I got up after a bit and said, "Harvey, I am gonna take this shotgun in with me for 24 hours." I saw Marvin nod his head at me. "You can come down to the station and get it tomorrow." I picked up the ejected rounds on the manicured grass.

"You got him, Marvin?" I asked.

"I got him. I got him," Marvin said.

We used to have a policy where we would extract guns from a hot situation where there might be more violence or suicide and lock them up at the police department. Just a local practice. The owner would have to go see the police chief and talk to him and retrieve the gun.

Ol' Harvey did. He picked up his gun the next day after Chief Hugh Lynch had a word of advice or two for him. Harvey remained quiet and behaved himself with the ladies from then on.

****

One morning some 10 years later, I was a detective; and we got a call of a body found near some undeveloped land in the southeast part of town. A cable man and a railroad agent were surveying land to bury some lines near a run of tracks when they stumbled upon a body not that far from the road.

When I got there, I was surprised to find EMTs feverishly at work at the scene. The railroad man walked up to me and said, "He wasn't dead! We thought he was dead, but he wasn't."

I walked past the agent and to the action. The techs were working on Harvey Wilson! Harvey was dressed up in a suit and looked like he was pulverized to a pulp. He was whisked to the hospital and lay there in intensive care for days in a coma before he could answer a question.

I went to Harvey's house, and neighbor Marvin and I tried to reconstruct his last healthy day. One thing for sure, Harvey's pickup was missing; and I put out a "BOLO" on the truck. We searched his house and found his insurance papers; and through a local agent, we got the license plate number. I was frozen stuck in a bad case with no leads and hoping the truck would show up somewhere and-or Harvey would wake up.

The hospital called days later. A nurse said Harvey was up and trying to eat. You know where I went.

"What happened, Harvey?" I asked him.

"John Wayne Williams. He asked me for a ride. Then he pulled a gun on me. That skunk fuck. He made me stop the truck out there on Morse Street. He beat me up with his gun and robbed me. Left me for dead meat in the woods."

John Wayne Williams. Local gangster. We'd gotten word of his recent parole, and no one would bet how long before he would be in violent trouble again. It was that inevitable. And he was indeed a skunk fuck. I got a probable-cause arrest warrant for Williams, and Danny McCormick and I hunted around and found him in about two days. He was a muscular 6 feet 5 inches smartass prison-weight-lifting, ex-con; and when we saw him in a housing project's parking lot, we both drew down on him with our .45s. We ordered him on his knees with his hands up and cuffed him quick.

At the station I interrogated him. He played dumb.

We never found that truck. In those days, they were easily stripped and sold for parts in chop shops either out in the county or in Dallas. With Harvey's court testimony, I sent him up for the "big bitch life," as this was his third felony.

Harvey was never quite the same after that near-death beating. Within a year or two thereafter, he died of natural causes. Heart attack.

Chapter 24: The Barefoot Policeman

Back in the 1970s I wanted to finish college, so I reluctantly requested a transfer into what was called the "relief patrol shift." I say reluctantly because I enjoyed my time with my regular rotating patrol shift, led by a Lt. Gene Green and Sgt. Eric Jackson. But the relief shift had the same hours each week, was partially created for college attendees, and was mathematically inserted inside the oddball eight-hour, rotating-shift openings.

But the relief-shift math wasn't completely perfect. There were shifts and days each week that had no gaps, and we of the relief outfit were just added to the manpower of rotating shifts. (This making any sense?) Week after week on certain nights, the regular rotating-shift Sergeant would look at us relief patrolmen and wonder what to do with us. We would often be assigned in the same cars as partners. Thus, for quite some time on Thursday nights, I was partnered with Sal, the barefoot policeman.

Sal and I always had a blast every Thursday night on the 3 p.m. to 11 p.m. shift. Sal was already a vet at the police department, and he was a hysterical fellow with a great sense of humor. He was a little bit buck-toothed and a real country boy. He was kind of shaped like John Wayne and would often wear his revolver like the Duke a click or two back on his belt. Not too near his back pocket but not right on the hip. He would casually rest his hand on his gun handle like Wayne did, which really stretched the leather holster through time. Eventually, it sort of flapped around back there when he walked.

They say that Sal started out a very gung-ho officer; but after being unfairly (his version) bumped on a sergeant's exam, his spirit was broken. Since then, he just wandered through his 40-hour workweek barely getting by and irritating supervisors and citizens alike. He left our agency for a while and worked out of state where one night he beat up a drunk driver and was fired. But we hired him back.

"That son-a-bitch kept reaching over and tearing up the DWI reports! I'd get half finished with one of them, and he'd lean over and rip it up. You can't pull that shit back here in Texas!" Sal told me. "So I hit him; I mean, that's what we'd do here. Hell, those pussies fired me."

That was one tale rehashed on many a Thursday night as Sal and I patrolled. It was not uncommon for Sal to ride shotgun and let me drive. In fact, I cannot recall a time when Sal ever drove. Too much work I think. It was almost a weekly routine for him to buy a big oversized bag of caramel-covered popcorn. He'd open the bag and start eating. Sometimes he'd eat Doritos, but usually it was the sticky brown popcorn.

We would drive around; and if we had a break in calls, eventually Sal would remove his cowboy boots. One at a time to let his feet ... breathe. Often, next off came his white socks. He would commence to pick his toenails, preen, and massage his feet ... and eat popcorn from the big bag. And, yes, absent-mindedly he would sometimes offer me some popcorn, which I would decline. He would sometimes produce silver nail clippers and with great intent carve away at his feet.

Meanwhile, I was still in my gung-ho stage and would aggressively patrol. Sal would curse at every call and gripe every time I dared initiate some action, especially once early in an evening shift. Just before sunset at rush hour, I spotted a car bust through a red light in a hurry. I accelerated after it, and Sal started in with his usual gripes, "What? Whatcha' doing, man?" he asked.

"They ran a red light."

"So what? Oh, come on!"

This was work, and he did not want to work; he wanted no part of it. I wanted to get into something. It wasn't the ticket I was after, but rather "what kind of shit I could get into" (as the common phrase said). I might not write him a ticket at all.

I had to blast the siren to let the driver know I was serious, because he seemed to ignore me at first. In the front seat next to him was a woman and another male at the passenger-door seat. When the car finally pulled into a business parking lot on Dallas Drive, I got out and approached the driver's door. Sal, barefoot with his bag of popcorn on his lap, remained in the squad car.

I collected the driver's license and returned to our squad car to run wants and warrants.

"What he say? Huh? What? What?" Sal was always over-curious and eagerly interested even though he took no action.

"Oh, nothing much," I told him. I started running the guy's name and DL on the NCIC. I sat in the driver's seat with the door open and one foot on the ground.

"Sixty-one," came the dispatcher.

"Go ahead," I said.

"The subject is wanted in Dallas for burglary."

"Damn!" muttered Sal. Work.

After getting some of the details from the dispatcher, I walked up to the car and asked the guy to get out and talk to me, which he did. I told him the bad news, and he started declaring that the system had made a big mistake, etcetera. I honestly cannot remember the guy's name and what he said. It's been about 30 years now. But what happened next? I couldn't forget.

When the driver complained loudly about the arrest warrant, the passenger door flung open; and the other male passenger got out. Sal popped his door. The guy took a few steps toward me, and then he turned and ran like hell across the business parking lots.

I itched to chase him, but what could I do about my burglary suspect? I couldn't leave him here. Just as the instant quandary hit me, here ran Sal ... barefoot ... in hot pursuit.

"Goddamn! Ya-little-mother-fuckin'-stupid-shit-son-a-bitch, I will shoot yer ass down, ya...." Sal emitted in one long cussing stream.

Did I tell you that Sal loved to play golf? Total addict. Daily. And he really wasn't in too bad a shape. He hotfooted across the A-1 Cleaners, Dallas Pawn Shop, and the 7-11 parking lots after this kid. The lots were too full of customers for Sal to shoot at him, which he had a hankering to do at those chase times.

"That officer has no shoes," the burglary suspect said calmly to me.

"The pay is a little low here," I told him as I cuffed his hands.

Off in the distance, Sal had caught the kid by the 7-11 gas pumps, had shaken him around a bit, and then cuffed him. He marched the kid back with a hand on the scruff of his neck.

Of course, many people stared in amazement at the barefoot policeman.

This second kid had drugs in his pocket. LSD I think, but I am not sure on that. Can't remember. But we arrested both of them. I searched the car and found nothing illegal. The girl had no record, and I let her drive the car off. On the way to the jail, Sal put his socks and cowboy boots on. No one said a word about it.

The next Thursday night? We had a few laughs, patrolled around town, stopped at a Gas-N'-Go, and Sal bought himself a big bag of caramel popcorn. Two hours into the shift he was happily munching away and picking at his bare feet.

And all things were right in heaven....

(P.S. Sal eventually left and became a golf club salesman.)

Chapter 25: A Nightmare Near Elm Street

I think the guy I confronted that strange night was a real pro, maybe more than any ex-con; maybe something else? And he played me well ... with his bullets....

"Armed robbery. White male. Armed with a handgun."

The address followed. A convenience store on the interstate. Usually means a high-speed getaway with a car, but not always. Not always. And not this time. I was one exit south, and the store was just out of my assigned jurisdiction. But I was near. Plus, I was the only available patrol car. It was a weekday night as I best recall, yet a very busy night shift; and the others were assigned their own little mandatory nightmares. The dispatcher sent me, and I was already in route anyway. Not too often you get this close to a fresh robbery. Still, by the time a victim gets free to call the police, the dispatcher answers, the dispatcher radios you, and you actually get there, precious minutes have ticked off.

"White male. Hat. Short hair, light-colored shirt...."

I turned on the interstate service road and floored the gas pedal. No red lights. No siren, as I wanted to get there as fast and as quietly as possible. To my left, the four-lane interstate highway. To my right, open fields, some trees, tall weeds, switch grass, and a horse ranch with rolling land. Beyond, way off in the distance, were older wooden homes on South Elm Street.

As I crested the hill that led to a full view of the store and the intersection off in the distance, WHAT? A white male! Before me. That was what I saw. A glimpse really. A second. A white male running up the service road toward me keeping tight to the brush in the field to his left. Hat. White guy? His hands...weapon? Couldn't discern them. He had to be over 40 years old. Maybe 50? Five feet, 10 inches? Short-sleeve pullover shirt. Muscular. Pants of some kind ... then he's gone! Gone. He took one look at me and ducked into this field! I don't recall a shocked expression. Was this a ghost? I slammed on my brakes. I could see the store down the road. Was there someone bleeding and dying in there? Was that the robbery suspect I just saw? On foot? Running away? What should I do? Proceed to the store as standard operating procedure dictates? No, I had to chase this guy.

"Dispatcher, I got a white male who dove into the brush. I am south of the store. He may be the robbery suspect. I will be in the field south and across Teasley Lane of the store. Older white..." I babbled the description and vague location into the car radio mike. Obviously I needed help, but there was no help available. Worse, back in the days of the 1970s, there was a shortage of hand-held radios! I had none.

I grabbed my flashlight, pulled out my Colt Python .357 Magnum, and ran to the field about where I saw this guy dive. I could not hear or see all that well. There was some ambient light. The highway behind me was full of steady traffic casting off the fleeting "sides" of headlights. Some distant, tall, gas-station tower lights were all around offering some glow. The whole place was varying shades of gray and was shifting about in a slight breeze. The semi-trucks and cars also caused a roaring hum to the landscape, especially the trucks. The tall grass and wild weeds ranged from heights of three feet to five feet or so, and the roll to the land made it taller and shorter in spots. I could barely hear myself scrape through the brush, which at times I had to part like I was swimming, light in one hand, and gun in the other. There were plenty of places for an armed man to hide and ambush; and, all in all, it was a real-life nightmare situation. And it suddenly got worse.

I got to a higher point and looked around. Nothing suspicious. Where could ... he! Gunshot! Ducked! What?

This guy popped up about 50 or 60 feet from me; fired a pistol at me. He popped back down. One second. I instantly ducked and dropped down on one knee below the grass line before I could digest what had really happened in that second. Less than a second?

"That mother-fucker shot at me!" I said to myself, astounded. And I could not see him or anything down this low! I felt the need to drop on my back, and I aimed my pistol up in his last general direction and at the wall of grass before me. Because what if he was moving in on me? I watched and listened waiting for a figure to peel through the tall grass or appear above the grass hunting me. That was the man I saw duck into this field. That time I saw him from belt-line high. He was maybe 50 years old and clean cut. Muscular and trim. I realized in a few seconds he wasn't charging me, and this prone position wasn't going to work for a host of reasons. I got back up to one knee. I looked back down the slope and saw my squad car parked on the service road. Still no help. No sense running back down to report in. That guy would get away.

I took steps to the left; and with my gun up, I popped up tall myself and scanned the grounds and then got low and moved off. No more Sunday stroll and noisy breast-stroke through this place! I circled in the direction I thought a fleeing man might choose to escape, which was the far east of the field, Elm Street, and the horse ranch. With each step I got further from the lights and roar of the interstate. I was in a crouched walk and sometimes low jog. I had chased armed men from time to time through the woods before, and it always sucked. This one felt different. My alert system was turned on full, full, full. This was lonely, scary shit! And I was ready to shoot at ANYTHING.

Bang! Him!

BANG! Me!

There he was again! He stood, shot, and ducked; and I shot back reflexively. No aim; just shot. One hand grip and no time to aim. I meant to let this guy know not to charge me while shooting at me, because I would pull the trigger on his ass. He was about 50 feet away this time? Maybe sixty and a bit closer to the horse ranch. "SHIT!" I cussed under my breath. I mean to say that this guy actually looked like a classic pop-up target that flipped forward and back before you could shoot at it!

I bolted off from the spot and peeked up again. Nothing. No sound. No bad guy. Just the wind whipping through the tall grass. The leaves rustling in sporadic trees. All in an area as big as three football fields or more. Distant lights. Distant traffic. Distant help. This was a cat and mouse game, and I couldn't tell you who was the cat or who was the mouse.

Two. He'd shot twice.

I continued the circle toward the dim lights of South Elm Street.

No one ever taught me to count bullets in any of the

police academies I had attended. In fact, there was talk to the contrary about NOT counting bullets because it would be a distraction. Many said you couldn't anyway. But I still learned it as a kid watching Westerns. It's all so situational. In a prolonged encounter like this, you had time to think about running a tab. Surely he had a wheel gun with six bullets? Five maybe? The gun flash there in the dark was larger than an enclosed semi-auto style, and the bang was bigger than one of those little Saturday Night Specials. Armed robbers usually do not bring speed loaders, but that word "usually" was the one that tripped me up here. Usually. We had caught robbers with loose rounds in their pockets.

It is hard to run in the dark on rough terrain in a poster-boy, classroom, two-hand pistol grip and hold a 1-foot-long, baton-sized flashlight. Heading toward my 12 o'clock in a sort of 10 o'clock direction and worried about the suspect to my 2, 3, or 4 o'clock, I had a lot to look at and think about. If I concentrated on where I thought the robber was in the classic, pistol-range pre-scribed, two-hand grip? I'd fall over something in about 10 seconds. Here in the dark, you couldn't focus on your sights or even spot the bad guy that way in the landscape! In real life, you have to let all that classroom stuff go. Let it go and just point, shoot, and run! I ran as low as I could crouched over in a combat position.

I dreamed for a moment of just shooting at the horizon. You know, filling it full of lead. I had five bullets in my gun, a speed loader, and 12 more bullets in loops on my belt. I could blind "field of fire" his ass and hope for the best. But I wasn't in the Tet Offensive here. This wasn't the Army. I couldn't. I was still the "good guy" out here, relentlessly brainwashed about when exactly or precisely to shoot and when not to shoot. He, on the other hand, wasn't so brainwashed and would shoot me in the back. But I reminded myself that while this wasn't Tet, it wasn't Times Square on New Year's Eve either. This shit was about to go all rodeo as the Elm Street backyards were fast approaching. When this went red again, I decided I was going to shoot a whole lot. DAMN! Why didn't I bring that shotgun with me from the car? That baby was right at the front seat behind my ankles when I bailed out of the squad!

Red it did! BANG! He did it again! From my right side about 4 o'clock and quite far away. I shot back where I saw the flash, but low because he ducked. BANG! BANG! BANG! I shot at nothing, nothing three times but where I thought he was. One in the center, one to the right of it, and one to the left. I stayed standing straight up. I held the high ground now! The tall view. Looked, looked, and looked. Gun up. Looked. Walked in.

I really thought for a moment I had dropped him. There were no escape sounds from the brush. No moaning. Wounded people may writhe in agony. Or not. I can't say if I did or didn't shout something. I might have. I slowly stepped forward scanning everything and hoping I'd soon see a dead mother-fucker robber right where I'd shot. But what if I'd clipped him and he lay back on the ground like I had lain moments before. Lay in waiting for me to stalk in?

Two bullets, two bullets, two bullets, two bullets. I have two bullets left in this gun. I stopped, shoved my flashlight into my right armpit, got out my speed loader, ejected six out from the cylinder, and dropped six in the gun. (Now THAT was important classic range practice!) He's got three. I've got six. Gun up. Moved forward. Looking up and down and all around but really hoping soon to see a dead guy laying where I'd just shot. I'd settle for near-dead. The rest could be arranged.

I looked down expecting to see my prey.

Nothing. For the first time that night, I put my flashlight on and scanned the ground. Body? Blood? Nothing. He was gone, or was I wrong? Distance can be deceiving, so I advanced more trying to second- and third-guess a downed enemy. Nothing! Damn. I crouched a bit more now and looked toward the horse ranch. I had no choice but to keep moving toward the fence line. I stepped my way northeast doing my best to look all around and stay low and get ready to duck and shoot.

A man! A man walked upright off in the distance at my 5 o'clock. My eyes scoped in on his grayish-black silhouette. I also noticed in the backdrop behind him wisps of the rotating red lights of a squad car on some trees and the sides of passing trucks. It was my backup. It was my Sergeant Dusty Mallard! And he was walking across this open kill zone like a stroll in the park. His car was back on the service road by mine. And he had no idea we'd busted a few caps out here already.

Damn it all again! My head swiveled back and forth. He'll be shot. He'll be shot for sure walking like that! I took off as fast and as low as I could in his direction.

"Hey, hey, Sarge!" I said in a quick half-shout; and Dusty looked at me. I was waving my hand for him to bend low. He saw me and turned in my direction. I pumped my hand dramatically, palm down, rapidly. We met halfway. I was on one knee; and he leaned over, a palm on his knee.

"Get down, Sarge!" I said. "This guy has shot at me!"

"Shot at you?"

"Yeah. Get down!" He leaned over a bit farther, and I told him what had happened. He listened as he scanned the grassland. In my opinion he was not low enough. It would probably take one round to whip and crackle over his head before he redefined the word "low."

He pulled his pistol out, and we decided to spread out and head for Elm Street. The good news was that Dusty, the Patrol Shift Supervisor, had a portable radio; and he asked for a unit to check out Elm Street. The bad news was a fugitive could easily spot and hide from a trolling patrol car on any street, least of all a semi-rural one like Elm with half a hundred places to hide.

With me doubling back to intercept Dusty, we had lost precious minutes by now. If a dedicated fugitive saw all this maneuvering over the geography as slick and cool as this one, he could turn this into quite a lead. I jogged and Dusty walked northeast until we hit the barbed-wire fences of the Elm backyards and the neighboring horse ranch. Through the houses, I saw not one but two squad cars with headlights off creeping down the street. If I saw them, he saw them, too. But if he shot at us now, he could be quickly surrounded; because the cavalry was here and would hear it. I walked the perimeter of the fence north, and Dusty went south. We finally both put our flashlights on and blatantly spotlighted the back of houses, porches, and driveways. Did I say half a hundred places to hide? Try a million.

Dusty and I met up after about 30 minutes or so and walked back to our cars on the service road. I stopped at the convenience store to check in with the patrolman who eventually responded to the report. The clerk recalled that the suspect was a white male in a ski mask displaying a large revolver and wore the short-sleeve shirt I saw in flashes. I added my report to the incident and then got back in the car and made multiple circles of the area, up and down Elm Street, up and down the service roads. A professional criminal knows how to hide and wait with a patience that lasts beyond work shifts. Many professional criminals know when patrol shifts change and commit crimes accordingly. I drove back to the area. I parked in the dark. I watched. I drove. I took a call. I returned. Meanwhile, a detective was called out to the scene.

At 11 p.m., we changed shifts; and the midnight shift was made aware of the mess in its briefing. Next, the day shift would know. When I returned to work the next afternoon, there was still no arrest made. I can only assume the detectives walked the field in daylight looking for any evidence like the ski mask, if the guy ever dropped it? I … assumed.

I thought a bit about this bad guy. Still do on occasion when, for whatever reason, I am reminded of him. Just who was this guy? A muscled-up ex-con who worked out in the prison gym? A two-time loser facing the big bitch, life, if I caught him? Was he passing through and needed quick travel money? Where was his getaway car? Why did he run so far up the service road from the store? Well, all questions remain unanswered. I also wondered where all of our bullets eventually landed? A few shots fired in the dark one night. Gone. Zipped away to who knows where?

Shots fired. You hear that term a lot in and around police work. Hear about "shots fired" on the news. And we have become so cavalier about it unless you are there receiving or doing the actual shots. Then the term has a whole deeper meaning and drama for you. They are not the empty words of a newsman, but rather they tend to cause a little rub here and there, a friction like a slow scratch on some matchstick in your esophagus or heart or head? Friction somewhere, as everyone's matchbook is just a little different.

I was telling this story to another cop a while back,

and he smiled and said, "Michael Weston!"

"Who?"

"You know, Michael Weston on ***Burn Notice*** (the now old TV show). You met up with a Michael Weston, and Weston doesn't want to shoot cops! He's a pro and he outsmarted you without hurting you."

I guess. I guess maybe he was, and I guess he sure did.

That was the 1970s. Today that area is jam-packed with buildings, apartments, houses, and businesses. Now in the 21st century, what was once the outskirts of town is just like downtown. Old and new completely attached. I drive by it once in a rare while in now in the 2020s, scanning the crowded "civilization" over, trying to remember where these fields were. Where these events took place.

Chapter 26: This'll Get Your Goat!

One balmy late afternoon, our PD received a very unusual call. A woman reported that several men with machetes were butchering a child in an alley. It was a very serious-sounding call. It was about 1978, and I was a patrolman whiling away the hours snooping around and was quickly ordered to the scene of this tortuous murder! I was sent from another district as backup. The dispatcher reported that the caller claimed the child was fighting and screaming, and the men were hacking away viciously.

When we arrived, the apartment complex was still and quiet as though nothing at all had happened. When we stepped into the alley in question, there was indeed a lot of blood on the cement. What? I radioed the dispatcher for the address of the caller. We got it, and we knocked on her apartment door. A terrified young black woman answered. She pointed to another apartment where the "foreign" men had carried the carcass of the child inside.

Well! The District Officer, my newly arrived Patrol Sergeant, and I charged over to that door. We drew our revolvers, and I kicked open the door after about three good thrusts and a power shoulder shove. After all, who could wait for a warrant with a potentially dying child inside! We drew down on the startled faces of four men busy on the kitchen floor. They were dressing out ... a goat.

A freakin' goat.

Those men were from Persia, actually you know... Iran, but to save political trouble, most Iranians back then (and still today) said they were Persian. Adhering to a certain feast requirement, they were killing and cooking a goat. We explained to them that they just couldn't kill goats on the streets or in the alleyways of the USA without some problems.

"But we paid for the goat!" one exclaimed innocently.

As my sergeant tipped his hat back on his head, he explained it was not about killing the goat so much as it was about *where* you killed the goat.

I slipped away from this one and drove back to my district. No need for a backup officer now; and, well, the ugly part of the "broken-door question" was looming. Somebody had to pay for the door since we found a dead goat and not a dead kid. If the residents complained enough, the division had money for such repair emergencies. But it was a hassle involving several supervisors up the Patrol Division chain, all desk jockeys who liked to throw their opinions, weight, and influence around and also yell a lot.

Our Detective Division also had a broken-door fund in the 1980s for just such problems and little "mistakes" back before each tiny misstep was fodder for some Federal Investigation and million-dollar lawsuit. We would quickly pay for the door (and a little extra for the trouble in case the frame needed painting or ... or something) and leave smiling. Only one CID Supervisor handled this door fund, and he was street-smart enough to dodge any brewing hassle. These quick, easy problem-solving funds were deemed inappropriate by the late 1980s.

Before I left, though, I stopped by the caller's apartment and explained to her what had happened. She said all she could see from peeking out of her window was the men grappling with something "child-size" and chopping at it. She was a college student from Des Moines and not at all used to such mealtime activities.

Periodically over the next few years that followed, we still had a few of those goat-killing calls caused by new immigrants; but then the problem died out. Soon the U.S. hostages were taken at our Iranian Embassy. Our city had two major universities, and many Iranians were in attendance. Under the disguise of calling themselves Persians to cover any retribution, they stayed quiet and low and seemingly skipped out on the public goat-killing festivities.

During the Iranian Hostage Crisis, this Persian moniker worked; and people smart enough to come to the USA for college were usually scared to death of the radical religious sects in Iran. Instead they were happy to hide out in the U.S. and get an education in the process. But the name change didn't fool our old warrant officer and former Marine we'll call "Mel" here. Each Monday during the Iranian Hostage Crisis, Mel would get a new list of misdemeanor warrants and shuffle all the Persian-sounding names to the top of the stack to be arrested first.

Today they would call it racial profiling I guess. Back then, we just called it "Mel's War." There was just something about the hostage crisis that got Mel's goat!

Chapter 27: This Illegal Immigrant Thing

This synopsis was re-vamped in 2024 while we here in the United States are overrun by millions of walkin immigrants, thanks to an open boder by empty, airhead president-puppet Joe Biden. Some 10 million people just walked in, with U.S. Border Patrol acting like a travel agency. Decades ago, things were different...

"Units 61, 63, 64, and report to the squad room," the dispatcher said, interrupting the 3 a.m. calm of a fall midnight shift, circa 1977.

"Ten-four," I answered as Unit 64. That was new to me. Several units called in like this? Such a thing not mentioned in the squad room briefing as a meeting or training? That was still my first year at that job in 1977, so maybe everything was still new to me? I drove across town, parked, and walked into the squad room as ordered. I did take notice of four large buses in the front parking lot of the police station.

Our Shift Sgt. Jacksboro and Lt. Wells were in the room with about a dozen or so other men and women dressed in brown and some in black. Border Patrol and Immigration. The Feds.

Sgt. Jacksboro spoke up and said the Feds were raiding several known illegal alien houses through the city, and we were to offer support. He handed us papers with addresses on them. There were three houses just off the interstate in my south-side district. I recognized them immediately. Very large, older wooden homes that we all knew housed illegal immigrants from Mexico. Many illegal aliens. Lots of them. The Feds were gathered to arrest them, and the buses in the front lot were for transport.

The other officers present from our agency had done this work before. As a rookie in Texas, I hadn't; but I gathered the Feds would be doing all the heavy lifting. I noted they were armed and badged. We all filtered out to the parking lots, and I introduced myself to guys hitting District 64.

"Anything in particular you want me to do?" I asked the senior agent.

"No, podna. Not really. Just be there in case something happens. We like to have local law enforcement present."

I nodded. Frankly, anything that didn't involve any extra paperwork was just fine with me. I mounted my squad and drove over to the first house on the list, leading the way. I parked up the street and waited. Several black sedans slowly drove by me, waved at me, and parked quietly by the house. Suddenly they all bailed out, and I followed suit. No car doors were slammed. They flooded the massive house front, sides, and back; and I didn't quite know which way to go to help? I was a professional sore thumb.

Silence shattered! Doors were kicked in and some windows busted out. Yells. Screams. I heard all kinds of intro shouts, "Federal agents!"

"Immigration."

"U.S. Border Patrol."

I had nothing to say to add to that. I dashed through the splintered and bashed front door. Once in the living room—well, it was once a living room—I saw quite a number of people were sleeping on the floor in makeshift beds. Mexican women screamed, and children cried as they emerged from various hallways and doors. They were not shoved by the agents. Herded. Some men busted a move for a door or a window. One ran for the front door, and I played a game of side-to-side tag with him until an agent grabbed him.

Honestly, it felt like I was in a science fiction movie where they rounded up the people for some reason, like Soylent Green or something. When you were actually part of the process, it was different. Agents outside were still yelling.

Everyone was handcuffed. Man, woman, but not child. Long lines were formed. Two buses were called in on a hand-held radio. I stepped out into the yard. The buses pulled up in front of the house making those old, big bus, brake-and-stop screeches and gush sounds of air brakes. The doors were shoved open by levers, and an odd hue of yellow and orange lights flashed on peppering the lawn and street.

I was surprised at the long line emerging from the house. That many people were in there? Sleeping? Living? They were seated on the buses. A bus and a half of Mexicans. The remaining agents jogged toward me and then passed me.

One said, "The second house."

Okay then, to the second house we go. I started my car and waited for the agents to get into theirs, and off we went. It was only three blocks away. The same game plan unfolded. The third house. The same again. I drove back to the station along with the last of the buses and agents. The diesel engines of the buses groaned and chugged in the City Hall parking lot as the agents said goodbye to us. They climbed into their cars and drove off with the buses full of Mexicans.

I stood in the lot beside Lt. Wells, who smirked at me and said, "They gotta do that every once in a while." He turned to the rest of us and said, "You all check back into service. Just fill out a general report for the dispatch card."

We wandered back to our squad cars. It was about 6 a.m. then, and a red sun was just barely cracking open a new day. I still had a few things to do before shift change. I got behind the wheel of my car but sat still for just a moment.

That was weird, I thought. Three houses raided. Crying women and kids. Men. Busloads of them. Carted off to Dallas where they would be "processed." I had an idea what that meant. Then shipped back to ol' Mexico? I'd probably see many of them back in three weeks.

Weird because about six blocks from the police station, about 20 or more illegal Mexicans would soon be gathering at a well-known street corner looking for day-work. Seven days a week. And nobody cared. Not us. We weren't raiding them. In fact, people needed the help. Nobody would raid them. We would not cram them in buses every single morning for deportation. Not us. I guess not the Feds either, because they only came once in a while.

I recalled every other Texas city I'd been to had these "street corners" of Mexicans; like hitchhikers waiting for a ride, they had waited as construction bosses or whoever drove by and picked up workers. Housewives drove by and picked out guys for landscaping. In all of my years, I couldn't recall a single problem from them.

In fact, we'd seen dozens of illegals every day everywhere. Dozens and dozens of them. In stores. Walking around. Everywhere. Did we arrest them? Why not?

The question this story begs, the thing most people wonder about the good ol' days, is why wasn't every cop in Texas, especially the border states, arresting busloads of illegal aliens back then. Just as the newer laws in states like Arizona suggested, back then you only arrested them when your paths crossed legitimately.

Here's how my old agency handled this. Back in the day, we were ... unofficially... required to do at least "five pieces of work" each shift. That is, let's say one ticket, one arrest, two crime reports, and an accident report. Or any combination thereof of any significant police activity. Too much of one thing meant you were obsessing about one topic. Well rounded was appreciated. There was no "mark," no piece of work for an illegal alien arrest on that basis alone. Such was uncounted and unrewarded. ANYONE could walk out into the street and fill a bus with people. We simply could not handle the enormous job and could not over-reward some obsessive officer who did five illegals a day to make his unofficial quota. So they simply went unaccounted for. The operative order was to leave them alone unless something happened that caused you to take such action. (And even then, it didn't count as an illegal immigrant arrest. It was an arrest plain and simple for a charge.) I certainly did not want to arrest illegals back then. Too much paperwork! You could investigate the immigration status. Sure. But such was used as a tool for some other goal.

I think in the late 1970s, the word came down from the Feds that we were to stop arresting them at all for those charges. At first it had seemed like a temporary legal issue. But it stands today.

I became a detective and discovered other related problems. Illegals were afraid to report crimes. Afraid to become witnesses. Fugitives fleeing to Mexico. Lots of problems. We had to work with the local so-called "coyotes" and then some of what might be called Mexican Mafia. Those were area people who transported, hired, and housed illegals. Some of those guys would take a percentage of their pay and sell them cars with never-ending payments ... it was much like the old coal mine stories.

"You load 15 tons and whatta ya get; another day older and deeper in debt."

We had a local kingpin who owned and operated out of a barber shop. I'll call him Mayan Cando here. The shop looked like the northeastern mafia pizza parlor or some such place the Sopranos would operate. Cando had a gaudy mansion in town with very old-school Mexican design architecture. He ran the runners, the housing, the jobs, and the justice. Made loans. Smuggled relatives in for fees.

Sometimes he would be a big friendly help to us, and other times he was a real pain in the ass. I dealt with him on a very grass-roots level. A personal level about Hispanic on Hispanic crime. Sometimes to chase down Hispanic fugitives. It was that classic, uneasy, creepy alliance. I never quite knew how I would be treated when I walked into the Cando Barber Shop on a case.

The USA had big problems now. Security problems. I wanted everyone to enter legally. I had no great solution to offer for this mess. I did like that expression "tall fences and big gates." That would help some to clean out the underworld, the shadow network that prostituted those poor people.

In my old city now, the Latino groups had constructed park-like picnic ground areas for those standing around seeking some morning "pick up" work. That evolved through time. Like a fancy covered bus stop. Almost daring the authorities to challenge the spot and the cause. It was an uneasy alliance. The cops drove by. They waved. We waved. The employers and housewives stopped, hired, and picked up. The Mexicans worked very hard in the heat and in the rain and on holidays. It was almost like the people ranted about in the news were not the same hard-working, friendly people I had known and seen and liked in our neighborhoods every day in Texas.

Yeah, yeah. I got the big picture. Yeah. It was important to remember this wasn't no "perfect union." Just a "more perfect union." One shot full of holes trying to be more perfect. But anyway, in this old gringo's mind, and I not the least bit religious, if I said, "God bless them all," you'd know what I mean.

Chapter 28: The Man Whose Head Was On Fire

Might I write a few words about the man whose head was on fire? It really was important and covered many aspects of human nature, training, and survival.

One night in the 1970s, I was dispatched to a house-on-fire call to assist the fire department in traffic and pedestrian control. It was one of our older housing additions full of huge, wooden, rambling-style homes. The fire trucks beat me to the scene, and I observed the usual residential shock and confusion. I parked sideways on my end of the street, and another officer did the same on the opposite end.

I began ushering people away from the house and immediate area. I saw the residents and the father of the family on the large front lawn, and firemen were pushing them back. The fire itself was concentrated on the back and second story of the house. When the firemen were distracted, I spotted the man dashing up the large front porch and right into the front of the house. I went after him.

Inside he was scampering about filling his arms with stuff. You know, family stuff.

"Come on! COME ON!" I ordered him. "You've got to get out of here." There was not much sign of fire in the living room and dining room, but there was some smoke and the distinct cracking of burning wood.

He listened to me, and we both left. I had other problems to deal with and took to them. But within 10 minutes I saw the man pacing his front lawn, and he dashed in again. That time, the house was further aflame and more dangerous. I cursed to myself and ran after him commanding him to leave yet again. His arms were full of more family stuff; and he reluctantly followed, but only after snatching two arm loads.

I thought that problem was over. The house continued to burn. I was talking to one of the Fire Captains, and he looked over my shoulder.

"Hock, your guy is back in the house," he told me.

I dashed onto the porch, the Captain with me. By that time there were signs of fire in spots in the front rooms and much smoke. The man gathered more belongings. But that time? There was a little patch of fire burning on the shoulder of his flannel shirt, and a small part of his long hair was on fire!

"YOU are on fire! Get out of here!" I shouted from the doorway.

He still ignored me, making his last collection; but when he passed the fireplace, above which hung a huge mirror, I saw his stern demeanor change into screaming fright when he actually saw his hair on fire in the reflection. He screamed in agony, dropped an armload of knickknacks, and this time ran past me so fast, well, like he was … like running from a fire! Finally! Two EMTs virtually tackled him down on the front yard and threw a blanket over his upper body. As they corralled him on the lawn and suffocated his body fire, the house fire suddenly roared with a roll of hot flame erupting from the living room. It blew across the porch ceiling and over the front of the roof.

We had all heard the Buddhist proverb about "living your life like your hair was on fire." But actually seeing or being on fire for real might not be such a good idea. And it smelled bad. But I did promise some related training ideas; and here are some on adrenaline, strength, shock, and pain tolerance.

Now seems a good time to talk about adrenaline. I suspected that the hot-headed man would have continued his emergency packing until sufficient burn from his head afire would have alerted him to his injury. But how long? As we knew, adrenaline bathes the body with many chemicals that give most of us strength and pain tolerance. Training programs in recent years have a tendency to over-sell adrenaline as an evil ogre to fear and overcome, but we need doses to survive. I do not completely trust the various studies and survey questions of the past about the negative aspects of adrenaline. For just one example: when exactly did tunnel vision and auditory exclusion become simple concentration and focus? Fast-breaking, new medical discoveries should enlighten us all on those aspects, in particular from the portable MRIs now being used in performance studies. Tailoring training around those new scientific truths will be our next big challenge.

Visual and mental shock. Thinking back when the man saw his head afire, and the shock took over his dogged concentration. Seeing yourself wounded usually has a very disturbing effect. Many of you had known that firsthand.

I was ambushed once, jumped by two men; and one was choking me on the ground, I presumed, to my death! In gasping desperation, I broke the pinky of the choker's hand at his knuckle. He immediately let go of me, stood up, and circled me, yelping and mesmerized by his broken finger and its new 45-degree angle.

If you were fighting a suspect who failed to react to pain, injury, or bleeding, perhaps you should call his attention to it! I remembered an old FBI instructor telling us that he once broke the forearm of a suspect in a fight in a tenement-building stairwell. In the scuffle, they both fell down the stairs. The suspect stood to continue fighting. The agent saw the man's bone piercing the skin, pointed at it, and shouted, "Look at that!" The man did, yelped, and clutched his forearm. The agent said the suspect lost about 75 percent of his will to fight. Further remarks like, "You need help with that right now. We can get it." Or, "You are going to bleed to death!" was certainly worth trying at certain times. The pain of a broken finger, broken arm, or any injury might not "hit" the brain right away from adrenaline, but the visual picture could in a non-pain manner. That was one form of what doctors have called "psychic pain."

We must specifically learn to expect and overcome that kind of shock pain should that happen to us. A common way to do this prep work would be by deep, almost self-hypnotic, visualization of such injuries. Then, we must learn to use that potential weakness on our enemies.

You have probably been thinking of several other parables about that man whose hair caught fire and how it related to multiple training issues and lessons. I had been telling that story in seminars for years now, and people would retell it with many other abject lessons. I would hope you would, too.

Chapter 29: Case of the Sleeping Gunmen

"Damn!" I cussed with my fingers drumming on my police car steering wheel. "Turn!"

The tan four-door sedan two cars ahead just ignored the green arrow to turn southbound on the interstate service road. The car right behind the sedan hit the horn. Nothing. That car pulled around the sedan and slipped southbound. Right where I needed to go.

The car in front of me moved allowing me in my car to move up one slot, but the light had changed. Okay. Lost that chance. A few minutes passed in this busy afternoon intersection, and our green arrow came again. The tan sedan sat there, and the guy in front of me hit the horn hard and long. Nothing. This car screeched its wheels and cut around the sedan, too, when it had a break in traffic. And now I pulled up behind it, knowing something just wasn't right.

I pulled the mike off the hook on the dash, opened my door, moved half out of the car with one foot on the street, and said into it, "Sixty-one, dispatch; I'll be out at Ft. Worth Drive and I35 on a … stalled vehicle" (I called it that for lack of a better term.). I reported the license plate info and car description, adding … "two occupants." I put my car flashers on. My car window was rolled down, and I put the mike through the window frame and hung it outside the door.

I marched up to the driver's side of the car.

"Hey. Hey!" I yelled out to the driver. His window was open, too. As I got near, pie piece by pie piece, wedging in step by step, I viewed the interior of the sedan. Two white males. Long hair. Big fat guys. And the driver had a pistol in his right hand! Resting on his right leg.

Holy … I instantly pulled my Colt out and pointed at the driver.

"HEY!" I yelled. No response. "Heeeeyyyy!"

I inched forward. This guy didn't move. There was another big pistol on the console between the front seats! And yet another pistol on the floorboard by his right foot.

What the…? My eyes scanned over the passenger. He was out cold, too. His head slumped to the side. A pistol, barrel down, between his legs. Another gun!

No matter how many times I would yell, "Hey," they were lifeless. Four pistols. Two guys sleeping? Dead? I saw no blood. No wounds. The engine was running, but it was in "Park" because the driver's foot was not on the brake. In the 1970s we did not have those little Star Trek radios police have today, and I simply had to walk backward to my car, gun aimed at the driver's door, grab the mike hanging on the door, and call in.

"Sixty-one, Dispatch. I need some more units here and an ambulance. The two occupants of my car are out cold. Be advised, they have four pistols in plain view. I need to extract them."

"Ten-four, 61."

I took a position near the front door of my car, aiming my gun in their general area. If those guys were faking? They could have lurched off for an escape. All those guns! I'd have to lock them up in my car I guessed. They would be too crazy and too dangerous to leave. I mean, why stop there like that in the first place and then fake it, all that sleepiness? Crazy. You thought about a lot of things waiting for backup. I also knew there was no way the EMTs could or should approach those armed men in the car. I'd have to get them out first. Make the scene safe, as they say.

Two other squad cars showed up and with pistols drawn, three of us surrounded the front of the sedan. I opened the driver's door, and the driver still did not move. Reluctantly, I holstered my gun, but the driver was under the business end of another officer's gun. I prepared myself to jump back as I grabbed the driver by the neck and shoulders and hauled (more like rolled) his giant ass out of the seat and onto the street. He hit the deck like a dead man, and the pistol in his hand tumbled onto the floorboard. I grabbed an arm and pulled him away from the guns and the car, rolled him over facedown, and cuffed one large arm and then the other. It wasn't easy.

Then back to the car. With some quick in-and-out lunges, I snatched the three guns from his side of the car. Now I myself was loaded with four pistols: mine in my holster and three large revolvers shoved into my Sam Brown belt. The other officer opened the passenger door and poked that sleeping beauty in the shoulder. Nothing. The officer reached in with his left hand and pulled the gun out from between the guy's legs. I went around to that side and grabbed this fat boy and tossed him to the street. He was sitting on a small semi-auto. (We would just call them "autos" way back then. Yeah, we all knew the difference. We just did.) The ambulance guys arrived and jogged up to my handcuffed driver on the island.

We dragged that passenger over to the island near the EMTs as they all scrambled around the pair to check all the vitals.

"They're alive," one responder told me as they feverishly ripped needles and other medical tricks and wonders from plastic and paper containers.

I walked back to my squad car, lifted the mike, and said, "Sixty-one, Dispatch, 10-95 two times. They're going to the hospital first. Need a wrecker."

Then I walked over to the sedan and had the free time to scour the total interior. A half-empty Jack Daniels bottle. Crushed beer cans. Trashed-out car. But it took more than some Jack Daniels and Coors to wipe out these hefty Bobbsy Twins.

My sergeant arrived, pulled over, and looked at the mess I'd made—three squad cars, an ambulance, a suspect vehicle, and two beached-whale-thugs down, all on one of our busiest highway intersections. And me with four guns on my belt. He approached me looking at the guns I was toting.

"Expecting trouble?" he asked. Clever bastard.

"Driver had three. Passenger had two, and I haven't popped the trunk yet."

"Well, then you'd better start your inventory," he said.

That meant look in the trunk. That was a vehicle search, incidental to a legitimate vehicle impound to secure personal property. As a result, all items found were legal and fair game. Just in case you were wondering.

I got the keys from the ignition while he ordered yet another officer to come and work traffic. This little production was wreaking havoc with the area traffic flow. I opened the trunk. It stunk like so many bad guy cars and trunks. Luggage in there, and under all that—drugs. Bricks of drugs. I pushed all of it around for a good look. Marijuana for sure and probably cocaine. You know we didn't do that Miami Vice crap "as seen on TV and the movies" where the officer taste-tests the … "product" with his tongue. Right. You actually tested it with a color-coded field kit, and most of us didn't have any such kits back then. The detectives did.

I approached the EMTs and advised, "We got a trunk full of dope over there. Those guys have probably OD'd."

"Yeah, yeah, makes sense," one said. "We need to transport now."

The sergeant aptly took control of the mess. "Hock, you stay with the car," and he sent the other two officers on to the hospital to guard and oversee the prisoners, who were now under arrest for drug possession. I would have to await the wrecker and then escort it to city impound where I would unlock the impound gates. Next, I would take an official inventory of the vehicle. Under this inventory process, all contraband would be legally seized as evidence. It was a significant drug bust, and detectives were called out with those little field-test kits. You opened the top of the kit, dropped in a sample, closed the top, and crunched the thin plastic tubes inside the kit. Shook it up. The colors changed and tipped you off to what drugs you had. (Note: Those were not and are not infallible. A proper lab must later confirm those findings.)

The two guys were put in the hospital. Severe overdoses. The narcotics detectives did some follow-up and told me later that the two had stayed in a local hotel the night before. They were in route to a drug deal and obviously became so wasted on their own product that they couldn't complete it.

Five recovered pistols, and I think two of the guns were stolen. The two guys lived through their overdoses to be prosecuted months later in a plea-bargain deal. I got a bit of backslapping and "nice work" comments back at the station; but as you could plainly see ... I had stumbled upon all that completely by accident.

But this was by far the safest felony gun and drug arrests I had ever made. Because the gunmen were asleep the whole time. In fact, I never once saw either of them awake from start to finish, which made it very weird. The case of the sleeping gunmen!

Chapter 30: The Tireless Chase! Roll Over Beethoven!

I like this essay because it is such a typical, fun patrol story...

"We were in hot pursuit, flying through the streets at incredible speeds of 15 or maybe 17 miles per hour!"

Crickets and gnats were all I saw or heard. A rampaging car wreaking havoc through this neighborhood? Smashing lawn furniture, knocking down mailboxes, tearing up fences and yards?

Where? But where?

I got out of the patrol, squad car and walked out onto the wide streets of the residential intersection. Four a.m. has its own kind of quiet.

Surely, I would hear something! The dispatcher had received too many calls for this not to be true.

Then I did hear something, though it wasn't at all like a car, it was more like a grinding hum, a high-pitched, cutting whine, and getting louder by the second. The noise was coming from the east, a street that went uphill then curved out of my sight toward the north.

"Is this some kind of new street sweeper, or garbage truck maybe?" I thought.

Ah, but it wasn't. I saw its sparks first, as it sliced

around the curve tearing asphalt as it came. It was a car, only it did not have a right front tire. Nor did it have even a wheel, just a drum ripping a scar on the street like a skater on fresh ice. I started out for the center of the street, intent on flagging him down, until the lights of the street corner revealed his ashen gray face. Two wide, white eyes glowed from behind white knuckles that were wrestling the steering wheel out of the turn. He glared straight at me, but I could tell he didn't see me.

The guy was nuts. I jumped out of his way, and he never once looked back, just swung wide and wild down the street in a flurry of sparks. Needless to add, he ran a stop sign. I ran back to my squad.

"I'm in pursuit, southbound on Nottingham," I told the dispatcher the details, "he's now turning east on Archer."

Ron Atkins was also in the search, racing to intercept this vehicle, no doubt envisioning me whipping through the streets, sliding around corners, etc., etc.

"Sixty-two, what's your location?" Atkins asked, needing to know where I was now.

"Still on Archer, approaching ..." I replied.

"Still?"

We had been on Archer for some few minutes, you see we were only going about 12 or 14 mph I coasted up beside this knucklehead, blowing my horn and veering at him hoping he'd pullover.
No way.

I aimed my spotlight on his profile and his wild curly hair made him resemble that famous bust of Beethoven. Shoot his tires out?

Ha! Do you think that would stop him? He was already cruising along on three tires. I was feeling lucky that he hadn't crashed into any parked cars, private property or me, although he came close with all three.

"What's your 20 now?" asked Ron.

"Still eastbound on Archer!" I told him.

Suddenly, Beethoven yanked the wheel hard to the

right, pulling into a dirt alley between the backyards of houses. Before I could radio in the change, Atkin's red lights magically appeared at the alley's only exit. With no place to turn and me in the cloud of dust behind the car, Ron was sure we had him trapped. I wasn't. I had seen his eyes. Apparently, Ron did too, and seconds before the sedan would have bashed into Ron's car, Atkins kicked the gas pedal and bolted clear of a head-on collision into a driveway.

Even at 12 mph…who wants a head-on collision? Then we were back on the streets in hot pursuit, racing at the incredible speed of 15 and 17 miles per hour. I drove up beside the ol' boy one more time and again inched him over to the sidewalk.

Closer and closer came my right rear door to his left bumper.
There were parked cars ahead, if only I could…he hit his brakes. A car door slammed. Beethoven's gone!

I jumped out of my car and saw him running at Ron's squad car. Atkins was half out of his car when Beethoven cut to the left and dashed to the sidewalk.

I ran around the front of my car, Ron the back of his, thinking that either way this fellow would run, we had a head start. He came my way, cutting across a front lawn for the backyard, but I had swung wide enough to block his path. He turned and charged for a tall row of hedges, cleared them in one bound, landed on all fours like Spiderman and dug out for the next yard with me and Ron behind him. Ron took the sidewalk. I made for the hedges and jumped. Knucklehead did it! Why shouldn't I? There's an insider "foot chase" rule in policing, every officer should know. The escaping suspect has more of an emotional motive to escape, that the pursuing officer has to catch him. This makes the escapee jump a little higher and run a little faster and further than first anticipated.

This age-old mandate came through once again. As I leapt, just a few inches worth of hedge raked my ankle.

Hedges will give way, but you know, chain link won't, and that's what was buried in this leafy hedge. A chain-link fence. While the suspect had landed on all fours, I made a fabulous one-point landing right on my face. Spitting out grass, I had to roll up and off again. To "the game afoot" I went.

Beethoven was gaining a lead, running far faster than his car traveled. Ron had one last ace to play. Just before Beethoven stepped completely out of Ron's reach in this foot chase, I saw Ron go airborne into a diving tackle, but all he could do was barely get a light touch of his hand, just a fingertip really, on the small of this fellow's back. This slight and magic contact however, pitched Beethoven off balance. He flew completely airborne himself. Ron hit the grass on his chest sliding to the left, and Bee? Bee flew some five feet more! And, with an alarming, sickly loud thud, slammed into a short, brick garden wall...headfirst!

He collapsed to the ground motionless. I thought for sure he was dead. He had to be dead. No human could have survived such a airborn blow to the skull. No one. Ron scrambled to his feet and Beethoven flipped over! He came up fighting at me! Wild man, hooking punches from left and right hands.

Duck, cover, and I punched his body back. Not his damaged head for fear of killing him. He wasn't feeling much. We clinched from the mutual charge. Ron scooped an arm. I got the other arm wrapped, and together we dropped him heavy on his back. He was kicking and screaming. I couldn't help but search his head, looking for that caved-in, brick wall injury. None. We restrained him rather easily, cuffed him and checked him out further.

"Should we call an ambulance?" I wondered, sitting on Bee's back as he kicked and screamed.

"I don't know. Looks OK to me," Ron said, lighting up his customary post-arrest cigarette.

We were both already thinking about the DWI paperwork. Ron's magic takedown touch qualified him as the "first-box" on the arrest report, arresting officer, so the health and well-being of this idiot was really his to decide. I would be in the arresting officer, "second box" and could dodge some flak? I had been left with picking up the pieces in the neighborhood, rather than face possible negligent homicide or brain-damage charges, I opted for the broken lawn chair and mailbox crimes reports.

Some drunks are invincible, and Bee was no exception. His head, or at least his skull anyway, was fine. He was, we learned later, wasted on a precise mixture of drugs and booze. When this wore off, he would be very sore. While Ron took him to the station, I checked out his lopsided, three-wheel car. He owned the vehicle and it was impounded.

The rest of the night didn't take a Tom Brown tracking course to re-create. The guy had cut about an inch-deep path into the street with his blown wheel. Several of us followed his carved, asphalt trail through the neighborhood, filling out crime reports for each singular act of damage until it all quieted down to just the crickets and gnats, 7-11 coffee and summer sunrise.

Why the three-wheel, 4 a.m. joyride? Your guess is as good as mine. When Beethoven rolled over in his jail bed the next morning, he couldn't remember a damn thing.

Update: This guy was shot and killed in a violent confrontation, many years later by our SWAT team.

Chapter 31: The Great Train Stoppery

"65, this man says his car is stuck on the railroad tracks behind the Motel Greenview," the dispatcher said. "We have a wrecker en-route."

"10-4," I replied, being the active sergent that night.

On the tracks? I guessed he had two tires stuck between the tracks. Glad the tow truck was on its way. The tracks could get slick and maybe a car tire can't get over them. Odd though.

It was Saturday night, almost Sunday morning, circa 1978, and we were too busy for me to be on a call like this for too long. The guy was probably drunk and lost control of his car. I started dreading the thick paperwork of DWI. In a few moments I was driving through the Motel Greenview parking lot to the field behind it, then onto a road where some railroad tracks ran north and south.

Our squad cars had big spotlights mounted by the driver's door just above the side mirror, with a handle inside the car, so that we can twist the light and aim the beam around. I spot-lighted the tracks. Lo and behold, there sat a cream-colored car. But the car was not positioned as I suspected. The front two wheels were not stuck inside the tracks. Nor were the right two wheels or the left two wheels stuck inside. The right two tires were on the right rail and the two left tires was on the left rail. On them!

After driving as close as I could, I got out and saw a thin fellow in ridiculous plaid red pants and a short-sleeved shirt. He was near 30 with short blond hair. As he approached me, I could tell that he wasn't drunk and my curiosity was instantly aroused.

"How…how did…?"

"You're gonna think I'm stupid," he said nervously, "but, I got my car stuck on those tracks. Ya' see, that's a company car, officer. That's a new, I say, a brand-new K-car, and I heard they had the same wheelbase as a railroad track and, and …"

"…and you wanted to see that?" I said. "To check that out?"

"Yeah, yeah, yeah, to see if I could ride on the tracks."

"Uh huh," I said with a wince. This was no normal dude.

"You've tried?" I said and waved my hand toward the K-car.

"Oh yes, yes, tried and tried. I just can't get over the rails … you probably think I'm stupid. I let some of the air out of tires to hug the rails better."

"Really?"

"Really. I am in town on business. I'm staying at the hotel." He pointed to the Greenview.

I smiled. I saw his wedding ring. Usually a businessman away from his family on a work trip gets in the usual veins of trouble that involve the police. You know, hookers. Drugs. Bar fights. Once in a while, a murder even. Not like this cat.

"Listen, there isn't a train coming is there?" he asked. "I mean, my boss would fire me if this car was wrecked like this." he said, anxiously following me back to my squad car.

"Well, we are trying to call the local railroad station now. A wrecker is on the way," I told him.

"I just hope a train doesn't come!" he shouted again.

"Me too." I really didn't. Too much paperwork.

As I got back in my squad car I wondered how many times a day a train did come through here, anyway? Four? Five? Surely the odds were with us. I leaned into the open door of my car and grabbed the mike.

"Dispatcher," I said, "are we getting through on the train phone call?"

"Be advised," she said, "the Lieutenant is on the phone now."

I knew that would be a complicated process, calling night personnel, identifying track routes, calling the train radio office, then calling the train itself.

"Ten four."

"What's your name?" I asked him.

"Charley Barrick."

"I need to take a quick look at some ID."

He pulled out his wallet and handed me his driver's license. Charles was his name. He lived in Houston. But I nicknamed him Casey Jones in my mind. In the meantime, I ran computer checks on ol' "Casey Jones" there, this salesman who dreamed of a night run down the railroad tracks in his K-car/train. He was "clear" of any priors, no wants. No warrants. And Chrysler's unexpected answer to a small locomotive was indeed registered to a business in Houston. In the distance, Casey was churning circles in the stones around the track, his car stuck to the rails like one of Pauline's Perils. Since Pauline was a machine this time, only a mechanical hero could come to the rescue, as in the wrecker.

I recalled a time several years ago when Officer Jack Warden and I were dispatched to a body lying on some railroad tracks right near this very spot. When we arrived, we found a drunk stretched across the rails. He said he wanted to die and was waiting for a train. We hauled him off to jail. At least the drunk had a reason for being on the tracks. Suicide! What about Casey?

I finally saw the wrecker's headlights drive up the track's access road and Casey was overjoyed. They exchanged words and I can only imagine the conversation. Similar words to mine with him no doubt...

"You are probably gonna think I'm stupid but..."

The wrecker began backing up on his narrow journey to the car. Getting into position was really tricky as the track was on elevated ground.

I started writing my report. Just what we called a general report. No DWI! When suddenly, an ominous roar disturbed our peace, rolling across the flatlands west of town.

I looked up.

The wrecker stopped.

Casey froze.

Casey's worst nightmare had come true. A single, glaring light appeared around a turn of the tracks, still quite a way off on the horizon, but it was a coming. And fast. A train was a coming, and it wasn't just coming, and I mean it was bearing down on us like a non-stop express line to Alaska and here we were in Texas! The wrecker spit gravel all the way back to the road, bailing on the rescue, despite Casey's frantic pleas and stumbling chase.

"Sweat Jesus!" Casey Jones cried out. "Oh my Lord."

"Jesus ain't got nothing to do with this," I said to myself.

Apparently, Casey had read the story about the two old women who had carried a huge piano down a burning flight of stairs, all thanks to adrenalin. He raced to the back of the K-Car, bent down, and grabbed the bumper, hoping that nature's rules of physics and gravity might momentarily turn its back. With a huge groan, he tried to pick up the back end of his car. Alas, if he were expecting to turn into the Incredible Hulk, he was stricken only with a very mild case of Mark Ruffalo/Bill Bixby.

The car rose only an inch off its shocks. Casey whimpered in desperation. Onward roared the giant, black, auto demolisher. I got back in my car and drove down the access road, parking still somewhat near, but a safe distance from the tracks (I'm no fool), in case the explosion would be greater than I imagined. I did flip on the red lights and aimed my spotlight beam in the direction of the engine.

Casey ran to my car window, and begged, "Have you contacted the train yet?"

"I'm trying to now, get out of the beam!" I said while waving and flashing the spotlight. Realizing my primitive method of communication, a bright light, a new, deeper sense of futility filled Casey as he stared at my modest, simple torch. That was the best I could do.

He ran across the tracks to the wrecker, now parked on the other side of the tracks with its emergency lights on. I could hear Casey beg the driver to rescue his car. No chance.

Onward barreled the one-eyed Chrysler Cruncher! It screamed, it roared, it wailed into the night's flatlands around us.

Closer. Closer. Then suddenly an ear-piercing screech tore at our senses, followed by the bashing sounds of hundreds of boxcars. That train had discovered we were there, either by our lights, or from the LTs phone call. But, was it too late?

With all the weight, speed and force of a run from Ft Worth, it did everything it could to slow down. I envisioned every loose crate, every free object, each person thrown violently forward. Still onward it came, slowing only in sparking fractions, sliding closer and closer.

200 feet, 150 feet, 140 feet, Casey was in shock.

Good God! A beat-like metallic howl.

80 feet, 60. I was hypnotized, absorbed by this colossal struggle of brakes and momentum. 50 feet, 45, would the Chrysler be destroyed? Would mighty metal hit cheap plastic? Would there be a dramatic explosion? Casey fell to his knees a few feet away.

"Get back!" I yelled.

I felt obligated to get him back. What if there was an explosion? Flying debris? I ran around the front of the squad car, dashed the few more feet and up the grade. 40 feet. SCREEEECHING!

I got him by the shoulders and yanked him up and back. Back and back and we both fell. 30 feet, 20 ... a sense of control appeared, a calm, the iron horse's reins were pulled back, 19, 18, a blast of smoke, 17, 16, rolled to a stop hiss ... like a harnessed bull, it rested....only 10 feet or so from the car.

Railroad men and engineers poured off the train, each with their own individual style of anger, growling, cursing, flashlights shook violently in the dark. The wrecker backed up again and hooked the car and yanked it free.

Casey Jones ran to the near crash. I leaned against my car, watching the show. I have to admit, a small part of me, the unprofessional part, would have enjoyed seeing that massive crash this close. Come on! Who wouldn't. But, as I had all the info I needed for a general report, as in "car stuck on tracks, train stopped," I got behind the wheel of the prowl car. As I backed away, I could hear ol' Casey Jones explaining to the crew,

"Well, you're gonna' think I'm stupid but..."

Well Case, wherever you are, I never had the chance to tell you this but...yes, I think you were very stupid.

Chapter 32: Bad Night at Broken Wagon

One crazy Saturday night in the 1970's in Texas was a very bad series of bar violence and a sad event I'll never forget. I was working a Saturday evening, patrol shift...

The action all kicked up about 6 p.m. Units and an ambulance were dispatched to the infamous Broken Wagon Country Western Club inside the borders of what was once called District 64. I was assigned to District 61, but physically on the map these beats were side-by-side. 61 and 64 routinely backed each other up on hot calls.

"Sixty-four. Knife fight at the Wagon. Sixty-one, you're backup. Ambulance in route."

I got there just as Unit 64 did. The parking lot was crawling with cowboy hats and jammed full of parked cars and trucks. The ambulance had beaten us there. Back in those days, EMTs courageously went right in whether we were there or not. Inside the Wagon, it was packed. This was during the heyday of the Waylon, Willie and the Boys Outlaw movement. The bouncers had already corralled the knife assaulter, and the EMTs were patching up the victim.

These bouncers at the Wagon were pretty tough characters. One named Rick had a reputation of "stomping" heads with his cowboy boots if he got an unsimpatico patron down on the ground. As anticipated, the knife guy had already been "softened" up by the security crew. Bravo, amigos! They were holding him down on the floor, a hand against his face, face first when we got there. We cuffed him. Sixty-four dropped the bloody knife in a carry-out, paper bag, and took the bad guy to the jailhouse. I lingered to round up some witnesses and steered them to the police station where the detectives would begin taking statements and building whatever case could made.

The dust on that mess settled early, but there were a few more shit storms to come. I slipped back into the prowl car and turned towards District 61. Within the hour the radio declared,

"Sixty-one. Fight at the Broken Wagon. No further details."

I was tagged as primary on this one as 64 was still busy with the earlier call. Back up would have to come from afar, if there would be any available. This was a Saturday night.

So I headed back over the border. Running inside the club, I could just feel in the smokey air that the prior knife fight had fired up the crowd. Rick, the bouncer shouted to me, and I peeled my way through the onlookers. The new fight was just brewing when the call came in. It had progressed and as usual, since it doesn't take long for fighters to get exhausted, they gassed out. Rick thought he'd calmed them down, but it took off just seconds before

I got there. Two guys were down fighting on the dance floor. I pulled my blackjack from my back pocket and rapped the left side ribs of the top guy. Not too hard, but his head would be next if he didn't quit.

"Hey! Break it up! Okay, break it up," I yelled. Rick grabbed the back of the top man's shirt collar, then shoulder and yanked him back. His torso came up, and that's when I saw the knife in the bottom guy's right hand. Though the top-side guy was yanked up, he still kept a death grip on the bottom guy's knife hand. Smart idea.

"Come on now, drop that knife," I said, and smacked the knife hand with my blackjack. "Drop it!"

He didn't. The bouncer pulled the top guy back and away, even more and I saw an opening. I cracked the knife guy across his cheekbone, a pretty good smack, with the blackjack. He wanted to act as though he didn't feel it, but the results were obvious. His face turned all unusual and rubbery askew. It was a short smack. When he saw me rear that jack back a little further for another crack, he dropped the knife.

Another bouncer arrived and took the topside guy off. Rick and I hauled this knife man over on his chest, and we both put knees on him. I snatched the knife off the floor and stuck it in my back pocket (these things have a way of disappearing in a crowd). I cuffed our bad guy with difficulty as he was still resisting me, but Rick was a big help. We stood the guy up. Another two bouncers got there and grabbed my guy and walked him to the front hall.

I looked the other guy over.

"You are stabbed!" I yelled at the topside feller. He felt of his chest and had a jaw-dropping look of shock ripple over his face. There were holes in his side. The bouncer hauled him to the side of the dance hall by the front office hallway and laid him down on the floor. Steve, the head barkeep, a college kid we all knew and really liked, stretched over his counter to see the action. He was still perched there when I shouted for him to call an ambulance. Steve quickly broke for the phone to make the call.

"Whatcha got here?" I asked, straddling the wounded cowboy. He had some slashes and stabbing opening by his left rib. No wind came and went from the hole. Not near the heart. No blood from the mouth. Steve pitched me some bar towels, and I pressed them onto the spot. A girl in the crowd stepped up and held it there.

The EMTs slid up outside, charged in and took over. We pulled the suspect to my car. A back-up unit arrived with the task of rounding up a few witnesses. More work for the detectives.

Now my night was full of paperwork, checking on the victim at the hospital and booking in the suspect. We had no jailers way back then, and the typical, book-in tasks were all ours. While handwriting my way through all the forms (computers were found only on Star Trek back then) I heard another call broadcast of a big fight at, you guessed it, the Broken Wagon! Sixty-four was still doing paperwork on a squad room table beside me, and we both shook our heads and traded sarcastic, sardonic remarks.

Within an hour, units were hauling three cuffed guys past us in the squad room from the Wagon. Two wore bloody shirts. Curious, I stepped into the booking room, and I learned that one of the three pulled a knife after a fight broke out and stabbed and slashed four patrons at the same country and western night club.

FOUR of them! That's a total of six people stabbed and or slashed there in one night. Three knives. All the knives were folders, but not like the "tactical" kinds you see today. They were wooden, or imitation, ivory-like handled, working, folding knives with no pocket clips. While some of the wounds were very severe, nobody died. The motives varied, all of which I cannot remember decades later, but I can tell you that they all were stupid reasons.

I got through the paperwork about 1 a.m. and headed home. Stayed up late, slept late, ate, and returned to work the next afternoon-the normal life of an evening-shift copper.

Once in the patrol shift briefing, I heard the really,

really bad, sad Broken Wagon news. The sergeant reported that at about 2:30 a.m., the Wagon's bartender Steve had counted the club money at closing, put it in the safe, cleaned up, barred the doors, and hopped on his motorcycle to head home. For some reason, he lost control of his bike on North Helm Street and hit a utility pole. It killed him. Poor kid.

Years later, while I can't remember the names and faces of all he stupid men fighting in bars, I still recall Steve.

It was a real bad night for the Broken Wagon.

Chapter 33: Fiery Grab-Assing!

One in the Top Ten, Crazy-Brave Police Moments I've Seen! Only it ain't what you might imagine!

One of the bravest things I have ever seen right before my very eyes wasn't in the military and wasn't performed in the act of battling criminals. This particular act of incredible courage was performed by one officer, Glenn Bell at the secluded police gasoline pumps on a Texas city service complex. I worked very closely with Glenn for several years back in the 1970s. He was a fastidious, do-gooder and the senior officer on our squad who really did take responsibility for the shift, and I mean seriously. This night it almost rendered him into a ball of fire. We had to keep this heroism secret for decades. Decades! Until now, whereupon I reveal it right here.

Not many citizens know that before the end of a patrol shift, just about every patrol car in the country, perhaps the world, has to go to a particular place to get gas. Most agencies drive to a city, county, state, federal complex or compound to refill their fuel. Or, they have a credit card arrangement/or some form of credit arrangement with a commercial gas station. This way the next shift takes over the car with a full tank of gas. If it's a take home police car so common in today's world, then the officer can refuel at his or her discretion.

When I worked patrol in the US Army in several states and countries, not only did we "fill er' up," but we were expected to "hose er' down." Clean the car. Unless the temp hit freezing, we grabbed a hose at the "Mike Poppa," as in the motor pool, and did a quick clean off of the car when getting gas.

At first, these chores were a personal affront to my immature, ignorant, self. Starting in the military police in garrison patrol duty, ("garrison" duty as in police work like in a major city, not like in the "battlefield") I perceived myself as an armed and elite agent of the law and thought for sure, subservient, attendees would flock to my squad car and service it when I pulled into the motor pool. Pretty much a NASCAR, pitstop treatment. Gas. Wash.

Oh, not so. We did it all. In my next assignment in South Korea, 90% of it was foot patrol, or standing around looking cool at various assigned places. When we used a jeep we actually did have such vehicle caretakers from time to time, like Koreans with their palms out for cash, to either drive us around, or spit-shine the jeeps. To you younguns' out there? These jeeps were not the Humvees of today. Oh, no sir. These jeeps were right out of an old War World II movie. I've had a misadventure or two in these jeeps, but those are the fodder for other stories. And I still have a fondness, a nostalgia for them.

By the time I went to work in Texas, the Hochheim "elite-ness" had been totally kicked and spit right out of me. No longer was I special and delusional about my position in the universe. You realize in the Army that you are a totally expendable grunt. The famous quote is "you are all equally worthless." With this lot in life, I learned to whistle gladly as I pumped my own gas, and hummed contentedly as I took the squad through the hosing or car wash whenever it was needed, for I was a professional in both social sanitation and vehicular maintenance. I just wondered what part of the totem pole I was. The part under the dirt? Or the part just above the dirt? No matter what, it involved dirt.

Back to the Texas filler-up, story. These petrol fill-ups were usually within one hour of the shift's end. And, on evening shift and certainly midnight shift when the world was blissfully in stage-three-REM sleep, these fill-ups are often congregations of squad cars getting gas and or waiting in line at the same time. This stop usually led to gossip sessions, comedy corners, bullshit speeches, major league complaining and many crazy shenanigans like stun gun duels, baton fights and if the fuel compounds were remote enough, Trick shooting and target contests. Many "cool" sergeants joined us in these sessions, but some anal-retentive patrol sergeants would watch these gas pump meetings from afar with binoculars, hiding in the dark, taking notes and charge officers with wasting precious city time. I mean, come on!

What harm could a little 6 a.m., on-duty, trick shooting contest bring? Even with shotguns! Hey, come on! We replaced the ammo, Lieutenant? Captain?

Generally speaking the local, Texican police colloquialism for such horseplay at our pumps was a simple, catch-all phrase, "grab-assing." Grab-ass became an official term connected with the gas line, but could be inserted when needed when officers foolishly misbehaved and were caught. You had to be caught at it of course, else it never existed. We learned this institutionalized nomenclature from the periodic and official warnings in squad meetings from the staff.

Solemn looks and wags of the finger and:

"This grab-assing at the pumps has got to quit."

"No more grab-ass at the pumps."

"We are setting up surveillance at the pumps to put an end to this grab-assing."

"This is the end of this grab-assing."

"If we catch you grab-assing at the pumps, we'll..."

And, the occasional, soon ignored mandate: "Three car limit. No more than three cars at the pumps at any time, to cut down on this grab-assing." (We would groan at this because we needed at least four to party.)

The Einstein algebraic equation seemed to prove that cosmic grab-assing statistically begins at the collection point of four officers. It's just science! Now, you understand that no one was officially, actually, really grabbing anyone's real ass, (though there were incidents of male and female officer huckle-bucking out in the further, darker reaches of the gas pumps, service compound. (I wouldn't know ANYTHING about this huckle-bucking!) But, a scientific combination of three or more of us congregating there at any time meant the potential for...official..."grab-ass."

The Night in Question.... near the end of one unforgettable, midnight shift, at about 5:50 a.m., four of us wound up getting gas at the city pound at the same time. FOUR! Me, Glenn Bell and two other officers. One name I forget. One, I will change his name to Ron Bapkins because his damn fool move is about the only, really super, dumb-ass thing he has ever done (well then again, I have seen some of the women he's chased...but I digress). Anyway, among our numbers, now four, was one person over the department commandments for the official possibility of grab-assing. Science!

Said night in question, I happily hummed a Waylon Jennings tune as I started pumping gas. Glenn was pumping his gas at the next row with this other officer waiting nearby. Bapkins was behind me in line and leaned against the front end of his car. Bapkins, a smoker, was holding a book of matches. Yes. And he was striking them for...fun...and tossing them on the ground. At the gas pumps. For...fun! You heard me.

Yes...gas pumps...while gas was being pumped...lit matches.

Yes. Yes, I know what you are thinking. But remember, we are not ourselves. We had entered into the bleak and twisted, mind-dumbing, twilight zone of Pump Station, Grab-Ass.

I started to complain to him. He taunted me.

"Wha? Ho Che Min? Chicken? CHICKEN are ya?"

Bapkins grinned, possessed by the Evil Specter of the Grab Ass syndrome.

He started tossing lit matches closer and closer to me.

"Are you nuts, are you..." I yelled at him, but it was too late. A tossed match came too close. Too close! For some reason as it flickered through the air and the entire rear side and trunk of my car sort of...blew up before me. The air actually became a rolling ball of flame before my eyes.

FIRE!

I jumped back, pulled the gas pump handle out with me, and thank goodness, releasing the gas pump handle shuts the gas flow off, but not before I shot some gas over the back of the car. I know a potential, freakin' fireball when I see one! And, the gas cap WAS STILL OPEN! The rear of my prowl car seemed to be on fire, like a layer of fire in a reddish wave. The fire danced around the gas cap and back trunk area of the car.

If the car blows up, one pump station blows up. Then the other pump stations blow up. I could see that in one primal, instinctive instant, the whole outfit would explode in something right out of a spy movie.

I swear my eye lashes were singed! My ape man brain said,

"Fire! Run! Run! Foolish primate! Face on fire!"

I took off at a dead run. Bapkins took off at a dead run in another direction. Officer Unknown took off at a dead run in yet another direction. But Glenn? No, no, not Glenn, senior officer on the scene, feeling responsible for my car and the other three sedans, the pumps and who knows what all would explode next, charged in, at a dead run! He obviously had a brain evolved beyond ours, I guess?

My keys were in the ignition. Glenn jumped into the driver's seat of the flaming car. He started the car and stomped the gas pedal. The engine roared. Over my shoulder, I saw him, driver's door held open for quick escape (perhaps the blast would throw him clear?) roar my fiery car across the compound parking lot some 40 or 50 feet. He jammed the car in park and dove out of the car, hit the pavement, rolled and ran for his life. He somehow drove my flaming car away from the gas pumps! I think that Glenn, as senior child-care officer, knew he would be blamed for the mess.

Bapkins got his fire extinguisher out. We jogged to my car like a grunting pack of monkeys, unable to speak, thinking the rear quarters and trunk would at least be irreparably charred if we could get there in time? He dosed the car. As we paced and mumbled like nervous chimps, the flames that licked the back of my car slowly...slowly...extinguished. We were amazed.

"Fire...gone!" one of us mumbled.

Indeed, the fire went out. Officer Unknown got an emergency blanket from his trunk and wiped the deck lid. The charred black came off! Wiped right off and the pure police, white goodness remained and shined though. We exchanged glances and mumbled. Oh, oh but return it to this pure, police state again! Especially poor arsonist Bapkins wished for this! Whose fault doth lie upon his window break! He'll have his Shake-speared but good!

But with the once-again, scientifically proven, Grab-Ass Equation of four or more officers present? Alas! We too shall roll with this tide as once again, we are proven to be little more than mischievous monkeys stuffed into polyester blue, playing with matches near 1,000 gallons of gas and staring curiously down the barrels of our guns, tempting fate itself on a daily basis.

But can monkeys accidentally type an encyclopedia? Glenn wanted us all to avoid these slings and arrows. He told me to get to a car wash fast as dawn was breaking. He would join me, and we would see if we could clean off all the smokey mess before being summoned in for day shift change. Quarters? Did we have quarters? Yes, we pooled our quarters.

Perhaps...just perhaps we did not need to report this flaming mishap to the supervisors! This would save us from the indignation of reporting to the police chief's office next morning and having him...yell at us... "on the carpet" ... and wag his finger at us...and...and suffer the psychological damage of this horrifying experience! Save us from the walk down the day-shift, admin hall, that hall of shame gauntlet where all admin sneer and whisper and cluck their tongues at us and, and... oh, the horrors! The potential, charge against us?

"Grab-assing at the pumps!" Almost blowing up the damn pumps. And this, after so many warnings.

Fearing this shame and embarrassment, and fear of creating a legend for generations of storytellers, Glenn and I raced to the nearest car wash and plunked in quarters. As senior officer, Glenn took control of the wash wand as the severity of the clean-up job was not to be left to a mere junior, patrolman such as myself. Too much was at stake. This job required zest, zeal and experience and he was clearly the Tarzan of the group. And I'll be damned if the black soot didn't come right off the squad car! It was somehow as good as new. Pristine again! Oh, wonder of wonders.

Car and souls again washed clean, at 6:50 a.m. we turned over our squads to the next shift, and no one was the wiser that Bapkins almost blew up my car and the surrounding compound. And that Glenn Bell had performed one of the most heroic, selfless acts I had ever seen. And it had to be held top secret. Until now.

Secret until now. For you see, the *Grab-Ass Statute of Limitations* is about 35 to 40 years, even if none of us work there anymore. The regime in charge must have either passed away or at least be in assisted living facilities before the event can be revealed. Their power! You don't understand their long-lasting power! One or two of my captains, I fear, will be positioned at the Pearly Gates, frowning, in the admission process! We kept this heroism secret for decades! But now you know. The world knows.

Glenn told us the next day or so that he discretely talked to some buddies at the Fire Department. The FD experts said they guessed only some of the gas was affected/lit and mostly gas fumes were actually on fire. The fumes would produce this look, linger on the car while it flashed away, and explain the soot that we wiped off.

While me, Bapkins and Officer Unknown, Misters See-No-Evil, Speak-No-Evil, Hear-No-Evil were busy dashing for our primal lives, I remember seeing Glenn driving away from us in my flaming car, trying to outrace our destruction.

Oh, and you want to know some irony? Years later, Glenn became the fire chief of a smaller city. I'll bet he did a fine job too.

Now, pass me a banana.

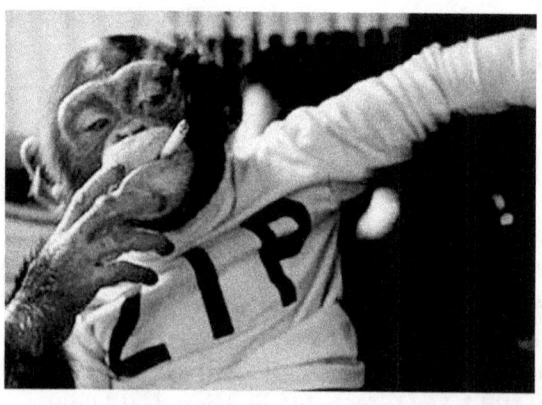

Marines practice the throat punch, but in lethal force situations.

Chapter 34: The Christmas Throat Punch

Christmas time and time to spread good cheer. In this holiday spirit we dust off this great Christmas carol of family love and togetherness, and from a solid throat punch.

"Twas Christmas day and all through the town, not a creature was stirring...except the Bellamy Brothers who were beating the Be-Jesus out of each other...

Christmas Day, 1977. I was on patrol with Gary Billings. Day shift. It was customary for we uniformed unfortunates back then on holiday duty, to work "out of the house," so to speak. That meant, one made roll call and briefing at the beginning of the tour, and then one could spend most of the day at home with one's family, but ever ready by the phone, squad car outside, to answer any calls. This was not an uncommon practice in the good ol' days, at police departments across the country on such big holidays. Might still be true in some places.

And there were always some Christmas day calls, a few accidents, domestic disturbances, etc. Only the most evil of cops were out hunting their daily traffic ticket prey on the big day...but then you know how the sick and obsessed are. Back then, Gary and I were single guys and we decided to just "drive around" as if it were any usual day. Gary was the senior officer on the shift, a position entitling us to rove the whole city, usually backing up other officers on calls, then being dispatched when all other units were tied up. But this Christmas Gary and I decided to handle as many calls as possible ourselves, and let our friends stay at home near, or at the yuletide (whatever the hell a yuletide is).

So when the radio call came out about trouble at the Bellamy Brother's house, we went straight away. The brothers, Jeremy and Joe, both in their 20s were chronic problems and would, a decade later, score big sentences for violent crimes. Jeremy sold crack for years and eventually killed someone. Joe did a little dope and just robbed people. In the 70s they were just blossoming thugs, experimenting with law breaking. I became one such experiment.

The neighbors, trying best to enjoy their own yuletides, had reported a front yard Bellamy family brawl. The brothers were arguing and bashing it out.

The parents took sides, and the three sisters were there to add piercing screeches to the overall holiday soundtrack. As we pulled up, the brothers were pushing and yelling at each other. Dismounted from said prowl car, I got between them, palms out shoving Joe back by way of an open palm to the throat area, and I held him at bay with this one hand. Gary marched right up to Jeremy and well…started his "Jack Webb" routine – you know, that whole robotic, riot-act reading thing in a monotone voice.

Jeremy took one look at him and belted him right, square in the Jack Webb nose. Gary launched back like a solid piece of wood, his gold-rimmed glasses ejecting into the air. Bam! Gary hit the turf, apparently knocked cold. Okay!

Lonely are the brave! Just in case you ain't keeping score, that'll be me lonely…versus the Bellamy clan. Jeremy turned his beady eyes next to me. He rushed me, and I got a palm across his chest too! So, there I was, tottering between the brothers, stretched out and in the middle of a big squeeze. Honestly, I don't know if they were after me or still after each other.

But I got the gut feeling they would kick anybody's ass at this point, since Gary was already out cold on the lawn, like a stump. I turned to Jeremy and pushed back hard, then spun and punched Joe right in the throat. Joe staggered back up against a big elm tree, gripped his neck, whereupon he remained gagging and gasping.

The three sisters, the father (who, looking back now, I think was secretly rooting for me) and the boisterous mother (who was not on our side) circled us uttering a chorus of curses.

Jeremy's arms flailed away at me, which I batted away as best I could, but he did get a few deflected shots in on me. I was able to step in and trip him down onto his back, in a mixed-bag, unidentifiable, takedown technique. Jeremy landed on his back hard with me on one knee above him. I snatched his right arm as he tried to hit me in the face, and I tried punching him back, but he used his other arm to take out the sting and deflect each of my shots. Then with the fingers of his free hand busy pushing against my face, my new free hand got the cuffs off my belt and I cuffed that big left arm.

One limb down. One to go. Glass half-full? Or half empty? Suddenly, a screaming banshee leapt half on my arm, half on my back, spider monkey style. It was the big, fat Bellamy mama.

Cussing me, she yanked on my arm and pulled hunks of my hair off my head! I shoved. She tumbled back and ripped my grip free of the handcuffed hand. Jeremy's emancipated arm quickly clocked me a good one in the jaw. Me no likey, cause it was a good one as I recall. I saw the Constellation Orion for a second. The loose, open end of the cuff smacked the top of my head.
Unfortunately, the cuff end was open. It cut into my confused head's scalp.

As Momma and I rolled back, me landing between her open legs, her house dress way up to her butt. It was an ugly scene. She scratched at my face and pulled out even more of my long Glen Campbell hairdo. AND she held me back. I tell ya' she was a spider monkey! Worse, Jeremy was still down and kicking viciously at my legs. I spotted Gary as he slid an unsteady leg up under himself to stand up. Given my "rear mount" predicament, I got a little pissed when he stumbled away from me and back over to the squad car!

Big Momma and I wrestled while Jeremy bolted up to his feet and started after me while his mother was clawing and clutching me. She was like a wasp squadron attack! He circled to stomp me as I pulled free from his Spider Momma.

Gary got there just in time to scoop up one of Jeremy's arms before it pummeled down on me. It spun Jeremy off his course. Then I scrambled to get up. As Gary wrestled with Jeremy in a wide spiral dance, I snatched the last handgrip of the mother and pried it free. Thank God she hadn't wrapped those hairy legs around me! Once up, we double-teamed Jeremy into cuffs this time, and we chunked his angry, Christmas-ass face down on the frozen ground.

Now who's kickin' who, Santa? Jeremy was down for the count. Next, Gary raced over to "ol coughin' Joe," still gagging back by the elm tree. As he shackled Joe, two squad cars roared up.

Seems Gary's little dash away from me was a dash back to our squad car to get on the radio and make a quick call for back up. A fine idea! I guess that's why he was the senior janitor in this social sanitation business we were in.

We marched the scuffling brothers into the back seats of the squad cars. The shift Sergeant took a look at my messed-up uniform and hair, then took a hard look at big Spider Monkey Momma, then back at me. "No," I said, "no, let's not arrest her."

Tough decision, since she was 10 feet away streaming artistic quatrains of curses right into our faces, and probably had evidence (my Glenn Campbell hair) still stuck to her fingers. And, my face flesh under her fingernails.

But it was Christmas! She was protecting her…babies! Albeit scumbags. Hellions. That, and ahhh really… who needs the extra paperwork of a third arrest? Joe was still gasping, but calm. I must admit that early on, in my so-called police career I was a throat-puncher a few times. Like a young fool, I didn't really truly understand just how dangerous it was to punch around the windpipe of somebody's neck. And good God it worked so well. But I settled in for the carotid artery strikes, which many cops called the Brachial Plexus Stun, and stayed away from the windpipe. I swear it's a wonder I didn't kill somebody, but each time, like Joe, they recovered. Imagine killing somebody on Christmas Day!

Jeremy was busted up real good by that point. He fought us and we kicked his ass until he stopped kicking back. Simple use of force.

Back then, if people were injured while fighting us during an arrest, we didn't even give them so much as an aspirin. They sat in their city and county cells and suffered. So soon sat these Bellamy brothers, ensconced in our piss-ridden, foul city cells, awaiting a trip to the similarly adorned county jail cells. But the rest of this yuletide afternoon Gary and I spent at the hospital, having been ordered there by our lieutenant when he saw our blood trickles. Me from my forehead and jack-up face, neck and arms, and Gary's from his flat nose. "Check up!" He ordered.

"Damn!" I said, "Lt, we are okay!" But to no avail.

Neither of us wanted the stigma of a trip to the hospital. Gary and I felt like idiots being wheeled around in the mandatory wheelchairs for exams and x-rays, all precautionary requirements.

Routine. It's no wonder we avoided reporting injuries

whenever possible. That, and the subsequent harassment from one's ...for lack of a better term...peers...

"Ohhh, does Hocky-Wocky have a whittle boo-boo on his wee, whittle head?" And the inevitable, "Did Gary boy hut' his nosey when the big bad man knocked him...ON HIS ASS!" HA! HA! HA! Or in this holiday case...HO! HO! HO! This would go on for days until the next troop scored an injury and then focus shifted upon them. I got a few butterfly stitches from the open end of the cuff tearing my scalp.

You would think all that VO-5 hairspray would protect my scalp, at least just a bit! Few know that the most common "edged-weapon" injury to a police officer is from the open teeth of a handcuff, his own or that of his buddy's, flying free in the frays of a fracas. At one point, Gary and I found ourselves wheeled into a hallway, sitting about 20 feet apart in our wheelchairs, our nurses having abandoned us momentarily while in route to our perspective "treatments." We stared at each other silently for a moment, then...

"Merry Christmas, Gary," I said.

"Merry Christmas, Hock," he said.

Naahhh...we didn't say any such damn thing to each other. I thought it would sound nice and "holiday-ish" for you all here and now. Actually, we cussed up the fucking Bellamy clan like big dogs.

And so, boys and girls, to ALL a good night. And that's my Christmas Story, a little something to warm up your yuletides. Whatever in Sam Hill they are?

Chapter 35: CPR at Sambos

"Sixty-five…fight on the Sambos parking lot," the police dispatcher announced, as Glen Nowles and I prowled the midnight hour, wintery north Texas streets in our squad car.

"Ten-four," I replied, and off we went to yet another pain-in-the-neck family argument, or redneck versus hippy, or disco versus cowboy, or, or…you get the picture and the numerous combinations.

Sambos Restaurant. Odd name, huh? It was a chain like a Denny's restaurant we see so much today. The names were changed to be more politically correct, but some historians say the name was never a derogatory black theme. It actually came from an abbreviation of the owners Sam Battistone and Newell Bohnett.

The logo was of an Indian boy, as in, India. Open 24 hours, near the Interstate and always a hotspot for the drunks after the bars closed. When the country western bars and discos closed, many of the drunk patrons flooded into the all-night and late-night restaurants. And of course, we had our hands full with these knuckleheads. Quite a mix. Roy Rogers at one table. John Travoltas at another. I've had a few knock-down and drag-out fights and arrests in places like this.

When Glenn and I rolled up to Sambos, we did not see any fight in progress, but rather a downed woman and the Sambos manager out front on the wide sidewalk of the restaurant. He waved us over with a motion of desperation. As we ran from the car, he yelled,

"He hit her and she fell. She's dead! I think she's dead!"

Probably knocked out when her head hit the pavement? Typical, I first thought. I went to her head and lifted it to see or feel for a wound as Glen grabbed for her throat and felt for a pulse.

"You call for an ambulance, too?" he asked the manager.

"No, just the police."

"Call an ambulance," Glen ordered, and he looked at me. "No pulse. No pulse," he told me.

We began CPR on her. Glenn started working on the mouth and I took the chest, as we were taught. We switched positions, but worked non-stop, for what seemed like an hour, but it wasn't. Both

Glen and I recognized her as someone we knew, an emergency room nurse at one of our hospitals. She suddenly gagged and coughed, and her body started to spasm. She even started to mumble. Glen and I dropped back on the ground beside her, pretty well exhausted.

She sat up in complete shock, babbling about where she was. I wanted to say from hell and back but refrained. Who knows, maybe she went the other way. We all three sat there on the sidewalk. In the distance, we heard the sirens of an ambulance.

"Your heart stopped," Glen said.

"My God, my God," she said.

"What happened?" he asked.

"My husband and I…. had a fight. That is all I can remember."

"He hit her!" the manager piped in. "He hit her, but she fell when he hit her in the chest. Hard in the chest!"

Apparently, it was a heart-stopping strike to the chest. Not all that unusual really. The ambulance pulled up and EMTs charged out with gear. They began checking her out as Glen and I stood up.

Typically, we follow the ambulance to the hospital and get all the complainant's contact information to fill out a crime report. The next day, detectives would work the assault case, domestic or
otherwise, and that is the typical routine of that age and era.

"Did you see the car the husband left in?" I asked the manager as I stood up, and as the EMT crew readied the woman for transport.

"Left? He didn't leave," the manager answered.

"What? Where is he?" I asked.

"Well, he is right there," and he pointed to the first booth in the corner of the front door. Through the huge glass windows, there sat a man with a menacing expression, smoking a cigarette, facing us with a cup of coffee on the table. He was right at the front window; directly facing us and saw everything we did.

"Him?" Glen asked, about as astonished as I was.

"Him," the manager replied.

"He watched us do all this?" I said aloud to myself mostly.

"Yup," the manager said. "Sat there the whole time."

Glen and I exchanged glances. Now, getting someone's heart to beat again is an emotional experience. It is a ride unlike no other. A ticking time bomb that must be diffused before explosions occur in the head and then in the body. It is a race. Then somehow, if it works, the magic of the universe kicks in. The spark of life. The heart beats yet again. So, to think that the husband sat and watched all this. Death, and life again.

I think I was the first to march toward the door. I was quite young then, and I was ready to destroy this guy with my bare hands. I am sure Glen, a bit older, was also.

But, as so called, professionals we put the "skids on," the adrenaline before we entered the establishment. I sat at the table. Glen stood. The husband barely looked at us.

He looked like an unshaven, smelly scumbag, an uneducated, middle-aged drunk waste of air, time and space. Of course, that is such a prejudiced, snap judgment on my part, huh? I just wanted to toss that hot coffee right in his face, the cup too and smack him out of his seat. Couldn't. But if he made so much as the wrong move? My dream would come true.

The conversation went, to the best of memory, something like this:

"Coffee good?" I asked quietly.

"No," he said.

I nodded.

"Any guess where we're going?"

"Jail," he said.

"Coffee's not much better there either."

All that angst, as actor/writer Billy Bob Thornton would call it years later - "angst and shit," and it came down to a calm, few lines about the coffee. Iconic. Laconic. Ironic.

I stood. He stood and Glenn cuffed his hands. Glenn searched him as I watched. We marched him to the squad car. No chance for a fight. There is no telling what would have happened if this sorry bastard tried a shove or a poke at us. I guess he could tell that Glen and I were about a thread away from going rodeo right then and there.

Instead, we booked him into the city jail for aggravated assault and the rest is history in a set of books I ain't read yet.

I guess they call us professional when we keep our cool at times like these. Sometimes it ain't easy, but it got easier as the years rolled along. I grew a callous on my hide that was once three inches thick. But I see that cover peeling away now, that bare unpredictable nerve coming closer to the surface again. I hope I can keep some of it, but that's why many call such survival skills like callouses - "perishable."

We saw the nurse at work for another year. She got a divorce. With each encounter, behind the curtain of our conversations, was some kind of a bond. Funny feeling. She told us she was back in school. She graduated with another medical degree and moved away. So, the nurse got a divorce and moved away. That ex-husband by the way? Turned out he really was an unshaven, smelly scumbag, an uneducated, middle-aged, drunk, waste of air, time and human space. A lot of my snap judgments do turn out.

Imagine that. Now as the years went Glenn, I and others did save a few more lives out on the proverbial "streets." We weren't EMTs, but we did. Decades later when our police department became more modernized and larger with the times, a new police chief instituted a medal for lifesaving. The first recipient had rescued a woman from a burning car wreck as I recall, and the young officer deserved some creds for his actions. Sure. This medal was awarded at a big, department ceremony with the news media. Great rounds of applause. Yipee.

But some of us older hands sat quiet and could not help but think of the times we had saved lives in the past years. A quick, accidental exchange of glances in the ceremony between me and other vets said it all to me,

"Oh well, guess the new kids get medals now," one vet said later.

Such is life. And death. Imagine trying to reward all those deeds retro-actively anyway. How exactly would you do that? And who among us would walk into an admin office and ask, "Can I have a medal, please?" Not me. Not the other vets either.

The medals are a good idea, though. Good for morale but also it is a special moment to do such a thing. Real heroes doing real work. Movie stars and sports stars aren't piss ants in a puddle to these real people. Not even piss ants in a puddle.

But the across the street? EMTs are saving lives all the time. Way, way more than any of us every did.

Even CPR has changed these days, emphasizing more on the chest pumping and way less on the mouth to mouth. Check out the new courses. You never know when you need it.

Chapter 36: Knife Fight and the Jailhouse Superbowl Ring

Our city in North Texas boasted two Superbowl player residents. And the two of them were as different as day and night and as racially typecast as one could imagine. One was a retired white guy in a very big house with many investments. The other was a black guy from what one might call our slums, or projects. He had no such monied investments. And no such home. He was older than most players but still playing ball. And every off season, he would return home to Texas. And every off-season he seemed to get into trouble of some sort. Both these guys wore the big brash and legendary Superbowl ring. I never met the white guy, but I did meet the black guy. In fact, he kind of saved my ass one Saturday morning, back in the 1970s…in a knife fight.

In one "hood" in our city we had a old drinking place called The Wine Tree. It was a bar, but not a bar. It was an open house with a jukebox and the booze flowed (illegally sold) along with the drugs. An old, crippled man named Willie lived in the back room and "ran" it with a henchman or two.

Through time you learn, either by emergency calls or by investigation that many of that area's crimes, at some point started, ran through, or ended up at the Wine Tree. Did Willie have a liquor license? A business permit? No. It was just a house. An open house party 24/7. The neighbors didn't care. Hell, they hung out there, too.

The attendees parked everywhere and the dancing and drinking and conniving and hustling spilled out onto the pounded-down and dry front lawn, and out onto the streets. There was even a jukebox in there.

The next mornings, especially after weekends, The Wine Tree had a hang-over. There were always stragglers still hovering on or about the property. One Saturday morning either a neighbor reported a fight in progress out front of the Wine Tree, or I drove up on this fight. I just can't remember. I was a young turk back then and worked this district. I was just as fearless as I was dumb. As I drove up to the Wine Tree, I saw at least three men arguing and another two others apparently interceding and peacemaking. The peacemakers weren't doing so well. In total, five knuckleheads bandied about.

Two of the arguing guys started a sloppy fight. The other three guys started in cheering or jeering. Some in the general area scattered. Some remained at a distance, on-looking, rubber-neckers in the general area.

I got out of the car and tried my hand at this peace-keeping routine too, but these men were charged up on who-knows-what-all from the night before and pissed off. My Gestalt therapy training just wasn't working, and the two main men crashed in on each other. I dove in trying to separate them. And wild fists flew. Then a third guy jumped in, and I'll tell you it was a free-for-all. Everybody against everybody, and I wasn't winning. I wound up half-wrestling, half-punching with one of them as the other two, struggled off a few feet and bumped into us.

Then one of them pulled a knife. It was a switchblade. He was cursing up a storm, and this whole event was going south very badly. He was not cursing or pointing the knife at me, just the other guy he was originally mad at. Then, to satisfy the arms race, one of the onlookers passed the other unarmed man a knife!

"Put down those knives!" I ordered.

They did not. The peacemakers and a few gathering onlookers did bail back about 15 feet when those knives came out. Some onlookers got involved and grabbed my arms. I think, as if, to stop me from shooting their friends I think. They tried to keep me away. They tried holding my arms as if to protect their fighting friends from me.

HA! So that "drop it," command of mine didn't work and I had this gut-crushing feeling this would end with my gun out, maybe shooting somebody and it all turn, six different kinds of crazy bad. I pushed back, got free and damned if they didn't re-grab me.

These two armed goons cursed a blue streak and were dueling as in a comedy of moves, slashing and stabbing at each other in uncoordinated, wild lunges and swings. But a knife is a great equalizer from fools to kings.

Then suddenly a stout black man charged up. From the proverbial "nowhere." He was not drunk. He hit the guy hanging on my right arm, using his shoulder and we both pushed this pain-in-the-ass off of me. Without hesitation, he pivoted and ran up to one in the knife party dance and belted him in the side of his head, with a fist, a forearm, or an elbow? I can't say which. It was a blind side, sucker shot. The man did not see it coming and was so stunned, he dropped the knife on impact, stumbled off and fell.

Arm now free, I pulled my Colt Python pistol. The onlookers gasped and cursed and groaned at its sight. I stepped before the other armed man and told him I'd kill him if he didn't drop the knife. I got in such a position that the other drunk that was first fighting with me, now shared my gun barrel time too.

The guy with the knife just stood there, tip of the knife aimed at my face, his eyes all google-eyed, bloodshot and watering, his lip busted open and bloody. He was wavering before me like a heat wave on booze and drugs. It would have been funny, but for the knife, the jerks around me...well, frankly, actually I guess it wasn't much funny at all.

"Don't even think about it," I warned him.

Good God, was I going to have to shoot this stumbling drunk? I decided I would if he lunged at me.

Meanwhile, this hard-charging citizen hero snatched up the loose knife from the ground and walked right up to the man before me and removed the knife from his hand while the drunk just stared at me. I ordered the two men on their knees. The first was already grounded.

The hero stood there like my professional backup! And, I wondered by the way, where my official back-up unit was, speaking of backup. They didn't get there in time. One thing I could tell was, everyone there, knew this hero guy and were obviously more afraid of him, than me....me being the PO-lice! Who was that unmasked man?

Two pair of handcuffs hung on my belt, and I had three men to shackle! I cuffed the bystander guy fighting me with one pair, figuring if he were damn fool enough to fight with me before, I needed both of his hands linked up now. Then I split my second pair of cuffs with these two so-called, "knife fighters."

"There ya go. Now go on and beat yourselves to death now," I told the two handcuffed together slobs. "See if I stop you again."

At this point I didn't care if they clobbered each other down. One cuff to one's right hand, the other cuff to the other man's right hand. This way if they both ran off, it wouldn't be too easy to run. In theory, one faced one way, one faced the other, (but in actuality, one of them could have crossed their arm over for them to run. Anyway, that didn't happen.)

Other units arrived, and we carted the men away. I had to get the name and address of this hero for my crime and arrest reports. I thanked him profusely. He was all smiles and told me everything. I'll call him "Ray Wilson" here.

At the station, our Patrol Lt. Gene Green wandered into the book-in room and wanted the sitrep. After my report, he said,

"Ray Wilson? He plays for the Chiefs. Ya' met Ray! Ya' see his big Superbowl ring? He comes home every off-season and stays with his momma. He gets into some kind of trouble every year."

"Well, he sure helped me out of a mess here!" I said.

"Just wait," Lt Green warned. "You'll see him in here for somethin' er' another." By "in here," he meant the book-in room.

"He comes home every year and sorta cleans up after his relatives' and friends' bad business. He has a helleva' family. Always in trouble."

That Wilson clan. Oh, yeah. Those kin folk! Well, I saw his point. What a shame. The guy just charged right in and helped me.

About a month or so later we were on midnight shift, and I walked through the station to the squad room. The old headquarters was situated kind of funny because you had to walk through the book-in room of our jail to get from the front side of the station and into to the back squad room. There on the book-in room bench, sat a handcuffed Ray Wilson. My Wine Tree hero.

He was arrested for assaulting some men with a baseball bat! Some kind of a family, revenge/vendetta, just like Lt. Green had suggested would happen. Ray nodded to me as I approached and passed through. His possessions were laid on the book-in counter, ready for safekeeping collection. A worn wallet. Some pocket change. An old watch. A belt…and a big, golden, Superbowl ring.

"Take care of that ring," Ray asked cordially.

"We always do, Ray," the arresting detective said.

He retired in our city, took over the family's, older home and then years later died of old age, but a poor man. He was one of the regulars I would stop and talk to, once in a while, through the years. He was a really good feller from and in a bad place.

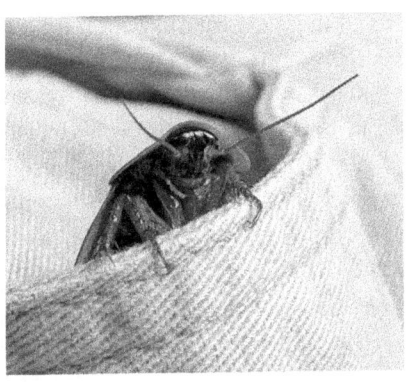

Chapter 37: A Roach Story

Ever hear of Chairman Mao Zedong's "Four Pests Campaign?" In 1958, Mao decided China needed a pest extermination, namely mosquitoes, flies, rats, and sparrows. Every person had to kill a certain number of flies and present these little carcasses to the neighborhood government agent or be punished. Grandchildren caught extra flies so their elderly grandparents would be safe.

Every week we read about another this-or-that species that is going extinct. You know, from evil mankind. No one seems to keep track of bugs. Insects. The visible bacteria of our world. I operate under the motto that, "The world is a better place with one less insect," and I try to do my share by squashing these things before they multiply. Imagine the planet overrun by ants. And don't doubt for a moment that they would love that. Love to have their way with our terrain into an eerie landscape of giant ant hills. Planet of the Apes? HA! We have apes under control. More likely, Planet of the Ants. Chuck Heston wouldn't drop to his knees and declare, "They blew it all up." He would say instead, "They ate us all up."

Kill as many ants as possible. Make it a daily chore. Did you know that when you tiptoe up to an ant hill to drop weapons of mass destruction upon their headquarters, they feel the vibrations in the ground of your initial approach and start saving the queen?

That's right, hundreds of little SAS/Green Beret ants start saving the queen, and you haven't even unscrewed the ant killer container yet, so fearful that a little whiff of the atomic insecticide will give you lung cancer and kill you. You then will die early and if not hermetically sealed? Bugs will eat your corpse. And that damn queen will still be pushing out baby ants.

Even overpriced coffins can't last forever as bugs gnaw away at them through the ages. There is a certain bug that likes everything.

Wood. Plastic. Whatever it is, it will be eaten by some kind of bug that delights on that kind of substance. Look at the dung beetle. If God made a bug that eats shit, He's made a bug that will eat anything. Then bugs will enter your expensive, sealed tomb like obsessed miners discovering an underground vein of silver and start a feast on you. No! No, only cremation saves you from this fate, my friends. Don't you see the dramatic struggle for survival? I do not have a bug phobia! I have just seen their extreme work and I'm telling you, it's ugly and they need killing.

Let's not even talk about fleas, chiggers or mosquitoes...or roaches. They would eat you alive if they could. Don't think so? Just stay still long enough. They'll eventually crawl up on ya and start eating!

I remember numerous homes I have been in as a cop that were covered with these bugs. David Stewart and I were starting a search of a house once and fled it like screaming psychos, suddenly overwhelmed by thick waves of starving fleas. Shrieking, we about stripped to our underwear on the street, flagellating ourselves like repentant Iranians.

Everyone knows about mosquitoes. Once on an outdoor assignment, I was bitten more than 80 times on each forearm in the open space between my gloves and short-sleeved shirt. God's little vampires. Didn't expect it. Couldn't leave for any spray. Why God? Why? Why did you make the mosquito? I am a bit stung on that point, as if it were a litmus test of the religious universe. Imagine the moveable feast on Noah's Ark? The insects also came in two-by-two! Then they quickly multiplied. Somebody had to keep watch on the termites because they love them some ark wood. But the mosquitoes! An ark full of critters was flesh and blood heaven.

Let's prepare our own little ark. Inside the cubits of every cop's trunk, there must be a kit containing emergency bug or mosquito spray or lotion. One never knows where one will suddenly be assigned a scene or surveillance.

In my official days, I've seen some big bugs. (Snakes? That's another essay.) I recall the day I saw the biggest roach in my life. And it wasn't in the Asian, African or South Pacific jungle! No, I don't mean a marijuana joint, but a genuine, bona-fide, all-American, even George Soros' house has-em', been-here-since prehistoric times, cockroach. A roach so big, it was first mistaken as a pet.

On one of my dinner breaks, after my food was delivered, I glanced up to see several local salesmen enter. All in a neat, pressed, hot-combed (remember "hot combs?") group they joked and sauntered their way up to the ordering counter.

But one of them stood out of the crowd, a man among men, with a particular unique characteristic, something each and every human should easily notice upon first glance. There on his shoulder, much like a parrot might perch on a sailor, like a falcon on a hunter, sat a huge, curious, cockroach. I say curious because his incredibly long feelers were in constant motion and his head appeared to be jerking around as if scanning the menu on the wall. I say huge because I could see its damn ribs.

Now, several thoughts flashed through my mind. First came the instantaneous loss of a once ferocious appetite. Then, I wondered if this was some sort of joke that his fellow colleagues were playing.

Either they had superhuman, self-control or they simply hadn't spied the bug? Perhaps it was a pet? No, I thought, it must be there by accident. It was just a question of time...

An elderly woman, going for a cup of coffee, approached the salesman and with an impatient disgust reported, "Sir, sir, there is a large roach on your shoulder!"

Shaken from his thoughts he said, "Huh?"

"There is a roach on your shoulder!" she growled.

The others turned to the salesman and like a bunch of school kids whined and chimed in with this announcement like a drunk choir.

The salesman's face turned white as his peripheral vision caught this parasite's visage atop his torso. With uncontrollable, epileptic motions, he spastically began slapping at his shoulders.

The other salesmen, knowing this action would surely send the roach flying, dodged and lunged around the man as if he'd suddenly become a germ-passing leper. Meanwhile, other customers began watching, interrupted by a series of snorts, helpless grunts and gags the other salesmen made.

A hero nearby made a dashing sweep, both cuffing the salesman on the back of the neck and striking the roach forward, but it took a few seconds of searching on the part of the group to discover that the long brown antlers protruding from the salesman's breast pocket was not the new design for the top of a BIC pen.

This hero had knocked the large bugger right into the salesman's shirt pocket. The creature, either desperately frightened, or calm and cozy, remained perfectly still there, just a Banlon layer away from the salesman's heart.

The crowd gasped. "There IT is!" they yelled. The salesman's helpless, animal grunts suddenly became louder. He began shaking his overweight torso, striking at his chest below the pocket. He banged into a table and sent a napkin holder, salt and pepper shakers, as well as his several pens and a small scratch pad flying, but still no roach! The prehistoric survivor was probably clutching on for dear life.

With a country-western, two-step through the eatery, the salesman began a grotesque disco-flamingo macabre march that would rival Michael Jackson. I'm sure all he really wanted to do was turn upside down, but even in such a crisis, we all must adhere to some social graces.

As an officer of the law, duly sworn to protect and serve, even I was frozen in shock, repulsed as this bug opera unfolded before my eyes. Finally, out the hideous creature flew. It apparently had enough! Ever resilient, ever strong, it flipped through the air, cracked to the ground and sped off.

First, it started in my direction. I thought for a second about drawing my revolver, but knew it was foolish. I might cause a ricochet on its hard shell. It turned and ran toward some shrieking woman, her hands to her face, her feet in a pathetic, aerobic routine, reducing contact with the floor. Then it disappeared into the woodwork of the restaurant, setting up a new residency and future roach empire for all time until the establishment gets nuked in the next world war. (Even that is questionable as many bugs actually survived Hiroshima and Nagasaki.)

The manager, circling the incident was at least relieved that the imported roach hadn't originated from her eatery.

"He brought that in!" she cried to no one in particular. "He brought that in!"

I guess her herd of critters was branded and easily identifiable? The salesmen settled down, and our once hungry victim carrier had only ice water for lunch. I quickly finished my meal, left the place for the elevated safety of my squad car, checked both my shoulders in the mirror, and drove off, feeling really, really itchy.

Calling all cars! Calling all cars! Kill all bugs you see. Repeat. Kill all bugs. Kill them before they multiply. Before they eat us all up.

Chapter 38: Me and John Paul Hale, from Fistfights to His Death

John Paul Hale started out a thug amongst thugs. A couple of burglaries. Drunk or drugged in public. A little dealing. A few fights. We patrolman of the busy and oft times violent patrol district all knew Hale.

My first encounter with him was on a Juneteenth. Juneteenth is the southern, summer celebration of President Lincoln freeing the slaves. In various parts of the U.S. it is often a day filled with picnics in parks and special events. So it is in Texas.

In our city, this meant an annual festival in a park, and in the 1970s, an era where racial politics cooked in a weak oven, the order of the day from the
police chief was to stay away from the park and avoid ANYTHING that could lead to a racial disturbance.

I made it my directive to patrol well away from the park. But as we know, about 5% or so of any race, creed and color, is made up of ignorant, punk criminals. Late in the hot afternoon, the five per-centers wandered into the park, making a scene, pushing some folks around, etc. People wandered across the street from the park and started calling the police.

"Sixty-one," came over the radio. This was not the usual dispatcher, but a rare audio appearance of our shift commander, Lt. Gene Ray Green. "Hock, John Paul Hale is making a scene at the park. I want you to go down there and get him, but YOU DO NOT make a scene."

"Ten-four," I said. Then they next dispatched, from way across town, a female officer I shall call here "Sarah." Sarah, in particular, was known as being a lousy backup and just a terrible fighter, but I knew instinctively, the idea was that the presence of me with a female would be less offensive than two, bully-cop males.

When I drove up, the multi-acre park was in full swing with hundreds of folks milling about. The bandstand rocked with a black group singing soul songs with a horn section. On the grounds, I saw Hale yelling harshly at some women and their husbands trying to intervene. As I approached, I saw all the good people in neighborhood discreetly pointing to Hale. The female officer drove up.

"John Paul!" I said, "Hey! I need to talk to you!" I tried to get him away from the picnic area.

His answer was a quick, snappy, "Fuck you, mother fucker."

I took his elbow and tried to walk away with him hoping to het him away from the park and talk. He flung his elbow into my chest. This is what we usually call "assault." I grabbed him again and a little wrestling match began to erupt. So did a crowd.

His buddies started in,

"Hey, hey leave him alone!"

I caught a few "honkeys" and a "pig" or two. Up till now I was tiptoeing around, doing the best I could not to make a scene, but the scene was under construction.

In all this, Hale gave me a hard shoulder or another

elbow or two just enough to spike my blood pressure. That ol' reptile voice in my brain, declared,

"That's about enough!"

I rammed my forearm across his chest and stepped behind him, swept out his leg and body slammed him as hard as I could onto the grassy, ground. BOOM! It was a shocker to Hale as well as the aghast crowd now surrounding me. I rolled him face down as he still flailed and struggled.

Then I grabbed his arms and tried to get his wrists close enough together for my partner to use her cuffs on his wrists. A bad case of isometrics set in, and Hale would not allow the movement.
Any other time I would've rabbit punched the son-of-a-bitch or ground my knee real good in his back, anything to break his concentration, and his isometric, but I was surrounded by unfriendlies and still trying to look friendly to the friendlies.

His friends started pulling on my hair. They stole the handcuffs right off my belt. They pulled on my shirt and belt. I felt the telltale tugs on the handle of my pistol! I tucked an elbow over my pistol, which made any handcuffing mission even more difficult.

FINALLY, I got the wrists close, and Sarah, her hands shaking, closed the cuffs around them. I grabbed an arm and pulled him up, yanking him across the park and across the street, leading a parade of cussing miscreants as I went. I looked into the faces of the good people there as I passed. None had helped me. None. Probably they feared Hale and his group at a later date. But I feared for my pistol and it could have gone way rodeo out there in an instant. A little help would have been... nice. I tossed Hale into the car, and we got out of there.

The charge? Class C: Disorderly Conduct, and I had to be the complainant because no one else probably would. In those old days, if you wrestled and fought with a cop and not much damage happened to either of us, we wouldn't automatically charge folks with bigger charges of resisting arrest or assault. We just didn't. It was just another slice of cop-life.

In the book-in room, I realized I was a disheveled mess and minus most of the gear off my belt. A local, popular, black businessman had called the station, talked to Lt. Green and reported I properly did what I had to, plus he appreciated us. He thanked us. So, Green wandered in with his big,

"Well-done," with his country smile.

"I'm going back!" I declared. "I want my speed loaders and my cuffs back and get some of them that assaulted me."

"Ohhh, no," Lt. Green said. "Hold yer horses. You ain't going back. You ain't! You'll cause a riot out there. Getcha' a Dr Pepper and sit down. Write the report and relax. We got a boxes full of handcuffs and bullets."

"Yeah," I said, "yeah," but I was neck-wringing, pissed at that point. I thought even more about how easily I could have lost my gun.

"It's over for today," Green said.

But it wasn't over for John Paul Hale and me. About a year later, the next thing he did was try to burn some people alive.

"Sandra Deagan married John Paul Hale?" I asked, not believing the gossip session in our squad room. The Deagan family members lived throughout our city and were a law-abiding, prosperous and religious clan. Mr. Deagan, the main living patriarch was the father of six or maybe seven kids of all ages, of which Sandra Deagan was one. All of them good kids. Mr. Deagan would have been one of the people at the Juneteenth party that would have called cops on Hale.

"Yup, married last Sunday."

Was this the bad-boy syndrome gone mad? Sandra

was no doubt bound for a very professional career somewhere. The fact that she married an unemployed dirt bag like Hale was unfathomable for us.

"Well, how did ol' man Deagan let that happen?" another patrolman asked. No one answered because no one knew.

"That won't last long," another officer said, and he was right.

Sure enough, within three months Sandra fled Hale and moved back into the Deagan house, in fear of Hale's craziness.

Then, one midnight shift, Detective Doug Norman spoke at our squad meeting...

"Mr. and Mrs. Deagan (Sarah's parents) have been getting death threats from John Paul Hale. He's tried to visit Sandra Hale at their house and they refuse to let him in. Hale stood on their porch and said that he will kill every Deagan in the city. So, we have posted the addresses of all the Deagan families on the bulletin board, with a mugshot of Hale. Be on the lookout for him and cover these houses as often as you can."

I took a look at the handwritten list on the board. The main, large Deagan house was on the outskirts of our inner city back then. Then there was the grandmother's house, all the brothers', and a sister's apartment.

Just a few nights later, at about 4 a.m. I got the radio call:

"Sixty-one. Assist fire department at 140 McKinney." It was the Deagan grandmother's house.

The fire department beat me to the scene and they were busy extinguishing a fire on a corner of the old wooden house. There on the sidewalk was the elderly Grandmother Deagan in her robe. Mr. Deagan and his brother were arriving and walked up beside me.

"Looks like it was started, like someone splashed

gasoline on the wall," a fireman commander told us.

We all knew what that meant. I asked the dispatcher via the radio to alert the on-duty detective. Hale was obviously the major suspect. I also asked for a BOLO-"be-on-the-lookout" for Hale. But of course, we had all been on the general lookout for him anyway, but this time we would stop and question him.

How the grandmother was awakened in time to escape the house I do not remember. But she was lucky as these houses were old WWII "salt-box" design and would have easily flared up like a tinderbox with her inside.

About two nights later, the Deagan brother, a minister, had his house doused with gas and set afire about 3 a.m. They were alert enough to quickly call the fire department. So far, two arsons and no injuries. Just property damage. No real evidence to arrest Hale.

The intensity of the search for Hale intensified. Question him. Scare him. There was still not a lick of new evidence that linked Hale to the fires. Some detectives prowled the streets at night. My patrol shift rotated over from midnights to evenings, but I was still "in the hunt" too, for this trouble-making, son of a bitch. A day shift rotation would have probably taken me out of any action on this. No probable cause. No arrest warrant. This must have accelerated his rage and courage, because...he started shooting next...

It was a snowy, dark evening when an alert neighbor, also on the lookout, spied a prowler at the main Deagan house. Our dispatcher sent two cars, two officers. I was one. Ron Stratler was the other.

"The neighbor reports a black male in dark clothes walking around the Deagan house and looking into the windows," the dispatcher said.

"Be advised, it looks like he's holding a stick or a long object. Or, a gun. The neighbor suggests it might be the son-in-law, Hale."

As I got close to the street I turned off my car headlights and coasted up, hoping to catch him there. (Remember this, I said that their house was on the edge of the woods that was soon scheduled to be a large housing edition. Roads were cut but no houses built yet. Just trees.)

From the very instant I opened my car door, Mr. Deagan was doomed. He'd sat at his kitchen table, surrounded by his large family eating dinner, with his back right up against a dining room window, right in front of the very window where the mysterious figure stood. Suddenly, as I cracked the car door open, I heard the window erupt with a giant explosion. A shotgun blast cut through the screen and glass. It shredded Deagan's head and some of his upper body into ribbons, kicking him across the table full of food and family. Face down. Dead right there.

The blast rocked the night landscape just as I put one foot on the street from the car. I rounded the front of my squad. I saw the man by the window some 30 yards away as he turned and ran into the woods. The sound and object in his hands told me it was a shotgun. As I charged up the lawn and hill, I pulled my pistol. As I ran by the window, I saw the utter nightmare through this blasted picture frame, a family horrified, chaos, shrieking and grasping their faces and throats. A figure lay face down on the table. A one-second look told the tale. Stratler had pulled up behind me and entered the house while children were exiting the doors screaming for help.

The figure with the gun was ahead of me as we ran into the woods. It was the worst of all foot pursuits. Dark. Snowing. Uneven, hilly terrain full of trees. I saw him darting between trees and it dawned on me that he could stop behind any one, wait and then cut me down with that scattergun as I ran by or just got close. I instinctively flanked a bit off to the left a bit to escape this and maybe get a glimpse of him from a position that he might not expect, yet still advancing forward.

Then...red taillights! An engine roar. He hadn't stopped to hide after all. Instead, he'd jumped into and started a truck many yards, maybe 30 yards ahead of me. Skidding in the snow, the truck raced off. In my chase, I fired two shots from my Colt Python as the truck flashed into view between the trees. Shots of anger and desperation. Wishful shots of hope that I might cut down the distant, fleeing criminal. But, the truck turned south on the street and sped off.

When I reached his point of departure, I discovered he'd parked on what was a newly cut, cul-de-sac road for that future housing addition. A perfect, new "flat" place to park and creep up on the house through the woods. I sprinted down the short road to the main residential street but the truck was long gone, out of sight. I ran to my squad car and reported the escaping pickup truck on the police radio.

Old? New? Color? It was so dark, through so many trees, I couldn't even offer a description.

Inhuman screams emanated from the house. The front door stood open. I ran into the living room and saw teens and children literally banging off the walls, clutching their faces, a mother, all in a frantic state of mindless shock. In the kitchen, I saw Stratler talking on the phone. He looked at me and shook his head. Mr. Deagan was dead, stretched across the dinner table. The back of his head and neck a red mush. A freezing winter wind blew in from the blasted window. I still remember the sheer, shredded, dining room curtains blowing. The screeching family, the kids seemed to bounce off the walls and furniture, like electrified zombies.

Then and there I felt the familiar, great, third-degree burn of personal frustration. I was seconds behind a psychopath. A murdering bastard. Seconds. Just seconds.

The ambulance arrived, but it was way too late. Half

the man's brains were on the table.

Two detectives showed up, and we walked out to the cul-de-sac and stood in the fresh, light snowfall with flashlights, staring at the disappearing snow prints of the suspect's tire treads. A detective took 35mm pictures of the tread prints with a wooden ruler next to them, while we silently knew that somewhere, new, 1970s technology existed to create a delicate, plaster cast of tire snow prints. Somewhere? New York City? Beverly Hills? FBI headquarters? Star Trek? Somewhere. But, not in a mid-sized city in North Texas. But, we all just knew John Paul Hale had to be the shooter. And worse, this new snow landed on the tire tracks and the few footprints from the frozen dirt to the vehicle.

We tried to retrace the chase, look for shoe prints, which I could not do well. I barely saw him and the ground under the traces had only traces of snow.

Maybe, just maybe one of my .357 rounds hit the truck and could tie him to the scene. Or then maybe, as I was running and shooting, did I just shoot two trees instead? We looked at the many trees in the dark with our lights. No bullet holes could be found. I hoped I had clipped the bastard in his escape. (Remember, this was Texas, in the 70s and you could pretty much shoot at fleeing murderers.)

The detectives hunted Hale on a probable cause warrant that didn't really have much probable cause in it. It was all vey sketchy. They eventually caught him holed up in a friend's house. No bullet holes were found in him or any trucks belonging to him or his friends. Nor could they match the poor, snow track photos with the tire treads with any truck. No footprints were found. The results were…inconclusive.

So, A smug Hale sat in jail for days denying everything and remained perfectly silent. After a week of sketchy incarceration, John Paul Hale was set free. He kept a low profile around town, no doubt proud of himself and his successful revenge, killing the one Deagan family father.

Then, about 8 months later...

"Sixty-one, you've got a fight outside the Soul House. Sixty-four and sixty-six to back," ordered the dispatcher.

There were usually more people hanging around outside the Soul House than could fit inside. On Saturday night the Soul House was a swinging place and anything could happen there, but that would be the subject of many other stories of killings, carpet-knife cuttings, busted heads and so on.

"Ten-four," I responded and tooled on off to the familiar trouble spot.

When I turned east off of Belton Avenue, I could see something wasn't right. Usually when there's a fight, the crowd ran in to see the action. When there was a killing, everyone ran … away. Fast. Or, every witness later interviewed was in the "baffroom." A hundred people seem to fit in the three-person, bathroom.

As I drove up, scared faces jogged past me and the crowd was quickly dispersing. Not good. Smacked of a killing and I fully expected to see somebody dead. Also not good, because anyone fleeing could be the suspect, but one man can't stop 40 or 50 people running in every direction, nor stop about 10 cars squealing tires to make their escape.

I pulled right up to the front and bailed out of the car. I saw a man on the sidewalk on his back and another man slowly climbing off of him, backing off of him. I knew that backing-away man to be Augustus Drudge, and Drudge had a look of astonishment on his face. Something told me to draw down on Drudge and I did, pulling my revolver and ordering him to freeze.

"Hold it! Freeze, Augustus! Stop right there!" I yelled as I ran around my car and over to him.

He never looked at me, just glared at the body on the ground, but he did stop. Keeping my gun barrel trained on him I got over to the downed body, on his back.

It was John Paul Hale, giving a last twitch and a stammer. A knife was rammed into an eye, at such an angle I could tell the blade was also deep in his brain. The two back-up officers crashed into Drudge, took him down and cuffed him.

I holstered my gun and knelt beside Hale. The knife handle in his eye was slightly wavering, which I took to interpret as his heartbeat. When it stopped it's ever-so-light "ticking," ticking down to his death. Then, Hale was dead. It was his turn to be "dead right there."

I stood up and walked back to the car and by the open door, I spoke into the radio mike,

"Got a body here. Roll an ambulance, Call CID. Need 60 out here (the patrol Sgt). Ten-ninety-five one time (that meant we had arrested one person)."

I heard chains clanging from inside the Soul House door and ran to the door and started hammering on it, "Milly! Milly Pete!" I barked. "Don't you lock this place up!"

Milton Peterson was famous for shutting down his club and even leaving town for a few days whenever ANYTHING happened at the Soul House. Worst case of Milly's flight was one other night when a man was shot by his pool tables, and all the clientele scattered. Milly hauled the dead man across the club, outside, across the sidewalk, and left him dead in the gutter. Then he locked up the House and fled town. A woman walking by about four hours later saw the corpse and called us. I got there and could see a thick, wide trail of blood coming from behind the chained doors. Milly was picked up out of town by some Dallas detectives and escorted back for questioning. I wasn't going to let Milly slip out on us like this again.

I heard the chains clamor again and the door opened.

"Milly, it's only 10:30," I said calmly and with a big smile.

"Closing up a little early tonight?"

"NO!" he said with a sneer. "you know…" He swung both doors open wide and shuffled back through the club, dragging the heavy door chains.

The EMTs arrived as I walked over to Augustus.

"What the hell happened, bubba?"

He was cuffed and leaning against a squad car. He already had one round of Miranda rights read to him, and I just wanted to know quickly what happened, in case we needed to do more work at the scene.

"We was fightin'," he said. "We hit the ground out here, and John Paul pulled a knife on me. Outta his pocket! I took it from him and stabbed him…in the head…like…like dat." he jutted his chin toward Hale

"He dead, huh?"

"He dead, Augustus," I repeated.

The EMTs kneeled around Hale, but they needn't do any work.

"What were you fighting over? What was the problem?" I asked.

"A woman. A woman we's boff wanted."

A detective arrived. Milly helped him collect some witness names.

We took Drudge in, booked him for homicide. I spent the next hour or two trying to run down some of the escaped witnesses. However, I was reminded that I was on the overtime clock and had to quit for the night. Such was detective work anyway.

When the dust settled, I learned that there had indeed been a shoving match about a woman that started in the club. Then it became a fist fight that rolled outside. They fell and landed on the sidewalk. On his back, Hale pulled and opened a pocketknife and, before he could use it, Drudge disarmed the knife, and shoved it into Hale's eye. The blade sunk in pretty much up to the hilt, and the blade plunged upward enough, into what little, twisted brain that skunk John Paul Hale had. It wasn't even a very big knife.

Drudge got a five-year sentence. One might think that Drudge acted in some kind of self-defense. But the whole matter was settled fast in a plea bargain with a public defender.

Two and a half years later, in the middle of the night, I stopped a reported stolen plumbing, business van. It was felony traffic stop so I pulled my gun out and approached the driver's window at wide angle. The driver smartly had both his hands high on the steering wheel.

"Augustus, is that you?" I asked, shining my flashlight in his face.

"Yep," he said with his hands held high.

"I thought you were in the pen?"

"I was…I'm on parole."

"Well," I said. "That shit's over. Step on outside."

And that is the story of John Paul Hale and me. I wasn't present at his birth. I tried to kill him and missed, but I was sure present at his death. This thought still gives me some consolation, even decades later. That punk son of a bitch.

Chapter 39: Caught in the Water Channel

(Another one of my favorite "typical day in patrol" stories.)

On the east side of our city, there ran a series of waterways, storm channels to handle the bad Texas rainstorms. I know some cities don't have any of these drains, but I guess everyone has seen storm channels in the classic movies and TV shows about Los Angeles. Just like those in the City of Angels, ours was an "open top" system, quite wide in parts, deep in sections and branched off into all parts of the city.

The channels were usually quite dry unless it rained heavily. But there was usually a skinny stream from somewhere. I have seen them flood and overflow. I have had a few foot chases, some fights, arrests, and a couple of mishaps down in the dirty ditches.

Here's one. My first real adventure down below in the water channels was back in the late 70s. There was a series of armed robberies plaguing us on the east side of town, and the detectives were doing the best they could with stakeouts and interviews to break the cases.

Solo actor. Big revolver. Black male. In his 30s. Afro. Cheap bandanna over the lower half of the face. We were all convinced that the suspect was a local. No one ever saw a getaway car, and each time the occasional witnesses reported the suspect just "melted" into the back lots and alleys behind the businesses.

Several nights a week back then, I rode with another patrolman named Clovis George, a very sharp and real funny guy, a prior border town/city cop down Mexico way. Even back then, the Texican border towns were all hotbeds for all kinds of criminal activity and, yes, drugs, drugs, drugs too. The interstate that split our city ran from old Mexico straight up the center of the US. A drug route then and now, but that's a whole other story. Clovis had seen a lot of street-level action down there on the border. The George family was big in our city and he returned home after several years to settle down. Our city produced one Miss America, Phyllis George, and she was his cousin.

Another one in this series of armed robbery calls went out late one weeknight while we were paired up in one car; and it had us and other cars running every which way, haywired, trying to find the suspect either running or driving away in a getaway car. Not a clue. A clean escape yet again.

When the dust settled, we drove to a taco outfit and got tacos and some iced tea, sat on our squad car hood, and ate, contemplating the world as it blew by us. We also contemplated the armed robber.

"I'll bet that squirrelly bastard is jumping down into these dry channels and running right home," Clovis said between bites.

"I'll bet we could jump in at one key point and cut him right off," I said.

"Yeah."

Sounded plausible to me, so we made a plan. A large percentage of criminals lived in the nearby projects in our beat, and we drove around to calculate possible routes from Tell Avenue, businesses to the government housing districts. We knew the CID stakeouts were spotty and all above ground and vehicle based. No way the detectives could cover all those locations every night, night after night. So if we were free and patrolling and heard a report of another east-side, armed robbery on our radio, and if our man was indeed a storm channel jumper, we would guesstimate the time and location where the robber would be running, jump in the drains at some point, and stake out that spot.

Well, within a few nights, a chicken restaurant was hit by our lone suspect. Handgun presented. Money grabbed. Masked. In and out.

And Clovis and I raced to our own planned stakeout. We parked the squad car and, in a huddled-over combat run, slipped into the open channel by a viaduct at a bend in the system where we couldn't be seen from afar. There was less than a small stream of water in there.

In less than one minute, we heard some splashing and footsteps, and we exchanged surprised expressions like ... "well, damn! That could be him!"

And sure enough, it was. He rounded that corner huffing and puffing with a paper bag of money in one hand and a revolver in the other. We spread out and hit him with our flashlight beams.

We pointed our pistols and started shouting, "Drop the gun, or we'll kill ya!" etc.... words to that general effect. You know what I mean. And they were true warnings.

Our man dropped his pistol and bag and put his hands up. Bandanna in his back pocket. We cuffed him, hauled him up the side, and "took him in," as the expression goes.

CID was kind of thrilled. They took over. Our suspect was not a local as it turned out. He was visiting locals and thought he'd run up some traveling money while in town. Mask. Gun. Money. Flight. Matching size and clothing description. Wow. Nice little arrest. Hey, three cheers for the Clovis George idea of ditch jumping, all over some tacos and ice tea.

Through the years together, Clovis and I were also detectives together on the same squad. First him, and then me. Starting back in the early 1980s, I had a bit of a reputation for getting a lot of confessions; known to "mix it up" when needed. Clovis often asked me to partner up with him when he had extra troublesome witnesses and suspects in his cases. Plus, I was his choice when he served an arrest warrant on some shady characters because we knew how to work in unison.

So, we worked numerous cases. Always had a blast, too. I remember he had an affinity toward the "Tonight Show's" Johnny Carson suit line. He thought he was really styling it in a Carson brand suit. You know what? He was!

We went out with our wives to various country and western establishments in those days, some Tex-Mex locales, and drank way too much as I seem to recall. Admin often made the mistake of sending us to various investigation training schools in Austin together, usually at DPS, the state police training academy or the state attorney general training symposiums, whereupon we had entirely too good a time above, beyond and outside the classes. We'd drive to Austin on Sundays to be in position for class on Monday mornings.

On some of the Austin training schools trips we'd bring a small camper's black and white TV set with us to try and watch the Cowboys games in the car on the drive down in football season. It was a war with the rabbit ears antenna, trying to catch the local channels as we passed through cities on the interstate.

Back then, you could legally drink and drive in Texas (not be drunk, just you know, sip until drunk?), and this traveling adventure always, legally, included Coors. One guy drove and the other guy operated the rabbit ears. What a team! (Imagine doing that today. We would both be serving life sentences.)

Clovis took a few promotion tests while in CID and

went back into uniform as a supervisor. He continued his professional career, while I, never testing for any rank, remained back in line operations working in the trenches, not unlike the stinky water ditch system where we made the aforementioned arrest.

Then he had a severe heart attack in the early 1990s. He recovered and became a supervisor for our communications division. He also became an avid runner. Then he suddenly died in 2002. The heart again. Couldn't outrun those genetics no matter how hard he tried. I was working out of the country at the time and missed the funeral.

Many years later, the next century actually, our agency developed a truly amazing, modern police academy. They dedicated the police library in his name, which I thought was just a damn fine idea.

Clovis George was a really good guy, a good friend, and we had a lot of laughs, tacos, beers, and margaritas. Plus, together, in patrol and as detectives we handcuffed a number of felons, too. What more could you possibly ask of a friend? I ask you? Seriously, what more?

Yours Truly, Clovis George and Greg Dunham. Three Musketeers of a strange sort.

Chapter 40: Everything But the Kitchen Sink

The predators came out on Friday and Saturday nights. Their hunting ground was a section in our city that once boasted scores of apartment complexes for college students. Somehow this district slowly degraded into busted up, run-down, graffiti-scarred tenements with those telltale, unbreakable amber streetlights surrounded by mesh. This set the stage for the abandoned cars, drug sales, prostitutes and all kinds of crime. These were mostly involved illegal aliens as victims and perpetrators, at the time. This environment brings with it a lot of police work.

I remember the odd, dull, orange-ish street lights, protected by a metal mesh that the city put up. Patrolling and investigating those streets at night gave you an eerie, warzone feeling. Back in the late 70's, a few of these residents decided to start robbing people for their pay-day cash on weekends.

The suspects were usually local, the victims usually illegal Mexicans in an illegal Mexican area. The victims would hesitate to call the police because of their status. Gun wounds and very serious knife wounds were usually reported to the police via the hospital.

On weekends, these street muggers armed with Saturday Night Special pistols or knives would hold up anyone they could. So, we started trolling. Slow and lights out if we could. My old buddy Greg Dunham and I were working this beat one Friday night, when we actually stumbled upon a robbery in progress on the outskirts of an apartment complex. From our squad car, we spied the startled reaction of a few people, and then looked deeper to see the drama of a street robbery at gunpoint play out before us.

A Hispanic male with a pistol bolted from the scene as we slid to a stop, and Greg and I bailed out, hollering a string of expletives about death and destruction should he continue to hotfoot away.

Hells bells, we still had to chase him. He dashed across the street with Greg and me, our revolvers drawn; young and fleet of foot (Greg was a marathon runner) after him. He slipped into an apartment complex and mounted a stairway. To lose sight of him now would be bad. But, quicksilver Greg was close enough to see him enter a specific apartment.

"Here!" Greg declared as I crested the second floor, and without hesitation, Greg and I, working like madman pistons, kicked the door right off its frame in seconds. In the eternal words and spirit of Sheriff Buford T. Justice,

"We wus' in HOT pursuit!" And a mere slum door shan't dally us!"

Greg and I attended the Texas Police Academy together, and we were search-school partners, and vets of numerous, subsequent, real-world searches. We knew what to do with each other. Gun barrel first, we peeled off to our respective sides of the living room. We fully expected to shoot down this armed son of a bitch right then and there!

Nothing. Dark. It was a cheap, one-room apartment, with a clear view of the bedroom ahead of us. We peered into the bedroom from the middle of the living room. Someone was in bed with the covers over them! What's this? We made our way to the bedroom door. The living room and kitchenette were clear. With a quick peek, I could see the one, small bedroom window was closed, nothing under it disturbed. Was the body in the bed our fleeing suspect? Was his pistol aimed right at us from under his covers? What of the half-opened bedroom closet door? The dark bathroom?

Greg and I exchanged glances. I started yelling commands in broken English/Spanish, "Get up! Wake up! Put your hands up!"

Greg took over with better Spanish. Nothing. No one could possible remain asleep with all this racket we raised. I looked around for innovative and new ways to "wake him up."

This was not the first time or the last time I was faced with this "pretend sleeper' situation. So, while Greg kept up the banter and pointed his .357 at him, I holstered my gun and grabbed some cups and saucers from the kitchen bar. Like Nolan Ryan in a play-off, I fired those babies a hundred miles an hour at the body in the bed. They hit HARD, bounced to the wall and shattered. Nothing. Not a movement. Not a peep. I got the frying pans and pots. I got the plates. Greg was starting to laugh and frankly, so was I.

"A-MI-GO! Wake the fuck up!" I ordered, heaving everything but the kitchen sink at him as hard as I could. With each object I flung, Greg and I got more cracked up. I got a dining room chair. I had to fully stand in the door, but I pitched the heavy chair as hard as I could onto the body in the bed.

Finally, he uttered a painful mutter. The bed covers went back and this doofus sat up, pretending to be confused and awakened from a sound sleep. The guy was fully dressed, and in the same clothing as the jerk we chased. Imagine that!

"Hands up!" we ordered in Spanish. He did. Greg moved to the closet. Empty. I cuffed our bruised Sleeping Beauty and rolled him onto the floor. I threw back the covers and there on the bed was his small semi-auto pistol.

We had our man, but we lost our victim! When we escorted the suspect out to the street, it was empty. The complainant ran off into the night, probably fearing deportation back to the homeland for his illegal status. A reason why illegals are prime victims for criminals.

We arrested Senior Rip Van Winkle anyway. Greg and I wrote up what we saw happen and what we did, summarizing the wake-up attempt methods. We submitted the pistola and a handful of squashed cash from the guy's pocket.

Still, minus a victim and within days, our detectives were able to amass some kind of charges on our gun-toting suspect. For one thing, he was an illegal alien. But armed robbery was not one of them. And of note, the robbery rate dropped just a bit, as this bandito was most likely responsible for a number of them.

There was always a bit of "tsk-tsking," and "cluck-clucking" by sergeants and lieutenants when a door was busted, but in the end, our old-school Police Chief Hugh Lynch always enjoyed a good action story. And besides, we were fully operating under that
Buford T. Justice "hot pursuit" doctrine!

As mentioned in other chapters and my books, we had a "door fund" at the PD and for about 100 bucks, front and interior doors were quickly replaced. The fund was mostly for CID, but the patrol division could dip into it for emergencies. I recommend such a fund for every police agency, but thinking about it, modern agencies might be too dainty for such quick, simple, common sense these days, and it would deprive so many citizens of hefty lawsuit material.

Through the years, this "hood" received rehabilitation and investors and once again became a college-based, residential area. Entire rattraps were demolished and replaced. Decent folk of all races took a stand and fought back. It's hard for me to drive through that area now and not remember the amber lights in protective mesh.

Dunham went on to become city manager in several cities in the US and despite all my bad influence, a respectable, church-going citizen and a true-blue, family man. He and I have had many, many misadventures together in the thrilling days of yesteryear. I can't repeat half of them, in case he runs for mayor somewhere, someday. Don't let his three-piece suit fool you, he is just as crazy as I am.

And, that's the hood update, and the Dunham update. Me? You already know where I am. Right here.

Chapter 41: Shoot the Car! I Need Me Some Relief!

I recall a time when cars did not have air conditioning, and when they did, many police cars still did not have the add-on feature. To save cost, skinflint supervisors ordered fleets of cars without AC, but of course their cars had AC.

In the Military Police, "back in the day," on day shift, we had to wear our class A uniforms. Whether tan or the green "suit," we had to wear that big-ass, white hat inside the car. The hat that rubbed on the interior roof if you were over 5 feet tall and turned the top of your hat gray. Yet, we'd see the Provost Marshal (like the police commissioner) driving in his sedan with AC on and hat off. His hair all blowing in the AC wind tunnels like a big dog. It's nice to be king!

Evenings and midnights we switched over to fatigues, but hot is hot in Oklahoma and Texas, and in the deep south.

Shoot the car! What? Wait, stay with me. Shoot the car for ventilation? Or for draining? Every once in a while some eager officer would draw out his gun too soon during a chase, hit a bump and shoot the car. The floorboards. Under the dash.

One time in Texas, an officer who shall remain nameless, held his gun, hit a bump, shot his car and killed it. Dead right there. I don't remember exactly where he shot, but it hit the engine and killed it.

This would also happen with interior "quick draw practice." Or the anxious officer would draw his gun out in a chase and lay it on the seat. Well, when you are driving at a hunnert miles an hour, a slight turn or braking, and that six gun would fling itself all over the car, along with the French fries and your burger. But back to shooting the car...for… draining?

A lot of these old police cars had bullet holes in their floorboards. On purpose. No accident. I was reminiscing with another old vet and we were talking about the ice bag trick. Various ice houses and stores back then often gave free big bags of ice to officers, or sold them, in the summer. Some ice houses just stacked them by their back, open loading doors, and cops would drive by and throw them into their cars.

The trick was to shoot the floorboard, you know the "center-mass" on the driver or passenger side. You just go out and drive over some soft dirt or sand, shoot the floor and the bullet went through the floorboard and buried into the ground. In them-thar days, the outside bottoms of cars did not have the Buck Rogers technology of today's cars. It just made a nice clean hole in the body, if you knew where to aim. Next, the big ice bags were plopped on the floorboards. The vent fan was turned up full, and walla h! Ice bag air conditioning. Primitive, but better than nothing.

The floorboard holes were needed to allow the condensation and ice bags to eventually drain. The driver needed a little makeshift barrier to keep his bags back from the pedals. Better than nothing, and your cowboy boots would keep your feet from freezing off, usually. Passengers could ride with their feet high up under the dash.

As I recall, you would certainly get into official trouble for shooting your car, but many veteran supervisors did this in the good ol' summer days, too. So, mums the word. If your supervisors were "cool" the word would get out about any pending inspections. And these were fleet cars back then, not necessarily assigned to anyone, two, or three officers. So finger-pointing alibis were engaged. What is that? Who shot what? And of course, the hole could be covered over by the floor mat, stored in the back floorboards. Hole? What hole?

Everyone knew where they could get their holes plugged if need be, for any planned inspections. You could just buy new floor mats and hope the captain didn't lift them to peer under. We had a day or two to fix things, and in emergencies, we all had a few midnight-shift, open garage/gas stations back then to race to when we had such a quick-fix-em-up emergency with our cars.
But that's another batch of stories.

Finally, cars were manufactured in such a way that it cost extra to remove the FM radios and remove air conditioners, frustrating sadistic administrators!

Playing FM rock in the cool breeze! And we peons ruled the day! Viva la revolution!

Chapter 42: Most Dead Ever, Right There

I have had unfortunate experiences in my life. I have seen groups of people freshly dead, and many more near dead, that died later. Not as many as some have, like veteran EMTs in big cities. Lord knows, imagine today working one of these massive shootings, plane crashes or bomb sites! More than me, but certainly more than most "normal" folks, I think. I have worked a few double and two triple homicides, but those are for longer stories that deserve a whole chapter, or maybe even as some of my friends suggest, an entire book.

Probably there is no bigger, common opportunity for a cop to see dead people than traffic crashes. I have seen a batch of them also through time. Most times single deaths. I could tell a dozen, extra-gross, traffic wreck stories. So could any veteran cop, or some non-police and non-military people I've known through the years chuckle when I combine the term "dead bodies."

"Well, Hock...HA! Aren't all bodies dead?

No. Like, there are busy bodies, nosy bodies, body builders, and there are dead bodies. When you are in the body business, you need these distinctions. Here are some shorter, more gross, odd tales I remember.

Here are three stories fairly unique to military police operations.

Most Dead 1 - The Dead Grenade That Wasn't Dead
1970s. North of our Army base in the U.S. was an enormous artillery range. Troops were constantly blowing up all kinds of big and small ordnance. For those not familiar, "ordnance" is defined as:

"All munitions containing explosives, nuclear fission or fusion materials, and biological and chemical agents. This includes bombs and warheads; guided and ballistic missiles; artillery, mortar, rocket, and small arms ammunition; all mines, torpedoes, and depth charges; demolition charges; pyrotechnics; clusters and dispensers; cartridge and propellant actuated devices; electro/explosive devices; clandestine and improvised explosive devices; and all similar correlated items or components explosive in nature."

A Dud defined: A dud is all of the above that didn't go boom. Now, enter the ordnance, the grenade. And enter then, the dud hand grenade story. Officially also –
"DUD-a thrown grenade that failed to detonate after the expected fuze time has elapsed."

As I said, artillery troops were always out on the northern ranges, blowing all kinds of stuff up. And a small percentage are duds. As the later investigations disclosed – One fine morning, out on a said field, a young private stumbled upon what appeared to be a very old hand grenade. He closed in on it and looked it over. No pin. No lever. Hmmmm. A dud, he presumes. What fun!

He threw some rocks at it. His buddies giggling nearby. Nothing. Deadness. He hit it with a stick. Then he kicked it and jumped back. It bounced across the rocky, dry terrain. He picked it up, tossed it up and down a few times and then stuck it in his jacket pocket. What a coup. What a toy.! A dud grenade!

The unit took a long, one-hour bouncy ride in the back of a deuce-and-a-half truck. The private pulled the grenade from his pocket and declared to those around him, "Look what I found!"

The others leaned away, aghast. But it became clear by his manipulations and juggling, it had to be a dud.

Once at their multi-story barracks building, they bailed out of the trucks, unloaded and hit the showers. The private went to his multi-person quarters and tossed the grenade on his bunk. He combed his wet hair, got in casual clothes – civvies – picked up his dud grenade and walked to the day room (TV, pool tables, a rec room, etc.) for some fun and games with his new toy.
He got to the day room door and peeked in. He saw many of his friends day-rooming about in there. Some were with him on the training day, and some not.

"GRENADE!" he yelled. He tossed the dud grenade into the middle of the room, then he ducked back into the hall, just for effect. Big joke. The so-called dud hit the floor and exploded. It blew with all its originally designed and planned intent. BAM! In the middle of the day room.

Our private and other nearby troops in the hall and other rooms ran to the door. The room was a bloody mess. Shreds of the room still floating in the air, they said. One or two seemed dead. Others wounded. Dying. Splinters everywhere. Lots of blood and guts and whines, yells and screams. The first instinct of bystanders was to call for an ambulance. Someone did, and the hospital called the police.

I was one of the units dispatched. I was assigned that day to the patrol district next to this one, or maybe as a rover? I just can't remember. When I arrived, I was not the first. The district police car and the patrol sergeant's car were there and several ambulances. At that moment, I was not clear exactly what had happened, nor was our police dispatcher clear either. We only knew that, some kind of a "bomb" went off on the third floor.

Hearing of a possible "bomb," as I parked, I looked

This was the very building, but on a much calmer day.

up to survey the building. I didn't know what to expect. Was the huge barracks building bombed? By whom? By what? I saw broken glass in some third story windows and curtains flapping in and out with the wind.

Soldiers were standing outside, looking up too. As I got close to the main doors, someone told me a grenade touched off up there. I entered the building, climbed the stairs to the third floor, and saw the commotion in the hallway.

When I stepped in the room, it looked like some 8 or 10 guys were pretty hurt. Another two or three were slightly hurt. Some laid dead still, mashed and abandoned. The room looked like, well, like a small bomb went off in it! I wandered around and tried to help out where I could, but the paramedics had done their triage assessment and were hard at work. Plus, some of the unit cadre were Nam vets and were already pitching in with the EMTs.

I walked out of the room and asked some Sergeants in the hall what had happened. They pointed to the kid who threw the "dud" in. I spoke with him. Our patrol sergeant walked up and listened to us talk it out. The kid was practically crying and in real shock. The district MP (military police) came over to us.

The Sarge pulled us aside and told the district MP to arrest the kid.

"For what Sarge?" the district MP asked. "What charge?"

"I don't know. For something. Charge him with something," he said. "We have to arrest him for this. Manslaughter. Something. Negligent something."

Then the Sarge's portable radio announced that, "CID was in route."

"Ten-four," he said into the radio, and told us, "Good. Okay. We'll let CID decide what to do with him."

We stuck around until two CID investigators (our FBI, more or less) arrived. We filled them in and pointed out the kid. They looked around and marched the kid off to one of the nearby offices. And we were ready to leave. As the Lone Ranger would say, "Tonto, our work here is done." A few hours later I had to go and give blood at the hospital. Three or four troops died, best I can recall.

I have thrown a few grenades. I have even qualified as expert on the old Army, grenade throwing range school. I got the targeting knack quickly. It was like throwing a football only heavier, so I aimed higher than the target to offset the weight, be it a window or whatever set up we were supposed to blow up. I always joke about how cavalier vets and movie actors are about these small bombs hanging off their uniforms, in comparison to the very first ones they hand you and you baby them like they are nitroglycerin.

But they are certainly no joke. Very generically speaking, the grenade kill zone is 5 meters or 16 feet. The injury range is 15 meters pr 50 feet. Shrapnel can go even further. A hand grenade, especially an older one, '70s and pre-1970s had a varying reputation back then. Some called them as devastating and some didn't. There are lots of fascinating, jaw-dropping stories. They weren't all always perfect like the distances described above. I guess it was situational.

But that "dud" took a toll on the day room and the unit that late afternoon, and also took a toll on my memory.

Most Dead 2: Big Army Wreck

Probably, the biggest fatality toll, the "most dead ever," for me, I recall was when stationed in the US, in the Army. A troop transport truck, hauling soldiers back from a distant, artillery range, lost it while navigating on winding, outback roads, sometimes asphalt, sometimes dirt roads, on the hills and small mountains up north. The driver took one turn too many, way too fast. The open-backed truck, in an odd shake of bad luck, turned over, flipped, and gutted, pinned, crushed, or otherwise dismembered soldiers. I think it was 15 dead?
Others hurt? But I could be just a bit wrong on that number. It was over 30 years ago.

I was among the first units to arrive on the scene, and it was quite a way from the main base. And it was a mess. A mess. Guys were screaming and groaning and dying. Ambulances came, and we all did what we could. Stop the bleeding. Guys were tossed down the side of a small, rocky mountain, on the road and still in the overturned truck. But I must say that the day was nearly a total loss when the body count was over. It might be comparable to a major bus accident in the civilian world, you might say.

In South Korea I was ordered to get a S.K. drivers license for one of these trucks and we made several runs/assignments with it. It's big, wieldy and in S.K. traffic (where we had to go several times, a monster. No power steering, and you already know my affinity for shifting gears!)

Most Dead 3: Whirlybird Down
Around those same times, I had been dispatched to a few whirly-bird crashes. "Whirlybird" seems to be a very generic term for all helicopters is some circles. For many of us back then, we also used that term for the double rotor, or "twin-rotor" choppers. That, or the proper name Chinooks. The US Army has a history of calling its helicopters after Indian tribal names. This is a tribute to their ferocity, not cute racism. I've been in them and flown in them on occasion.

And I have been around them, crashed. Just a few. These workhorses fly successfully all the time, but the rare crashes would occur well off our main post, yet still on the massive acreage of the fort . In a way, they were almost secret affairs. Sometimes we would see the red glow from these crashes in the distant, clear, flat, mid-west, night sky, if we knew where to look. We would hear the scrambling, yet low-key and coded radio traffic at times. Then other times these events would be dispatched and discussed over other radio channels we had no access to. Why we heard some and not others, I don't know.

At rare times, we were dispatched to them when extra help was needed. Usually the crashes were investigated by aviation experts and responding air/fire crews. And, the powers that be didn't like the civilian press to catch wind of these. The fewer who knew, the better. Need-to-know.

Eventually gossip of these crashes would travel down to us and we would learn what happened. One such crash, the federal/military investigators found six packs of beer in the rubble of the cockpit.

The suggestion was that the pilots were drunk. Sometimes these dual engine choppers would, more or less, fall right out of the sky, if the front end raised up too far, it would sort of "lose its balance" and with the rear end too low, it would slip down right out of the sky. The chopper would crash and crumble. This was explained to me right on a crash site one night, but I suggest you refer to a dual rotor pilot on this type of failure.

One gruesome night I recall, a bird was full of men and it went down north of the main fort. They call it a chalk of men. A chalk. Usually about a dozen, but this time there was almost double that number. It took a long time for us to drive out there that night. Fire trucks has already arrived There was crushed rubble and several burning fires, metal and people when I arrived. A small war zone. Burned people stink up the place with an unforgettable smell, you know? Unforgettable. How many people? I could not tell.

Most Dead 4: Car versus Bicycles

I have one haunting memory from a car "accident." In an early evening, a family of five, mother, father and three daughters were bicycling. They were sticking to the side streets but had to spend a few risky minutes on a larger, one way street to get back home.

A speeding, drunk driver plowed into *all five*, killing all of them. The driver fled the scene. Though these were "traffic fatalities" and usually handled by the patrol division, the next morning, our police chief turned it over to our detective division to find the killer.

I was a new detective then, and as fate would have it, I drove to the scene that night when I heard the catastrophic calls on the police radio, and I saw this nightmare of mangled bikes, children and adults. It is a vivid nightmare picture I hate to conjure up. They were all dead and mangled.

Several of us worked on this case, and within 24 hours we located the driver and damaged car in a suburb city.

We surrounded his country house and jumped him when he answered the door. A background investigation of his day proved he was ossified drunk before the crash. All vet cops and EMTs have seen horrific wrecks.

Dead bodies. Dead right there before you. Be they from these large scenes or other crimes, accidents and car wrecks, don't think them too much because they could drive you crazy.

Chapter 43: The Mudslide Fight at Hospital Hill

"I will jump on my head!" he yelled from the rooftop. My sergeant and I stared up at the man who stood tall at a pinnacle about three-stories up.

"Can you climb up there?" Sarge asked me quietly. I scanned the apartment complex building and mumbled, "How did that guy get up there?"

To wit, the Sarge mumbled back, "I don't know."

That rooftop guy was about a 20-year-old, white male perched on the edge, about to dive on his head. We knew his plan because he kept orating, "I will jump on my head," over and over again.

There was no safe way up there. Plus, it was lightly raining to boot! Plus-plus, I might add here for the record that I was not then, nor am I now, the social worker type. Deep down, I didn't care if some idiot decided to take a triple-gainer off a roof. Personally, I was in the policing business to hunt and catch criminals, and any chore on the far, side of that, I simply did not take to. This lack of "social urgency" and shallowness on my part did not inspire me to spread myself across a shaky metal railing and leap to a barely feasible catch on the lip of a two-story roof and try to haul myself up…in the rain.

My shallowness did not interfere with duty either. As Tennyson said in the 1850s *Charge of the Light Brigade*,

"Theirs not to reason why, theirs but to do and die" Military and policing indoctrination always pointed my way.

"Climb up...ahh, maybe with a ladder? Maybe we need to call the fire department," I said.

"But he did it! He got up there" the Sarge said.

"Yea, but he wants to die. What's a fall to him?" was my answer, as I wiped the light rain from my face.

"Call the fire department and get a ladder," he told me.

The Sarge, who was much more of a social worker type, continued his sensitive dialogue with the jumper. The jumper's life had gone awry and blah-blah-blah...another story in the naked city – to the youngsters here, that's an old joke reference to the 1950's cop, tv show, the Naked City, starring Paul Burke and...well never mind.

Meanwhile the Fire Department coasted up, no sirens, to the back half of the building on a side street. I watched them crank the ladder up to the roof. I looked at the firemen longingly, as if to say, "You rescue cats from trees, how about a crazy dude?"

It became apparent that it was yours truly who had to climb the fire ladder, in the light rain, and use various methods of therapy to, as they say, "Talk the jumper down." I got within 20 feet of said "jumper." Then, he saw me coming.

"Hey, I'll jump! I'll jump!" Mr. Jump proclaimed.

"You probably will just break a few bones. We are not that high up, man! You might just paralyze yourself if you jumped." I told him. "Then you'll really be miserable.

"I'll jump on my head!" he said...yet again.

"Yea, but you can't guarantee you'll land on your head," I argued. "Ever jump off a diving board into a pool? You can't guarantee how you'll land. I saw a guy fall off a building much bigger than this, and he almost got up and limped away. Just broke his ankle." I lied.

That puzzled him for a moment, and then the Sarge

took over from down below. His fatherly overtones and pleadings of "Now son-this and now son-that," coupled with suggestions of an unsure demise at that altitude must have worked. Jump stood up and walked over to me.

We both backed down the ladder. Him first. Sarge kind of embraced him at ground zero and walked him over to his squad car. It was the Sarge, not me, that yakked him off the roof. The next step was to get him booked into our jail on any charge we could concoct, such as disorderly conduct. We needed an arrest to start the mental health process of transferring him to the "Flight Deck," our nickname for the mental ward at Floyd Hospital. This "Flight Deck" moniker came after the "flights" of fancy some citizens took, for upcoming "flights" off to more serious mental institutions in Texas.

"Get in the back, Hock" the Sarge told me. Huh? The back? Usually, we cuff the suspect, put him in the back seat of a squad car. As patrol supervisor, he would drive off in his car, and I would be stuck with all the transport, paperwork and babysitting. I would next transfer him to the Flight Deck. This would take many, many boring hours. Suddenly we were bypassing this arrest process (no paperwork - so I was happy about that) and we are going straight to the hospital? And in his car?

With his two hands, the Sarge guided the shoulders of the jumper into the front passenger side…uncuffed! I am sure that the plan was not to cuff Jump so he would feel less threatened and hostile. This is a very common cop tactic despite the rulebook's "cuff-all-in custody," requirement. Sarge got behind the wheel of his car. I got in the back of his car, and off we went to the hospital. I would be driven back to my car abandoned in the apartment parking lot, hours later, I presumed.

On the drive the rain picked up and so did the nervous tension of our guest. He still had…issues…with mental wards. He had been to a few before. By the time we pulled up to the emergency room side of Floyd Hospital, he was getting jumpy. He sat in cold silence. Sarge got out and walked around the car to open the passenger side. I popped open my door and remained half-in until

"Jump" was out of the car, in case he remained in. Sarge then firmly guided the man up and out.

Firmly? Not too firmly because right then, Jump spun! By the sarge's own grip he became a victim of a child's whip game as Jump swung him around and around the parking lot trying to break free. I guess the Sarge thought that once he got his footing, he could regain control, but the lot was too slippery and he had to let go. I don't know if the Sarge hit the asphalt or not because I grabbed the Jumper's other arm just as he started a mad dash to escape.

Now, the west side of Floyd Hospital was very steep with quite a grassy embankment. To give you an idea, you can pretty much see most of the west and north side of the city and well beyond from the elevated ER parking lot. The energy of my catch, coupled with his dash, caused the both of us to fly over the edge of the embankment onto the grass of the steep hill below.

I did say grass? It was really mud from the rains. We rolled in the loose, muck for some 12 feet before we could spread out enough tentacles to actually stop. Maybe one more rotation would have been smarter though because he wound up on top of me. At first, he just tried to rip free, but when he couldn't, he started punching me. I instinctively put up my arms to block, and he used that as a quick ticket to escape. He lunged off of me, with me after him in another slippery dive. We collided again and slid another 5 or so feet.

Still trying to play somewhat by "cop-rules" at this point (as in not hurting the suspect much), I attempted a required control, submission, containment move by trying to wrap up an arm. But the slime on his arm, and his commitment to hit me in the face, made it impossible. We sloshed even farther down the hill. I remember well the kick he delivered into my stomach with a big, clunky, muddy boot. I tried to grab that leg but the cold, wet Levi pants did not allow for it. The limb slipped free and his foot pushed off against my groin, propelling him further away in the mud, and well… squashing my balls pretty damn good. There have come a few times in my life when a voice of determined and angered dedication echoed in my head, and this was one such time. The voice growled its powerful command into my psyche…

"This mother-fucker…IS NOT…GETTING…AWAY."

Obeying this reptilian command in my brain, I pitched forward again, this time fists flying. I remember pummeling him. Bad targets, good targets, passing aside legs and arms to hit anywhere, with him doing the same. Rolling a little more, he fended me off where he could. I now can only imagine that we looked like a crude, unplanned fight in one of those cheap 1930s westerns.

Then with a moan, Jump suddenly lay limp, gasping? Something in that chaotic mess must have landed. I turned him face down and handcuffed him.

Where was the Sarge during all this you ask? Well, considering that this whole hillside episode took probably 55 seconds or so, you could realistically assume he'd still hadn't gotten on his feet yet at the top of the hill, but actually he had run down the driveway beside us and was waiting for me to drag his flaky new "son" over to the concrete.

Wouldn't want to get all muddy now would we, Sergeant? I don't know what was harder, fighting Jump in a thick, free fall down the side of this hospital hill, or hauling his stumbling, dazed, mud-caked, handcuffed body the 20 or so feet to the driveway? Sarge was now pissed, and this time to jail with him!

Back at the station, I can't remember what we

charged him with, escape, or assault, or "conspiracy to head-dive," or something. I don't know. Didn't matter though because all charges short of murder and rape always got
dismissed to clear the way for the "Flight Deck" mental health ward to ship people off.

Squish. Slop. Squish. Slop. After booking him into a cell, I walked into the bathroom and stared at the mirror, studying my visage of thick, wet, clingy, polyester mud. My face was a brown-streaked camo, my hair glued up and out in some kind of bizarre, post-electric, punk rock, shock treatment. My pistol, then a Colt Python, and holster, was simply a block of mud on my hip.

Where and how do I start cleaning that off? I pulled my gun and pushed muck off with a paper towel.

The barrel was…

SWISH…bam!

The bathroom door burst open and hit the wall. It was Patrol Lt. Russell Trapp.

"Hochheim, get out to Loop 114. There's a three-car wreck," he said.

"I got a crazy guy in the drunk tank who needs to go the Flight Deck," I said.

"It can wait," he said.

"But…but my car is still back at the at the Pleasant Groves parking lot," I said lamely.

"Get a ride to it and go!" he ordered and left.

There is just no glory or respect for the champion of the "Mudslide Fight of Hospital Hill." No respect at all.

Chapter 44: Car as a Coffin

Back in the 1970s, the 80s and even the 90s, this phrase "the car as a coffin" was already a warning, a cop, training phrase, a "word to the wise" about being stuck in the car and being killed while stuck by an outside shooter. The advice was to…"Get out of the car! Because the car is a coffin."

When things got hot and you predicted bullets could/would fly, or while bullets were indeed flying, you have to try and get out of the car. Get out of the car because the car is an enclosed coffin. So, we got out if we could, because you know, sometimes you can't! We got out the driver's side, or we planned on traversing across the front seat to escape, low and crawling, to get out the passenger side if need be. OR, I have had friends successfully dive under the dashboard while under fire.

But alas, that was the good ol' days of big cars. Who can dive for cover under a dashboard in today's cars or worse, today's patrol cars? They have some small patrol cars today, and some big police SUVs too. But, have you seen the front seat of a police car lately? It resembles a miniature version of the bridge of the Star Trek Enterprise. Computer systems, like a Robby the Robot, if you will, sit in the middle of the front seat. You CANNOT traverse the front seat anymore! And in civilian cars, the popularity of the console traps you in the driver's seat more than ever.

I followed this golden rule, but even when you believe in it, you can still get caught there in an instant. Like I did this one disturbing Saturday, summer night in 1980.

"Sixty-one," the dispatcher said.

"Go ahead," my reserve police partner Joe Reilly said.

"Domestic. Brothers fighting in back yard. The Starnes brothers. Mother called it in. 615 Jasper Street."

"Ten-four."

"Ask if the two brothers are wanted," I told Reilly.

"Dispatcher, check wants and warrants on the brothers."

"In progress. They're clear."

"Ten four."

Damn. The Starnes brothers. Bout half-crazy troublemakers. Almost twins, born so close and virtually look-alikes. In just about the same kinds of twin trouble. Drugs. Fighting. Burglaries. It wasn't too late yet in the evening. About 8 p.m. Too early for the real trouble these neighborhoods brewed. We drove through the busy streets on the warm night. We didn't need to look 615 Jasper up on the map. We'd been there before. We pulled up, Reilly and I got out and heard the loud argument in the backyard, behind the long, old white house. We walked up the driveway beside the house, passed through the metal, chain-link gate and into the yard.

The mom was there in a house dress, arms folded. A neighbor we knew by sight, a very big dude was calmly standing by and when he needed to, pushing the brothers apart. The bothers were neck vein popping mad over something.

"Hey!" I said loudly. "What's going on?"

The mother spoke up and relayed the problem which, frankly, I don't recall to report here. We all talked it over for a moment, and I appreciated the presence of the neighbor. But, upon our very arrival, the brothers wanted to disappear. Afraid of being arrested again? Something else? I don't know. It seemed like our very appearance ended the fight.

Brother Buddy Starnes was shirtless and wearing very tight, light-colored jeans. This is important later.

Just about the time I was officially wrapping up the conversation, Buddy left prematurely. Looking back now, it was obvious he had something to hide or be worried about. He turned and walked away well before I finished, and I, casually, walked after him down the driveway. Reilly lagged back just a few seconds more to finish up with the mom.

I felt Buddy's exit was a little too soon, but I really didn't know what to do about it. He led the way down the driveway to the street, and I looked him over from behind. There weren't any clothing prints of weapons that I could see in those tight pants.

"Buddy, next time, don't leave until we're through," I said.

I wasn't trying to be bossy, or a prick, but I wanted to say something to…to see what he would say or do. He looked over his shoulder at me and gave me a real dirty look. Which, you know, "sticks and stones," and a look never hurt me. He strutted off onto the street heading toward a crowd of folks up the next avenue. I walked around the front of the patrol car, opened the door and sat in behind the wheel. The very instant my butt hit the seat and closed the door, I caught motion in the corner of my left eye.

Buddy was strutting back to me, his right hand borrowing into his right pocket.

Shit. Coffin. I instinctively, instantly pulled my revolver. The window was already down, and I laid the 4-inch barrel of my magnum on the top of the door. Barrel right at him. It's big, and he saw it.

"WHAT you pulling?" I growled.

He yanked his empty hand out of his pocket and stood

there. Expressionless. Looking at the hole in the barrel of my gun. Now, I tell you I stared hard at the pocket. It was flat, flat, flat and his jeans were very tight. I made a snap decision that he could not have anything at all in that pocket, or any pocket for that matter.

"Get the fuck outta here," I told him in a very quiet, very sinister way.

Expressionless, he waited in a stare down with me and the gun, then turned and walked away in his original direction. I did not holster my Python. I just watched him walk off.

Reilly slipped into the passenger side, sat and was shocked at my position. Gun out, barrel on the door.

"Wha...?"

"I don't know," I told him. "He turned back on me, and it looked like he was pulling something from his pocket."

"Okay!"

"But I can't imagine he had anything in that pocket. Those pants are skintight."

I put my gun away, started the car and drove off. Not even a half a minute later...

"Sixty-one, are you still on Jasper street?" the dispatcher asked.

"Just a block away," Reilly answered.

"Man shot on porch, on 619 Jasper. Ambulance in route."

What? I whipped the car around and blasted over to 10 Jasper.

We slid up in front, ran up the to the porch where an older woman was tending to a man lying on the porch. He was down and shot in the chest. I propped him up just a bit. We told her to get us a towel, and Reilly made for the trunk for our first aid kit. We plugged the hole. Applied pressure.

The old man could talk. He said he was sitting on his porch when "that boy" without a shirt in tan pants walked by, out in the street, looked at him and then shot him.

"Was that Buddy Starnes?" I asked while the ambulance sirens closed in on us.

"It couldna' been, but I don't sees real well. Real far. At night."

The bullet hole didn't look very big on his chest, but a chest wound is a chest wound. The EMTs got there and took over. Reilly and I jumped back in our car, and I checked in with the dispatcher. I put Buddy Starnes out on the air as the shooting suspect.

We and other units scoured the streets for Buddy. Reilly and I made every nightclub in the district. Asked everyone on the street. For hours. Nothing. And boy-howdy, I knew I screwed up. I made a snap decision to let that little piece of shit walk off. He did have a thin gun after all, must have, probably a small, semi-auto in that pocket. That bullet was meant for me. But since he couldn't shoot me, he, frustrated, walked off a few houses away and shot that old man. I should have stepped out and patted him down. But, I let a visual-search-only trick my judgement.

I met with the detective on call that night, and I told him what had happened. He also hunted Starnes with us in his own car. I can't remember which detective it was. He asked Reilly and I to write supplements to the shooting crime report when we got back to HQ.

CID worked up a case on Starnes. The old man lived. It was a
.32 caliber bullet that didn't do much damage at all. Within a day or two, the detectives found Buddy, but they never found the gun. He confessed to shooting the old man because he said he'd always had trouble with him as he was growing up. A cranky old neighbor motive?

But deep down, I knew what happened. I first ticked Buddy off.
He wanted to shoot me in the car but I got the drop on him. And since I let him walk off, he shot that old man

instead.

Months and a few years later, I would stop and talk to this old man a time or two, when I saw him on the porch in that same chair. Even years later as a detective. He frequently reminded me that he and Buddy had problems since Buddy was a kid, and that is why he was shot, but I still feel like I was a precursor to his shooting. I know I was. What…what do you say to this guy, to make any kind of amends? The old man died in the 90s. I still think about it sometimes. A missed chance. A missed chance!

"The car as a coffin." My good, trusty compadre and working Texas cop, Jeff "Rawhide" Laun, told me that even now, 40 years later, they still use that phrase in police work and training. Even though they are now more captured today on the driver's side of their cars with the techno systems in the middle of the front seat. No crawling across the front seat to escape! No dropping out the passenger door!

No diving under the dash! You are stuck. The coffin shrinks. But, this was as close as I got to being stuck in a car and shot. My friends have been shot at while inside cars and those are other stories. But, no matter how well I understood, and how much I believed and worried about that classic training line – "the car is a coffin" – in a single instant, I still got stuck in there.

I am alive today because several times over the years I got my gun out first and fast. I am not some kind of a quick draw artist, not at all. I am…just quick-to-draw. My gun just "appeared" when I needed it. Practice, I guess?

Can't drive off? If you have to shoot through the glass of your car? Shoot. Don't worry about the finer points of trajectory and how the bullets will go slightly up or down due to the angle of the car glass. You don't have time to run the math. Just shoot. Make a hole and shoot through that hole!

Chapter 45: Splittin' Hairs

Officer Bernie Staunch thought the top of his head was blown off. It all started on a quiet weekday afternoon when we received a call from a neighbor who saw a white male break a window in a house next door to them and climb in. In a sea of false alarms and mistaken calls such as any police agency gets annually, I thought this one had a ring of truth to it when I heard the dispatcher's words on the radio. The neighbor told the dispatcher that the man she saw was absolutely not the resident, and she had never seen him before.

She said he acted very suspicious. He broke a side window glass and he looked around in a paranoid manner as he climbed in. Officers started arriving at various times and Bernie was first on the scene. He tiptoed around the house in neighborhood of somewhat older, wooden homes. Sure enough. Bernie spotted a broken window on the west side.

Bernie duck-walked to and under the window, which was a bit higher than usual windows in this old house, and he put his hands on the lower frame and slowly lifted his head up for a peek inside.

What he saw was his unforgettable nightmare. Inches from his head was the barrel of a revolver. He looked down the dark hole. The gun fired.

A sudden, surprise explosion! Bernie fell straight

back on the alley grass. His immediate reaction was to clutch the top of his head. Then he looked at his hands and he saw blood! He began mumbling, stuttering and squirming, "I am shot, shot. Shot!" Covering the window, somebody clutched his uniform as a desperate handle and hauled him to the front corner of the house. Bernie grabbed his head and looked at his hands and saw blood.

"BOOM!" came another gunshot from behind the house! The bad guy went straight for the back door to escape, which was covered by Officer Peter Nilt. Peter said he saw the wooden back door slowly open and emerging into his view from behind this door was a snub nose revolver. The gun-holding hand appeared. Then a wrist.

Peter, about 7 feet away, took aim at the gun hand and blasted a .357 round at the pistol. He missed. This magnum bullet took a free, air trip across about 10 back yards and to a row of house fronts at the intersection. The shooter ducked back inside.

"I'm shot! I'm shot in the head," Bernie kept saying. More officers and now an ambulance showed up. Once hauled behind our squad cars, Bernie's head was examined. It was fine! His jaw remained dropped open in a silent scream and he was in predictable shock, but he was going a little bald and his head was clearly intact.

What was bleeding however, were his hands! It appeared that when he grabbed the lower window frame to stand up and peek inside, then bolted back and away from the gun and gun shot, he'd raked his hands over the broken glass still stuck in the wooden frame. This cut his hands open! He reflexively put his hands to his head and then looked at his hands for blood. He saw hand-blood, not head-blood.

"I felt the bullet go through my hair," he babbled. "I thought it hit me for sure." It was the 70s and we all had something of country-western pompadours. Tall pomps, thank goodness.

Now, squad cars pulled up closer to the house. I cannot remember who took over. A sergeant or lieutenant, but they started yelling into the house, "We have the house surrounded. Come out with your hands up. Or we're coming in to get ya!"

Sounds like an old Dragnet episode. No SWAT response you ask? There was no SWAT team back then. Our little gaggle of characters was the SWAT team at the moment. We began drawing up the ugly plans to raid the house.

Through the witness and neighbor, the dispatcher was trying to figure out a way to contact the absent residents at their jobs. Having some intel on the house and some front door keys instead of kicking it down would be a faster entry. If you've ever REALLY tried to kick a front door of an older, stout house? Well, I have. We have, and anything odd could happen. We didn't get door rams until years later.

But, after only 15 minutes or so, the burglar came out with…his hands up. As I recall, he had hidden the pistol inside the house and it took quite an extensive search to find it. He was charged with attempted murder of our police officer.

About a week later, on a dark parking lot at about 3 in the morning, Bernie and I parked our police cars and talked about this. He told me his trip home that day. He lived out in the country.

"That day I drove home from work and saw my kids playing on the front lawn," he said. "It was a beautiful day. My wife was out there doing something too. I stopped the car at the driveway, and I couldn't get out of the car. I just started bawling. I was so lucky to be alive. I thought the top of my brains were shot out."

Bernie was really affected by this close call. Within 6 months he quit the department and became an accountant for various state agencies. I last talked to him on the phone, oh, about 20 years later. We didn't discuss that day in the 1970s at all.

The burglar made some statements to detectives. He claimed he just reflexively fired at a head bobbing into the window. He claimed he didn't know that it was an officer, and it could have been anyone. He claimed he was startled and shot in an instant. I don't recall if that story worked in a plea bargain or in court. He did time.

Another picture lingers in my mind, too, an image from standing on the northwest corner of that house. I stood there that day and looked down all those backyards and the housing addition across the street from them. It was a weekday. Nobody home. No kids playing in the yards.

Pretty desolate. Trying to shoot the gun out of someone's hand? We all had .357 magnum revolvers back then, and the bullets were all jacked up to blow the hell out of anyone or anything they hit. I knocked on the wooden, back door to "hear" its density. Could Peter have shot through the door a few times, instead of aiming at the small, moving, gun hand? Would the rounds penetrate the door properly? Sufficiently? Would they be slightly deflected? Questions.

Questions. So many questions and split-second, geography. Haunting, nagging questions about living and dying and the…sheer, raw chance of it all.

Epilogue to the Book 1 patrol section...

Most of my 26 years in law enforcement, I was a "street" detective. Army and Texas. I guesstimate, my patrol time is only about 9 years. In Texas, I was happy being the "consummate patrolman" as I envisioned/defined it. I was very happy on the streets in Texas in patrol until my police chief (Hugh Lynch) asked me "do you want to be a detective?" in late 1980. (See Book 2!)

I of course said yes, having been one in the Army, but I really was happy at that very time concentrating on patrol. Patrol is in the true trenches. A detective has its own, other kind of deep, deep trench. I was always influenced and inspired by many things. Many...heroes. We all are, or should be. I am so old that "Adam 12" was a prime time show while I was on patrol.

But another show was...Joe Forrester. A lost show in time. A one-year show in the 70s. I watched this. I got it. Joe was a street cop. He knew his beat . People and businesses. He cared for and worried about all them. It didn't matter who or what you were. It was "his beat." It was deeply personal, admirable commitment. He was a protector. He was a hero I watched on TV and  was a tireless inspiration. He pushed me when I needed pushing even if I didn't know it. Art imitates life, life imamates art.

People all need this steady push. I know...I know...It was just a "show," but folks, stories are our inspiration in life, be they from the bible, fiction or non-fiction, or from wherever you can find inspiration.

See the hero.

Be the hero, no matter your life situation.

Stories true or otherwise teach us heroism.
In your life. In your trenches.
Be open to inspiration.
You know what a hero says.
You know what a hero does.
You are the hero of your life story, big or small.
And then be the hero, the inspiration for someone else too. To me, good cops will always be a hero.

(This ends this collection of Texas patrol stories. It is impossible to record here the many years of patrol adventures and misadventures. This book is becoming too voluminous. The few I have selected I hope you found entertaining and informative. Next we move on to the detective years in Book 2.

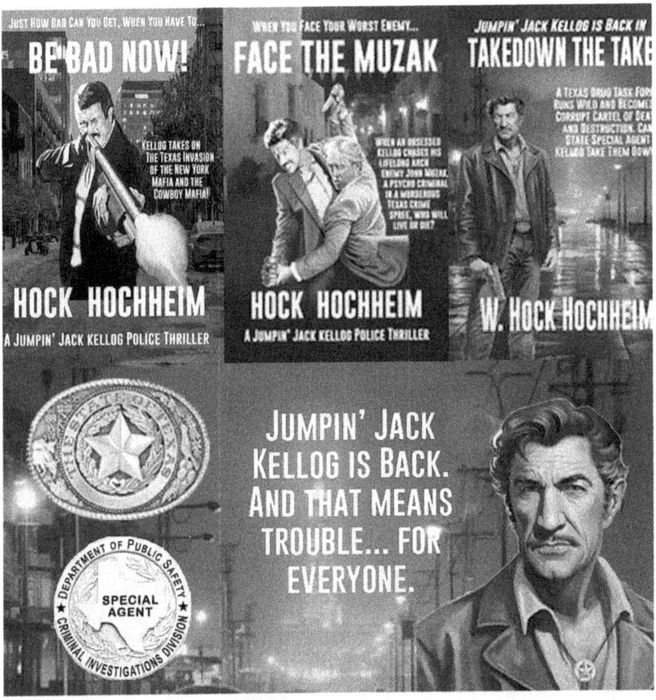

FROM WOLFPACK PUBLISHING. GET THE KINDLE EBOOK.
GET THE PAPERBACK.

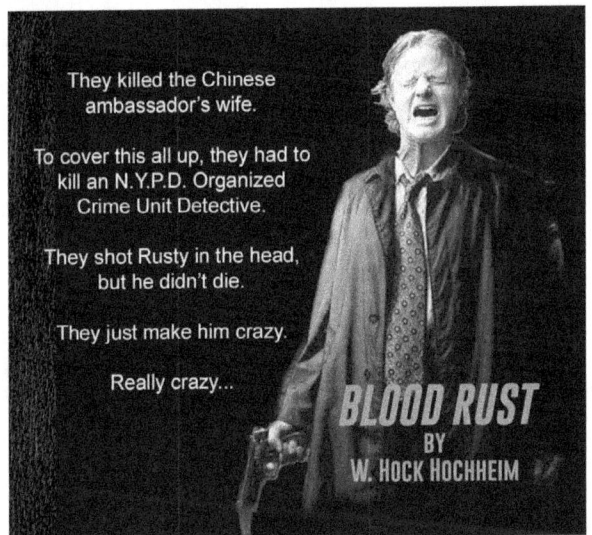

The Johann Gunther Western Hero Adventure Series. Ebooks, Paperback, Audio.

Coming in 2024

"The Horse Killers"

Find these books on Amazon and Barnes and Nobles, be they ebooks, paperbacks or hardcovers

www.ingramcontent.com/pod-product-compliance
Lightning Source LLC
Chambersburg PA
CBHW070803040426
42333CB00061B/1802